The Resume Makeover

50 Common Problems with Resumes and Cover Letters—and How to Fix Them

JOHN J. MARCUS

McGraw-Hill

New York   Chicago   San Francisco   Lisbon   London
Madrid   Mexico City   Milan   New Delhi
San Juan   Seoul   Singapore
Sydney   Toronto

The McGraw·Hill Companies

Library of Congress Cataloging-in-Publication Data

Marcus, John J.
    The resume makeover : 50 common problems with resumes and cover letters—and how to fix them / by John Marcus.
      p. cm .
    Includes index.
    ISBN 0-07-141057-0 (alk. paper)
    1. Résumés (Employment)—Handbooks, manuals, etc.
I. Title.
HF5383.M264 2003
650.14'2—dc21

2002156360

1 2 3 4 5 6 7 8 9 0 QPD/QPD 0 9 8 7 6 5 4 3

ISBN 0-07-141057-0

This publication is designed to provide accurate and authoritative information in regard to the subject matter covered. It is sold with the understanding that the publisher is not engaged in rendering legal, accounting, or other professional service. If legal advice or other expert assistance is required, the services of a competent professional person should be sought.

    —From a declaration of principles jointly adopted by a committee of the American Bar Association and a committee of publishers.

This book is printed on recycled, acid-free paper containing a minimum of 50% recycled, de-inked fiber.

McGraw-Hill books are available at special quantity discounts to use as premiums and sales promotions, or for use in corporate training sessions. For more information, please write to the Director of Special Sales, Professional Publishing, McGraw-Hill, Two Penn Plaza, New York, NY 10121-2298. Or contact your local bookstore.

Contents

Preface

I've been in the employment business for three decades. While most of my work has focused on executive search and outplacement, for the past dozen years I've been concentrating on writing resumes and cover letters for clients nationwide.

Throughout my career, I've spoken with thousands of people about the work they've done and how effectively they feel their resume presents it. The vast majority make these two statements:

My resume doesn't really do it. It just doesn't express how good I am.

I think my resume sells my capability, but I want my resume to be different, to be unique, so it will stand out in the crowd.

When I decided to write this book, I therefore had these two goals in mind. First, to show you how to write your resume so that it will make a compelling case for your qualifications, and, second, to show you how to prepare your resume so that it will be markedly different from all the others and get the attention you want.

One of the many things *The Resume Makeover* does to achieve these goals is discuss 50 common problems that job hunters encounter when writing their resume and cover letters. Because I plan to write a second edition of this book to keep pace with an ever-changing job market, I'd like to hear from you about any particular problems you've incurred when preparing your resume and/or letters. Whatever the challenges may have been, you weren't alone in having to deal with them, and addressing them in the next edition will make the book that much more valuable to its readers. Feel free to contact me at my e-mail address below.

Writing this book has been an exciting adventure and a great joy. I hope you derive as much benefit from it in the job market as the joy I have had in writing it for you.

The best of luck with your new resume, job search, and new position!

John J. Marcus
Sarasota, Florida
TheResMakeover@aol.com

Acknowledgments

Many people made important contributions to this book. I would like to thank in particular:

Robert Wilson, my agent, for encouraging me to write a third career book.

Michelle Howry, Barry Neville, Pattie Amoroso, Penelope Linskey, and Lashae Brigmon of McGraw-Hill—thank you all for improving the manuscript and transforming it into a wonderful book. Special thanks to Michelle, who conceived of the book and selected me to write it.

Frances Koblin, for superb editing.

Fred Dahl, of Inkwell Publishing Services, for marvelous design work.

Gail Marks, for your love and support throughout the project, especially while writing the manuscript.

Cory Perlman, with whom I will forever debate the value of the one-page resume.

All my clients—present and past—a never-ending source of knowledge and inspiration.

WRITING YOUR RESUME
AND COVER LETTERS

1

What This Book Is All About

A myth abounds among job hunters. Many believe that all they need to do to get the interviews they want is to prepare a resume that's well-written, attractively laid out, and that showcases their strengths and accomplishments. Then they expect this document to produce immediate interviews once they begin their job search. They usually start out by contacting a handful of friends, writing to some recruiters and prospective employers, plus answering Internet postings and print ads. As the weeks and months roll by, however, the positive response they were anticipating seldom materializes. Few interviews come their way, and they have no idea why.

The problem is that most resumes don't get read. They get glanced at.

Employers and recruiters are always swamped with resumes. In good times, job openings are plentiful, and people aggressively pursue the increased responsibility, large salary hikes, hefty sign-on bonuses, and potentially lucrative stock options that companies offer. When times are lean, many people are unemployed or fear they soon will be, so they aggressively circulate their resume. For example, a job opening posted on a leading employment Web site, such as Monster.com or Careerbuilder.com, or placed in the Tuesday edition of the *Wall Street Journal* or Sunday edition of the *New York Times*, can quickly draw over 500 responses.

The result of all this activity is that resume reviewers can't keep up with all the submissions they receive, and they're pressed for time as they go through each document. No one will give your resume their undivided attention and read it like this:

Now let's see . . . a unit manager . . . ah, the chemical industry. . . . Interesting set of responsibilities . . . wonder if he has any acquisition experience . . . yep, that's good. . . . Look at that, doubled sales . . . wonder how he did it . . . doesn't seem to say . . . oh, there it is. . . . I wonder if he entered any new markets . . . can't quite figure out what that means; maybe he did, maybe he didn't. . . . Let's see if he cut costs any . . . nothing said about that . . . maybe that's covered on the second page. . . . Did he develop any new products? . . . Can't seem to find anything about that on either page. . . .

Employers and recruiters won't read your resume with this painstaking care. They'll have dozens or hundreds of documents to go through, and your submission will be somewhere in their PC or in-basket. When it's your resume's turn, it will be given just a brief moment—perhaps 10 seconds—to see if it merits an in-depth evaluation or should be filed away.

This critical 10-second period is your opportunity to make statements about your background that have such a powerful impact that people will read your resume in its entirety.

A few years ago, I looked for a new way to write a resume so that my clients could capitalize on these precious 10 seconds and gain an important advantage over the competition. I experimented with different kinds of presentations in an effort to find a device—a hook, if you will—that would immediately spark readers' interest.

Reasoning that when most people begin to read a resume they start with the introductory section, this is where I focused my attention. I tried something new. I organized the section around a client's accomplishments versus the traditional approach of describing someone's capability, then listing a half dozen or so key skills. The traditional method *told* people why someone excelled. My approach, presenting successes, *showed* people why someone excelled.

This simple change made all the difference, and it produced miraculous results. Clients quickly reported a sharp increase in the number of interviews. Stating a client's successes was the hook I had been searching for.

This book shows you how to write your resume so that it immediately gains the readers' interest. It also helps you to present your background in such a compelling way that people will contact you for interviews.

Your resume will be evaluated in five areas—content, organization, appearance, word usage, and impact. By following the principles set forth in Part I, you'll score high grades in each category. Especially important, you'll learn how to begin your resume with an introductory section that will set your resume apart from the competition and prompt people to read your background in its entirety. You'll also learn how to write your resume whether you're seeking advancement in your field, pursuing a career change, or reentering the job market after a lengthy absence. Part I concludes with a discussion on how to compose high-impact cover letters to accompany your resume.

Part II contains 42 resumes and 8 cover letters, each exemplifying how you can avoid a problem area that reduces the likelihood of getting interviews. You'll see the "before" version of each document, including an explanation of the problem and how to fix it. Then you'll see the makeover, the "after" version, where the document has been rewritten to fix the problem. (In most instances, for reasons of space, only the first page of the resume is shown.)

The 50 problems that are discussed range in severity—from the critical, which concern content, to the cosmetic, which regard form. The key point is that you'll learn how to prepare your resume and cover letters so that they won't contain any of the problem areas (serious or minor) that continuously cause job hunters to lose out on interviews. For example, I know recruiters and employers who, when faced with a large number of resumes to evaluate, eliminate applicants on factors such as font or layout, just so they can quickly reduce to a manageable level the number of resumes they have to read. This book will ensure that you'll cover all the bases when composing your job-search materials. As a result, you'll set up a maximum number of interviews.

You can use Part II in two different ways: It can serve as a guide for solving any particular problem you're encountering. Just turn to the page that addresses your concern, and you'll find the solution you need. Or you can use Part II as a checklist to assure that you're not making any of the 50 mistakes that are discussed.

The resumes and letters in the book represent job hunters in a wide range of fields, from forestry to high finance, and at all the different levels of responsibility, from administrative assistant to executive.

As you read the 42 resume makeovers, you'll note that they look a good deal alike. There's a reason why. They all adhere to the resume-writing principles set forth in Part I, the most important of which are to begin with a powerful introductory section and then to describe work experience with bulleted statements that focus on accomplishments.

The format shown in this book is the most effective way to discuss your background, and I strongly recommend that you don't deviate from this approach. Not only will you make the best presentation possible, but its striking introductory section will instantly gain readers' attention. Then, as they read the sections that follow, they'll learn about your strengths and accomplishments, and your resume will generate the interviews you want.

2

Creating Your Resume

Your resume contains a great deal of information about your background. What you say about the different things you've done can be organized according to the following sections, depending upon how extensive your experience is and how detailed an accounting you want to provide:

Primary Sections

- Introduction
- Experience
- Education

Secondary Sections

- Objective
- Professional Honors and Awards
- Inventions and Patents
- Publications
- Computer Skills
- Professional Organizations
- Board Memberships
- Community Activities
- Clubs

- Foreign Languages
- Volunteer Positions
- Part-Time Jobs
- College Work Experience
- Hobbies and Interests
- Military Experience
- Personal Information
- Additional Information

The three most important elements of your resume are the introduction, the experience section, and the education section. Many outstanding resumes, in fact, are written using these three sections alone. The others are considered to be secondary, and they're used to provide additional information to enhance core qualifications.

We'll discuss the sections sequentially, culminating in a discussion on how to prepare the introduction. Even though the introduction is the most important part of your resume, it will be covered last. This is because it contains the most exciting points about your background, and what you say is taken from the other sections. Without a complete understanding of what you have to offer potential employers, you won't be able to decide what information to include in the introduction in order to achieve the greatest impact possible.

The resume of Joel H. Gregory (see pgs 10–11) is an example of the advice that's being provided. You'll want to refer to it often as you learn to write your resume.

THE EXPERIENCE SECTION

When most people talk about a resume, they're usually referring to the experience section that describes the work someone has performed throughout his or her career. For this reason, this section almost always appears first.

In the event that you're changing careers, however, your experience might be completely unrelated to the type of work you want to do, and your education could be more important than your work background. In this case, the education section should precede the discussion of your work experience. Likewise, if you happen to hold a position where specific degrees and licensure are prerequisites for employment, such as a doctor, lawyer, teacher, or healthcare practitioner, begin your resume with the education section.

The vast majority of job hunters are seeking a career progression, not a career change, and their work experience is what prospective employers and recruiters key in on. They therefore begin their resume with the experience section. Here's how to proceed.

Present your work experience in reverse-chronological order, starting with your current or most recent employer. Because you're organizing the resume this way, it's known as a *chronological* resume.

State the name of your employer, its location by city and state, and your dates of employment, expressed in years only. By omitting the months, you'll be able to conceal any gaps that may exist in your employment history. It's unnecessary to include an employer's street address, zip code, or telephone number.

Next, offer a one-sentence description of your employer, listing its products and/or services and, if possible, the annual revenues for the previous year. If you've worked for an organization that's extremely well-known, such as Microsoft or The United Way, it isn't necessary to describe what it does.

Now state your title, followed by a brief explanation of your responsibilities. If you held a management position, state the number of people you supervised along with the titles of your direct reports.

We now come to the most important part of your work experience: your accomplishments and duties. Describe exactly what you did and, especially, the results you achieved, showing how you benefited your employer and the value you added to the organization. Be sure to mention anything you did that was new or different. Nothing is more important in a resume than demonstrating innovation.

To make sure that you identify all of your key accomplishments, ask yourself these three questions:

What did I do that I'm the most proud of?

What did I do that I want other people to know about?

What did I do that I received a lot of praise on?

If you feel uncomfortable about "tooting your horn," understand that this is exactly what you're supposed to do in your resume. It's no place to be modest. Prospective employers and recruiters will be looking for exciting accomplishments, and if they don't see them, your resume will pale in the face of the competition.

There's no hard-and-fast rule for the number of accomplishments to discuss. Keep in mind, however, that your resume is not your autobiography, so it isn't essential to take a complete inventory of your work experience and state everything you've done. Focus on the job you want to hold, then describe your most important achievements as they relate to this position. Your goal is to provide enough information so that people will develop an understanding of your successes and capability and want to interview you. However, be sure to avoid background information that will bore a reader or that doesn't relate directly to your job target. As a general rule, the less you say, the greater the impact of what you do say. Use your best judgment in deciding where to draw the line on how much information to provide. If you have 20 or more years' experience, concentrate on the last 10.

By following a targeted approach, not only will you write a better resume, but you'll write your resume in half the time it would take otherwise.

In the event that you have a highly diverse background with several different jobs in mind, then write a separate resume for each one, where each resume is tailored to a specific position.

Joel H. Gregory
376 Rosemarie Lane
Georgetown, MA 01833
Tel: (508) 352-3806

Fax: (508) 352-7210
JHGregory17@aol.com

SALES DIRECTOR—INDUSTRIAL PRODUCTS

- **P&L Responsibility**
- **Strategic Planning**
- **Organizational Restructuring**
- **Turnaround Management**
- **End User & Distributor Sales**
- **Human Resources Maximization**

- Reversed 9 years of flat or declining sales for $90 million manufacturer, doubling revenues to $185 million in 4 years while increasing profit from 8% of sales to 20%.
- Turned around 3 years of declining volume for another manufacturer, growing revenues from $7.5 million to $10 million in 1 year.
- Elected to "Hall of Fame" twice; Won "District Manager of the Year" once, "District Manager of the Month" 11 times, plus hired and trained sales reps who won "Sales Rep of the Year" and were inducted into "Hall of Fame."

An innovative and energetic leader, skilled communicator / team builder, and adept negotiator. Proven ability to analyze products, markets, and growth opportunities, then introduce strategic and tactical solutions that improve competitive performance while increasing revenues and profits. Recognized for outstanding ability to develop and lead high-performance sales organizations that continuously exceed goals.

EXPERIENCE

New England Coatings & Chemicals, Inc., Cambridge, MA. 1998 - Present

$185 million producer and distributor of high-performance composite coatings and specialty chemicals, generating gross margin of 60-70%.

Sales Director

Complete responsibility for sales of 2 separate divisions, overseeing 80 independent distributors and 4 levels of internal personnel, including 2 product managers, 3 regional managers, 7 sales managers, and 20 sales representatives. Report to VP - Sales.

- Recruited by VP - Sales to reverse 9 years of flat and / or declining sales.
- Rigorously analyzed sales organization and markets, then instituted sweeping changes that grew revenues 100% in 4 years, dwarfing industry growth rate and expanding profit from 8% of sales to 20%.
  - Restructured both divisions, plus established separate sales organizations for each one.
  - Upgraded sales management and sales personnel; implemented time and territory management programs; created and instituted modular training programs; automated sales organizations; added new distributors and service partners; established OEM sales channel that contributes 65-75% gross-margin sales.
- Grew sales in the United Kingdom and Ireland 52% while on 18-month special assignment. Repaired damaged distributor relationships; hired new sales managers; performed extensive training of sales force; personally met with end users to strengthen relationship.
- Served as member of Strategic Planning Team. Personally established template for sales / marketing plan that was instituted globally.
- Initiated domestic product line extension program.
- Designed collateral material plus bottom-up sales and expense forecasting method that was implemented throughout North America.

- Present new and existing products to groups of up to 200 personnel, plus give presentations to prospective distributors and key accounts.
- Organize and conduct annual North American Sales Meeting and Global Managers' Meeting.

Rotanium Products Division, American-Industrial Corporation, Chicago, IL. 1991 - 1998

Manufacturer and distributor of premium-priced, high-performance electrical maintenance products, anchoring and drilling equipment, and specialty chemicals.

Regional Sales Head, 1998; **Zone Manager,** 1997; **Assistant Zone Manager,** 1996 - 1997; **District Manager / Assistant District Manager,** 1993 - 1996; **Sales Supervisor,** 1992 - 1993; **Field Trainer / Agent,** 1991 - 1992.

- Reversed 3 years of declining sales and delivered 1997 revenues of $10 million versus previous year's $7.5 million.
- Devised and implemented personalized training programs for field personnel, plus conducted advanced training seminars for developing managers at corporate headquarters. Selected by top management to teach sales rep training seminars at corporate level. Expanded collegiate recruiting program.
- Only Zone Manager to successfully train and promote 2 District Managers in Boston and New York City districts.
- Won "District Manager of the Year," FY 1997 (increased market share 115%), and "District Manager of the Month" 11 times.
- Recruited, hired, and trained 2 individuals who won "Sales Rep of the Year" and 3 out of 4 first-year inductees into company's "Hall of Fame."
- Twice elected to "Hall of Fame"; finished 8th out of 120 for "Division Sales Champion"; trained third-place finisher for "New Sales Rep of the Year"; developed and promoted 2 Field Trainers.
- Received award for most orders written by new sales rep in 1992.
- Developed new territory into second-highest producing territory among all new sales reps, 1991.
- Runner-up for "New Sales Rep of the Year," 1991.

MEMBERSHIPS

Industrial Distributors Association

American Supply & Machinery Manufacturers Association
Member, Young Executive Forum

American Management Association

EDUCATION

Executive M.B.A. Program, University of New Hampshire, Durham, NH. 2002
B.S., Marketing, Boston University, Boston, MA. 1990

When you list your accomplishments and duties, present them in the order of their importance to the kind of position you're seeking. Keep your statements short and to the point, since lengthy sentences lack power. Always begin a statement with an "action" word, omitting the pronoun "I."

Here are 220 action words to choose from. Reflecting on each one may also help to identify important accomplishments. For example, think about what you *planned, led, organized, increased, reduced, created,* and/or *developed* and see which achievements come to mind.

accelerated	collected	displayed	hypnotized
accounted for	communicated	disproved	identified
achieved	compiled	diverted	illustrated
acted	completed	drafted	implemented
adapted	composed	drew	improved
addressed	conceived of	drove	increased
administered	conceptualized	edited	influenced
advertised	conducted	effected	informed
adopted	consolidated	elected	initiated
advanced	constructed	eliminated	innovated
advised	consulted	enforced	inspired
aligned	contracted	enhanced	installed
analyzed	contributed to	enlarged	instituted
anticipated	controlled	enlisted	instructed
arbitrated	convinced	established	integrated
appraised	coordinated	estimated	interpreted
approved	counseled	evaluated	invented
arranged	created	examined	investigated
ascertained	danced	exhibited	judged
assembled	debated	expanded	launched
assessed	decided	expedited	lectured
assigned	decorated	experimented	led
attained	decreased	explained	leveraged
audited	defined	fabricated	maintained
augmented	delegated	facilitated	managed
automated	demonstrated	financed	manufactured
budgeted	designed	fixed	mediated
built	detected	formulated	molded
calculated	determined	founded	monitored
cared for	developed	gathered	motivated
charted	devised	generated	navigated
checked	diagnosed	guided	negotiated
classified	directed	handled	observed
coached	discovered	headed	operated

ordered	provided	revised	surveyed
organized	publicized	saved	synchronized
originated	published	scheduled	synergized
oversaw	purchased	separated	synthesized
painted	realigned	served	systematized
participated in	recommended	serviced	tabulated
perceived	reconciled	set up	taught
performed	recorded	shaped	tested
persuaded	reduced	sketched	trained
planned	reengineered	sold	transcribed
predicted	rehabilitated	solved	translated
prepared	reinforced	sorted	transmitted
prescribed	reorganized	spearheaded	triggered
presented	repaired	spoke	troubleshot
prioritized	reported	started	unified
processed	researched	streamlined	united
produced	resolved	strengthened	upgraded
projected	restored	structured	was awarded
promoted	restructured	summarized	was promoted
proposed	revamped	supervised	won
proved	reviewed	supported	wrote

Try to avoid beginning statements with "Participated in," "Involved with," "Active in," and "Contributed to." These words suggest that your role was minimal. A more powerful way to begin a statement when you can't take complete responsibility for something is, "Played key role in," "Instrumental in," "Played critical part in," or "Served as key player in."

Tips for Expressing Your Accomplishments

When describing your accomplishments, always use numbers to convey their extent. For example, it's much more impressive to write,

• Grew profits 300% in 2 years,

than it is to say,

• Dramatically increased profits.

Numbers show people *how well* you did something.

Also, use actual numbers; don't spell a word out. As above, write "300%," not "three hundred percent" and "2 years," not "two years." Even numbers below 10 should not be written out. Resume writing has its own set of rules.

What will add further impact to your writing is to omit the articles "the," "a," and "an." For example, instead of saying,

- Drove the territory to a record-setting year,

write,

- Drove territory to record-setting year.

If you're describing an activity and not an accomplishment, still try to use numbers as much as possible so people will understand the scope of your responsibility. For example, state the number of people you coordinated, or forms you processed each day, or sizes of the loans, grants, or contracts you worked with.

An accomplishment will also have much more power if you discuss by how much you exceeded your goal, mention any obstacles you were facing at the time of the success, or state how your accomplishment compared with the performance of your peers, as in these examples (the different things that could be said are underlined for your convenience):

- Increased sales 25% in 1 year <u>versus goal of 15%</u>.
- Increased sales 25% in 1 year <u>versus industry growth rate of only 4%</u>.
- Increased sales 25% in 1 year <u>versus company average of only 8%</u>.
- Increased sales 25% in 1 year <u>despite flat market</u>.
- Increased sales 25% in 1 year <u>despite recessionary environment</u>.

If you happen to be in a managerial role, here are two effective ways to begin the discussion of an accomplishment to "frame" it and add impact to what you're saying (again, the variations are underlined for your convenience):

- <u>Provided the vision, leadership, and technical direction</u> that drove division to best year in its history, growing profits 300% over 24-month period.
- <u>Rigorously analyzed operations, then implemented sweeping changes</u> that drove division to best year in its history, growing profits 300% over 24-month period.

These two statements not only convey a success, but they inform readers that the person has vision, leadership skills, and the ability to manage technical people or that the candidate is capable of evaluating a situation, identifying opportunities for change and growth, then taking action. Each of these is an extremely desirable attribute.

If you tried to accomplish something but either didn't succeed as you had hoped to or weren't in the position long enough for your work to have produced quantifiable results, you can express the accomplishment as follows (the words in parentheses represent other things that could be said):

- Planned and implemented strategy to increase sales (efficiencies) (output) 300% in 2 years.

While you're not stating how well you did something, by writing "to increase sales" you're conveying the results that you *expected* to deliver, and this adds power to the statement through implication.

Here are effective ways to convey accomplishments in the event that you're not able to state quantifiable results:

- Created innovative (business) solutions through applying leading-edge (technologies) (sales principles) (marketing principles) (financial principles) (manufacturing processes) (engineering processes) (business processes).

- Leveraged (sales) (marketing) (finance) (manufacturing) (engineering) (IT) background to improve (cite what you improved).
- Leveraged (sales) (marketing) (finance) (manufacturing) (engineering) (IT) strengths to outperform the competition in (type of product or service) markets (worldwide).
- Revamped and expanded (state what you were working on and then improved).
- Implemented effective tools for measuring cost, productivity, and process efficiencies.
- Achieved new benchmark standards using best practice models and continuous process improvements.
- Introduced new products that gained immediate market recognition.
- Introduced new (production) processes that immediately increased (throughput) (efficiencies) (quality).
- Optimized capital assets and capacity of core manufacturing business.
- Exploited core competencies to drive organization (department) to new levels of success.
- Reestablished company's credibility, product recognition, and loyalty from accounts.
- Streamlined operations and work flow, resulting in reduced response times as well as greater efficiencies during increased work loads.
- Expanded distribution activities and developed targeted marketing strategies.

These statements pertain only to management personnel:

- Provided strategic and tactical leadership in achieving performance objectives in organizations facing significant (personnel) (business process) (financial) (equipment) (technology) issues.
- Grew start-up to successful operating entity.
- Developed work teams, empowered employees, and rewarded innovation in identifying and implementing cost reduction, process improvement, and optimization techniques.
- Established accountability standards and encouraged risk taking and innovation among staff.

While you're not saying specifically what you did in the above, you're conveying that you made important contributions.

If you achieved something through implementing a new technology or process that's in great demand or by doing something that was extremely innovative, be sure to tell readers about this. Your knowledge of the technology or process, or the innovative methodology that you developed, could be as important, or even more important, than the actual result you achieved.

If your accomplishment didn't require taking any innovative steps, however, then don't tell people what you did to get there. Let them wonder. It could be an additional reason to contact you.

For example, the most impressive thing about the following accomplishment is that someone created new programs that made the accomplishment possible. The person did something innovative and didn't follow an established procedure.

- Reduced labor costs 25% through developing and implementing new training and motivational programs that increased worker productivity, enabling 25% reduction in staff.

If you were to state the accomplishment by omitting the training and motivational programs that made the success possible, the accomplishment would be far less exciting. It would read:

- Decreased operating costs 25% through reducing staff.

Anyone can save money by letting people go.

If all you did to reduce costs was, in fact, to let people go, then you'd be better off saying:

- Decreased operating costs 25%.

This lets readers wonder what you did to cut the costs.

Two Caveats

When describing your work experience, two matters require special attention:

Be aware of word repetition. Certain words automatically lend themselves to resume writing, such as *increased, reduced, created, managed, developed,* and *implemented.* Be sure you never overuse a word. Vary your language as much as possible so that your writing doesn't become boring. Look through the list of action words given previously for substitutes or use a thesaurus.

Use statements that are short and crisp. Avoid long-winded entries such as:

- Conducted research to identify potential customers, cold-called each prospect to introduce company and its products, set up appointments, explained features and benefits of products being offered, answered questions and overcame objections, and achieved closing rate of 50%.

The following succinct statement has much more impact:

- Identified potential customers, cold-called to set up appointments, and closed 50% of prospects.

It bears repeating that the less you say, the greater the impact of what you do say.

Key Words

When discussing your background, be sure to use what are known as *key words.* These are the words that denote the specific skills, activities, and/or responsibilities that pertain to your position.

Using key words is extremely important because an increasing number of employers and recruiting firms are using software to search for these words when reading resumes. If the software doesn't gather a sufficient number of key words that pertain to your line of work, your resume won't be considered. Here are examples of key words for two different fields. These are key words for financial management.

accounting	acquisitions	budgets	cost reduction
accounts payable	asset	cash flow	credit facility
accounts	management	corporate	divestiture
receivable	bridge loan	finance	DSO

expense reduction	investment banking	management buyouts	ROA
financial analysis	investment management	mergers	ROE
financial forecasting	IPO	negotiations	ROI
debt financing	LBO	P&L	SEC
equity financing	lending	private equity	spin-off
internal audit	leveraged buyouts	private placements	strategic planning
	loans	reverse merger	tax
			treasury
			valuations

These are the key words pertaining to the human resources field:

affirmative action	401k	organizational development	stock options
arbitration	gain-sharing	pay-for-performance	succession planning
benefits	grievances	performance appraisal	training
compensation	HRIS	performance management	union avoidance
cost-per-hire	incentive plans	recruitment	wage and salary
diversity	labor relations	retention	workers' compensation
EEO	manpower planning	safety	
employee relations	manpower succession	security	
employment	mediation	staffing	
executive coaching	OD		

Format

Now turn to Joel Gregory's resume at the beginning of this chapter. Notice that all the accomplishments are preceded by bullets, just as are all the accomplishments that appeared in the examples on the last few pages. These marks are critical to successful resume writing. They guide the reader's eye, make the reading and evaluation task much easier, and also automatically add power to what's being said. Information isn't nearly as exciting or as easy to digest when it's presented in paragraph form.

THE EDUCATION SECTION

Educational background is usually the second most important section. Here are the different ways to present your educational training depending on your individual situation.

If you have an advanced degree, list that degree first:

EDUCATION

M.B.A., Northeastern University, Boston, MA. 1985
B.A., Economics, Boston University, Boston, MA. 1980

If you're currently studying for an advanced degree, provide that information along with your four-year degree:

EDUCATION

M.S. Program, Advanced Registered Nurse Practitioner.
Will receive degree from University of South Florida, Tampa, FL, in 2004.
B.S., Nursing, University of Tampa, Tampa, FL. 1999

If you're a college graduate and have additional educational training that will enable you to advance in your field, include those studies. Here's how an insurance salesman described his educational background:

EDUCATION

Currently studying to obtain C.I.C. designation, with Property and Casualty portions completed.
Numerous industry-related courses at The College of Insurance, including Business Law and Accounting.
B.S., Business Administration, New York University, New York, NY. 1985

And here's what a sales manager wrote:

EDUCATION

Xerox Sales School and Xerox Management School, Cleveland, OH. 1995
B.S., Marketing, Villanova University, Villanova, PA. 1988

If you're currently studying for a two-year or four-year degree:

EDUCATION

A.S., Pilot Technology, Manatee Community College, Bradenton, FL. Will receive degree in 2005.

If you have college experience but don't plan on obtaining a degree:

EDUCATION

University of Southern California, Pasadena, CA. 1985 - 1987
Concentration in Economics and Accounting

If you have only a certificate in a field:

EDUCATION

Certificate, Hairstyling, Sarasota County Vocational Institute, Sarasota, FL. 1998
Diploma, Manhasset High School, Manhasset, NY. 1990

If you have licenses in a field:

EDUCATION

State of Florida Community Association Manager, 1994.
State of Florida Real Estate Broker, 1988.
Liberal Arts, Southern Methodist University, Dallas, TX. 1980 - 1982

If you don't have any college training or trade education, then list your high school education:

EDUCATION

Diploma, Port Washington High School, Port Washington, NY. 1985

If your only postsecondary education consists of workshops, seminars, and lectures, list these programs after stating your high school diploma:

EDUCATION

Staff Motivation, National Institute of Business Management, 1998.
Coaching Skills for Managers & Supervisors, Fred Pryor Seminars, Tampa, FL. 1998
Customer Service, Fred Pryor Seminars, Tampa, FL. 1998.
Files and Records Organization, Padgett-Thompson Seminars, Tampa, FL. 1998
Naval Weapons Center, China Lake, CA. 1989 - 1995
Certified annually in this military defense instructor's course.
Diploma, Sarasota High School, Sarasota, FL. 1988

When discussing your education, don't include any courses or programs you've taken that don't pertain to your field. This will just detract from your related educational background.

Other matters to consider are your grade point average (G.P.A.), extracurricular activities, honors and awards, and the fact that you may have paid for a significant part of your education. This information will be important to include, however, only if you have been out of school for approximately five years or less.

State your G.P.A. if it was 3.50 or higher.

EDUCATION

M.A., Education, Lynchburg College, Lynchburg, VA. 2002
G.P.A. 3.70.
B.A., Economics, Randolph Macon Woman's College, Lynchburg, VA. 2000
G.P.A. 3.65.

Extracurricular activities that pertain to your field can also enhance your qualifications. Here's what a graduating college student wrote who wanted to enter the public relations field or the advertising business:

EDUCATION

B.A., Communications, University of Arkansas, Little Rock, AR. 2002
Member, Public Relations Society
Committee for the Restoration of "Old Main"
Staff writer and copy editor for college newspaper
Member, Debate Club

Here's how to present your educational background when you want to include honors and awards:

EDUCATION

B.A., Economics, Denison University, Granville, OH. 2001
Cum Laude
Recipient of Lewis Newton Thomas Scholarship

If you're in the early stages of your career, it will always make a favorable impression if you state that you paid for a large part of your education:

EDUCATION

B.A., Finance, Florida State University, Tallahassee, FL. 2002
Paid for 75% of education through working summers
and holding part-time jobs during school year.

THE SECONDARY SECTIONS

Objective

Your objective is a statement about the type of position you're seeking, and you may or may not decide to include it in your resume.

Many people omit their objective because they feel it would limit the types of positions for which they can be considered. Instead, they begin their resume with an introductory section that summarizes their background. This discussion prompts readers to evaluate them for a variety of positions.

My recommendation is that you omit your objective unless you're seeking one specific position, with no interest in any other. If you happen to be changing careers and lack directly related experience for the kind of work you want to do, always state the type of position you're pursuing. (In this instance, you won't be able to create a compelling introductory section.)

When describing your job objective, word it so that it's short, specific, and to the point. Here are three examples of effective objective statements:

Outside sales position with a manufacturer or distributor of electronic components.

Editorial Director at a book publisher, responsible for nonfiction.

Vice President of Engineering at a plastics manufacturer in either a start-up or turnaround stage.

Be sure you never write an objective like any of the following, as so many job hunters do:

To apply my skills in manufacturing at a progressive, customer-driven company that is committed to innovation, quality, and growth and that also recognizes outstanding performance and rewards people commensurately.

To work for a dynamic, growing organization that will leverage my extensive talent base and ability to increase the organization's revenues and profits while rewarding me for my performance.

To seek a leadership position at a dynamic company where there are challenging opportunities to apply my business skills for professional growth, fulfillment, and advancement.

These statements focus on what the person hopes to get from a company and provide no information on what he or she wants to do. This begins the resume on a weak note.

Professional Honors and Awards

These kudos can appear in a separate section or be woven into your introduction. If you prefer the former, here's how a manufacturing manager in the automotive business conveyed this information:

PROFESSIONAL HONORS & AWARDS

"Supplier of the Year," General Motors
"World Excellence Award," Ford
"Toyota Partnership Award," Toyota
"TPM Award," Japanese Institute of Planned Management

Inventions and Patents

The inventor of a product used for alleviating skin irritation described his patent as follows:

PATENT

"Method for Alleviating Skin Irritation By Formulations Containing Superoxide Dismutase. "
Patent Number: 4,695,456. September 22, 1987.

Publications

Here's how someone in the information technology field listed her publishing credits:

PUBLICATIONS

Author of 6 books published by Microsoft Press, Faulkner & Gray, and Powersoft Press.
Extensively published in trade magazines, including "Internet Week," "EC.com," "E-Business Advisor," "Security Advisor," "PowerBuilder Advisor Magazine," "DataBased Web Advisor," "Internet Java and ActiveX Advisor," "PowerBuilder Developer's Journal," "Java Developer's Journal," and "PowerBuilder and Java Journal On-Line."

Computer Skills

An administrative assistant presented her computer skills as follows:

COMPUTER SKILLS

Microsoft Word, Excel, Lotus 1-2-3, PowerPoint.

Professional Organizations

Memberships in professional organizations demonstrate a sincere interest and commitment to one's career. People who don't engage in career-related activities outside their work day don't appear to have any real involvement in what they do for a living.

Here's how a social worker with a specialty in gerontology presented this section:

PROFESSIONAL ORGANIZATIONS

National Association of Private Geriatric Care Managers
Sigma Phi Omega - National Academic and Professional Society in Gerontology
Gerontological Society of America
Southern Gerontological Society
Gerontological Society of Florida
Sarasota County Aging Network - Secretary and Member of Steering Committee and Publicity Committee

Board Memberships

Senior executives are frequently members of their company's board of directors as well as of subsidiary and outside companies. The president of a financial services company listed his board memberships as follows:

BOARD MEMBERSHIPS

Chairman, Evergreen Capital Corporation
Chairman, Evergreen Financial Services
Member, Evergreen Investments
Member, Delta Capital Corporation
Member, Hawthorne Financial Services

Community Activities

Participation in community activities will always advance your qualifications when the activities relate to your career. Mentioning your involvement in your community will also be beneficial if the position you're interested in requires strong social skills. A hospital wellness coordinator detailed her community involvement this way:

COMMUNITY ACTIVITIES

Planned Approach to Community Health, Sarasota County, Florida
The Health Advisory Council, Sarasota, Florida
The Coalition on Child Abuse, Sarasota, Florida
The School Advisory Council, Sarasota County, Florida
Steering Committee on Women's Issues, Big Brothers / Big Sisters, Sarasota, Florida

Clubs

Another way to show that you're socially adept is to list your club memberships. Here's how a sales representative treated this section:

CLUBS

Bath & Racquet Club
The Jazz Club of Sarasota
Sarasota Rugby Club

Foreign Languages

If you have a foreign language proficiency, follow this example provided by an international sales executive:

FOREIGN LANGUAGES

Fluent in English, French, and Italian; knowledgeable of Spanish, Portuguese, German, and Dutch

Volunteer Positions

Recent college graduates as well as people who are trying to change careers will benefit the most from listing volunteer experiences. An accountant who wanted to become a fund-raiser used her volunteer experience to demonstrate her qualifications for her new career choice:

VOLUNTEER POSITIONS

Fund-raiser for numerous organizations, including Ringling Museum of Art,
American Heart Association, Asolo Performing Arts Center, and The Players Theater.

Part-Time Jobs

Career changers as well as people reentering the work force after an extended absence will find listing part-time jobs to be helpful. Here's how a housewife and former bookkeeper used this section to convey her recent bookkeeping experience:

RECENT PART-TIME JOBS

Allston Car Wash, Allston, MA. 2002
Bookkeeper
- Managed accounts receivable and payable, working 10 hours a week.
- Prepared payroll information as well as information for outside CPA.

Educational Press, Brookline, MA. 2001
Bookkeeper
- Handled accounts receivable and payable, working 8 hours a week.
- Collected past-due accounts.
- Performed computer data entry.

College Work Experience

Career changers and recent college graduates will find listing college jobs to be helpful. A graduating college student who was looking for an outside sales position described his experience as follows in order to substantiate his qualifications:

COLLEGE WORK EXPERIENCE

Sales Representative, Kirby Vacuum Cleaners, Atlanta, GA. 2000 - 2001
- Made sales presentations to residential accounts, following up on leads provided by Marketing Department.
- Consistently exceeded quota, closing 50% of prospects.

Sales Representative, Alpharetta Security Systems, Alpharetta, GA. 1999 - 2000
- Telemarketed throughout suburban Atlanta area.
- Set up appointments, presented features and benefits of security systems, and closed 25% of prospects, exceeding goal.

Hobbies and Interests

Stating hobbies and interests can advance the qualifications of people who are starting out in their career, changing careers, or trying to reenter the work force, when these activities directly relate to the type of work they want to do. An audio buff who wanted to transition from teaching into repairing home-entertainment equipment presented his qualifications this way:

HOBBIES & INTERESTS

10 years' experience designing and building tuners, amplifiers, and speakers.
Subscribe to "Stereophile," "AudioVideo International," "Audio / Video Interiors," and "Home Theater."

Military Experience

If the majority of your work experience, or the type of work you want to perform, occurred in the armed forces, include your military experience. Here's how a sergeant who was in the Army for 10 years and who was seeking a supervisory position in civilian life described his military background:

MILITARY EXPERIENCE

U.S. Army, Ft. Sill, OK; Ft. Raleigh, KS; Ft. Carson, CO; Camp Essayons, Korea. 1991 - 2002
Sergeant E-5
Headquarters Section Chief, 1998 - 2002
Crew Chief - Multiple Launch Rocket Systems, 1993 - 1998
Platoon Sergeant, 1991 - 1993
- Managed up to 18 personnel.
- Scheduled all daily activities, including classroom assignments.
- Trained personnel in Weapons & Tactics, Computer Data Entry, Combat Sustainment, and Equal Opportunity.
- Provided technical assistance in operating multiple-launch rocket systems.
- Supervised maintenance and construction activities, plus ensured compliance with safety procedures.
- Read, interpreted, and collected intelligence information.
- Evaluated performance of personnel, wrote performance reports, and made recommendations for promotions.

Personal Information

Omit personal information such as your date of birth, social security number, name of your spouse, and number or names and ages of your children. Don't state that you're single, married, divorced, or separated. If you happen to be pursuing work that requires extensive travel, however, and you happen to be single or divorced, then it will be advantageous to include your marital status, as in this example:

PERSONAL INFORMATION

Single; open to extensive travel.

Additional Information

Use this section for information you want prospective employers to have that doesn't fit into any of the other categories. For example, a manufacturing engineer who once represented his native Germany in the Olympics stated "A former decathlon record holder in Germany." No one can reach this level of excellence without an inordinate amount of hard work, discipline, and commitment. These attributes are relevant to all fields, not just to sports.

If you're pursuing a position that requires a great deal of travel, it can be beneficial to write "Willing to travel extensively."

If you're a world traveler or have lived in many different countries, and you think this information will advance your qualifications, include your international travels.

Some kinds of personal information, however, can backfire on you. Be careful about mentioning memberships in organizations that would indicate your race, religion, political preference, or any personal matters that could possibly be considered offensive or controversial. You don't want to say anything about yourself unless you're certain it will increase your chances of an interview. For example, someone might be proud that they belong to Mensa (an organization for individuals with high IQs and who have scored in the top 2 percent of certain standardized tests); however many people are intimidated by this level of intelligence or consider it arrogant to make reference to it in a resume. Recruiters and prospective employers are much more impressed with job-related accomplishments than they are with the fact that someone has a high IQ.

THE INTRODUCTORY SECTION

We now come to the most important part of your resume: the introductory section. As explained in Chapter 1, this is your opportunity to create a resume that will be different from all the others—in both content and appearance. Your introduction will immediately gain readers' attention and ensure that they'll read your background information in its entirety.

Before discussing how to write this section, I want to explain how to lay out the resume's heading so that you'll maximize the impact of your introduction. While the heading isn't part of the introduction per se, it's constructed in such a way that it leads the reader right into it.

Place your name, address, and home telephone number at the left margin, then additional contact information, such as your fax number, cell phone number, or e-mail address, at the right margin. Use the same font and type size that you're using for the body of your resume.

Your name must be on a line by itself. Otherwise computer software will read whatever else is on the line as part of your name. As a result, there will always be one more entry on the left side of the page than on the right.

It's best to omit your business phone number and/or office e-mail address if you happen to be currently employed. You don't want to appear to be looking for a new position on your company's time and at its expense. Don't be concerned that leaving out this information will cost you interviews. Employers and recruiters contact applicants at home all the time. (Once you've met with a prospective employer, you'll often be asked if it's okay to call you at the office, and that's when it's appropriate to offer your business phone number.)

The purpose of laying out the heading at the two margins is to create white space in the center of the page that will draw the reader's eye to the banner headline that follows, which is the beginning of the introductory section.

While you might be tempted to highlight your name by placing it in the center of the page in large, bold-faced type (as in most of the "before" resumes in Part II), your name is actually the least important part of your resume, and no one is going to interview you because of it. People will interview you only because of your capability, and the sooner you convey it, the more enthusiastic prospective employers and recruiters will be about reading your resume. Because of the value of using this split-heading approach, all the "after" resumes that appear in Part II use it.

Let's now discuss how to create the introductory section. Begin with a banner headline that positions you in the eyes of readers. Next, insert a horizontal line underneath the headline, and list beneath the line your key areas of expertise.

Then present two to four of your most impressive accomplishments that directly relate to the type of position you're seeking, preceding each one with a bullet. Conclude with a narrative paragraph that rounds out your background and further relates your qualifications. For an example of this introductory section, turn to Joel Gregory's resume at the beginning of this chapter.

Now here's how to create each of the introduction's four parts.

The Banner Headline

This statement immediately announces who you are and prompts readers to see you in a certain light. The banner headline informs resume reviewers of your level of seniority, functional specialty, and, if you wish, industry affiliation. The headline is set in bold, capital, italicized letters and is centered on the page.

The banner headline doesn't signify that this is your job title or job objective, although it could be one or both of these. Instead, it's a statement that positions you with readers and enables them to determine where you would fit in their organization. It also helps readers know in advance the kind of information to be looking for as they go through your resume. This makes their reading task easier. Here are some examples of banner headlines:

CEO / PRESIDENT

SENIOR GENERAL MANAGEMENT EXECUTIVE

CHIEF OPERATING OFFICER—TELECOMMUNICATIONS

SENIOR EXECUTIVE—GENERAL MANAGEMENT / SALES / MARKETING

VP - SALES & MARKETING—INFORMATION TECHNOLOGY

DIRECTOR OF MANUFACTURING

SUPERVISOR OF QUALITY CONTROL—APPAREL

SALES EXECUTIVE—SPECIALTY CHEMICALS

FUND-RAISING EXECUTIVE

WELLNESS COORDINATOR

CLINICAL PSYCHOLOGIST—PRIVATE PRACTICE

CLINICAL PSYCHOLOGIST—RESEARCH

DIRECTOR OF EDITORIAL SERVICES—TRADE BOOKS

EDITOR—SPORTS / BUSINESS / HEALTH

HISTORY PROFESSOR

CHIEF OF POLICE

POLICE OFFICER

DATABASE MANAGER

QUALITY ASSURANCE ENGINEER

AUTOMOTIVE MECHANIC—IMPORTED CARS

REAL ESTATE BROKER—COMMERCIAL PROPERTIES

REALTOR—RESIDENTIAL & COMMERCIAL PROPERTIES

LIBRARIAN

GYM COACH—HIGH SCHOOL

ELEMENTARY EDUCATION TEACHER

ADMINISTRATIVE ASSISTANT

Areas of Expertise

After you have set your banner headline, insert a horizontal line beneath it, then list the functional areas in which you excel. (It's important to use an actual line and not underlining. The latter doesn't provide enough space between itself and the characters above it for many computer scanners to be able to read the text. A line offers sufficient space.) By stating your expertise in functional areas, readers will have a better understanding of your capability and will be able to determine the different positions for which to consider you. This information should be presented in boldface, in upper- and lowercase letters, and be preceded by bullets. Here are three examples of how job hunters have presented their areas of expertise:

SENIOR GENERAL MANAGEMENT EXECUTIVE—CONSUMER PRODUCTS

• P&L	• New Business Development
• Strategic Planning	• Manufacturing
• Start-ups	• Mergers & Acquisitions
• Turnarounds	• Acquisition Integration
• Sales & Marketing	• International Experience

MANUFACTURING ENGINEER—ELECTRO-MECHANICAL PRODUCTS

Productivity & Quality Improvement • Cost Reduction • Lean Manufacturing • TQM • ISO 9000

EVENTS PLANNER / COORDINATOR

Client Development • Site Selection • Food & Entertainment • Logistics Management

---

Your Accomplishments

Your accomplishments are the core of the introductory section. You have successfully gained your readers' interest. This is your opportunity to hook them on wanting to read your resume in its entirety by demonstrating how you have excelled throughout your career. Past performance is the best indicator of future performance!

First carefully consider the position you're seeking; then go through the different sections of your resume to identify the two to four most exciting things you've done throughout your career that will best convey your ability to excel at this position.

Once you've decided what you want to say, present the statements in bulleted form and in the order in which they will have the greatest impact, not necessarily in the order in which they actually occurred. For example, the first statement could be an accomplishment that happened three jobs ago and the second statement an accomplishment that occurred last month. Additionally, a statement need not be restricted to what you did in one position at a company. It can be a composite of two or more accomplishments that occurred at different times during your career. For example, a salesperson might have opened up new territories at one company, added a large number of accounts at another, introduced new products at a third company, tripled sales in one year at a fourth company, and increased margins 15 points at a fifth company. He could then include all of these accomplishments in the following statement:

- Introduced new products, penetrated new territories, and added new accounts, increasing sales as much as 200% in 1 year and expanding margins as much as 15 points.

Describe your accomplishments so that the wording is different than in the experience section. For example, if in the experience section you have written:

- Introduced state-of-the-art production processes that reduced cycle time 50% and improved quality 25%.

In the introduction rephrase along these lines:

- Decreased cycle time 50% and enhanced quality 25% through implementing state-of-the-art production processes.

Notice that in addition to inverting the statements, "introduced" was changed to "implementing," "reduced" was changed to "decreased," and "improved" was changed to "enhanced." See the action words listed earlier in the chapter for alternative verb choices or use a thesaurus.

Also, don't be concerned about providing information twice. First of all, readers will want to know where and when your accomplishments occurred. Second, and more important, when someone sees the same accomplishments again in the experience section, it means that your resume is being read, and this is the whole purpose of the introduction.

In the event that your background doesn't lend itself to visible accomplishments, then state key elements from your experience that will immediately convey your capability. For example, here's how a nurse could begin a resume to quickly gain a reader's attention and interest:

STAFF NURSE
- Extensive experience in medical-surgical, urology, gynecology, the ER, and OR.
- Recognized by Directors of Nursing for providing exceptional patient care.
- Served as Preceptor.
- B.S., Nursing.

Narrative Paragraph

This part of the introduction adds the finishing touch to the introductory section. Use this paragraph to provide key information about your abilities, including information from the education and secondary sections. Advanced education, honors, awards, publishing credits, and speaking engagements are especially impressive.

Here are six examples of narrative paragraphs, with the entire introductory section appearing so that you can relate the content of the paragraph to the job hunter's background and successes:

SALES REPRESENTATIVE—High-technology / Hardware & Software

Start-ups • Account Team Management • International Experience

- Drove underperforming Cisco territory from 60% of quota to 126% in 1 year.
- Established European and U.S. sales for start-up software company, generating $2 million in first-year revenues.
- Negotiated and closed multi-million-dollar contracts for Octel, landing leading accounts, including J.P. Morgan, Pepsi-Cola, Chemical Bank, Phillip Morris, American Express, Merrill Lynch, Goldman Sachs, and The Boston Consulting Group.

An accomplished sales executive skilled at prospecting, accessing key decision makers, and closing business. Recognized for strengths in consultative / solutions sales, selling in fast-paced, rapidly changing markets, winning business at accounts previously dominated by the competition, as well as developing long-term relationships with customers built on trust and exceptional service.

SENIOR VICE PRESIDENT—MANUFACTURING

P&L • Turnaround Management • Organizational Reengineering • Multi-plant Experience

- Reversed $250 million manufacturer's 12% operating loss and delivered 6% operating income after 10 months; grew operating income to 15% level 8 months later.
- Reduced $75 million manufacturer's set up times 45%, boosted machine utilization 40%, decreased scrap 66%, and improved on-time delivery from 79% to 96% while decreasing direct labor 15%.
- Expert at leading-edge manufacturing techniques: Lean Manufacturing, JIT, Kaizen, Kanban, Flow Production.

An innovative and energetic leader, skilled communicator / team builder, and adept negotiator. Recognized for broad strengths in strategic planning, turnaround management, manufacturing, and human resources development / maximization. Accomplished at analyzing operations and growth opportunities, then developing and implementing strategic and tactical solutions that increase production and product quality while reducing costs. Successful in fast-paced, turbulent environments. Officer of numerous industry trade groups. M.S.I.E.

ELEMENTARY SCHOOL TEACHER

- Planned and taught full curriculum to 3rd, 4th, and 5th grade students, with classes ranging to 28 students in self-contained setting. Applied basal and whole-language skills to teaching methods.
- Planned thematic units that incorporated art, music, and physical activities to broaden curriculum.
- Worked one-on-one with students, assisting in numerous literature and language arts activities.
- Directed "Johnny Appleseed," the 4th grade play. Member of Core Knowledge, Science Fair, Grade, and Hospitality committees.

An exceptional teacher with the proven ability to create a classroom environment conducive to learning. Implements appropriate teaching strategies, utilizing multi-media tools, plus instructs students individually as well as in large and small groups. An excellent disciplinarian and motivator, who is patient, understanding, and adores children. B.A., Education; Certified Elementary School Teacher, Ohio.

FINANCIAL SERVICES EXECUTIVE

Retail Banking • Student Loans • Product Development • Sales • Compliance

- Established Consumer Product Development Department for $2 billion bank—introduced direct mail campaign that increased response rate 300%.
- Created Consumer Lending Department for $50 million bank, achieving $8 million monthly production with yields averaging 6.25 points above cost of funds.
- Started up mortgage production subsidiary for $100 million S&L, delivering profitability the first quarter.
- Wrote IPO business plan for start-up VISA card company--presented to Wall Street community.

A visionary financial executive with broad strengths in identifying growth opportunities throughout the financial services industry, then designing and marketing niche products responsive to customer demand and competitive factors. Twice won "Marketer of the Year." Published author with extensive speaking experience at industry events. Top-school MBA.

DIRECTOR OF HUMAN RESOURCES

• **Recruitment**	• **Training**
• **Compensation**	• **Multi-plant Experience**
• **Benefits**	• **Union / Nonunion**

- Developed and implemented recruitment program that slashed cost-per-hire 25%.
- Restructured benefits program and secured new vendors, reducing costs 15% while improving quality of coverage.
- Successfully negotiated 3 union contracts while thwarting effort to organize at key manufacturing facility.
- Created and instituted comprehensive training and succession programs to ensure sustained double-digit growth in sales and profits.

An accomplished HR leader who partners with executives organization-wide in the development of HR processes that drive organizational growth. Recognized for broad strengths in improving productivity, quality, revenues, and profits while reducing operating costs. A skilled strategist and change agent adept at building successful relationships with all levels of management, including providing executive coaching to support top management in attainment of corporate and departmental goals. M.A. in Management & Human Resources.

MERCHANDISING & SOURCING—APPAREL

High-volume Production • Cost Reduction • Quality Improvement • International Experience

- 10 years' sourcing, buying, and merchandising experience with leading retailers, including Lerner New York, Kmart, and Bergdorf-Goodman.
- Directed sourcing for up to 73 million units a year at cost of over $500 million annually.
- Reduced production in Northeast Asia and transferred to Southeast Asia, Middle East, Central America, and the US.
- Decreased vendor base 40% and cut quality issues from 5% to 3% while improving on-time delivery.
- Developed new products with design groups, including sourcing, sales / margin analysis, product- cost comparison analysis, margin targets, inventory levels.

An energetic leader and driven apparel executive with an uncompromising regard for maximizing growth and profit opportunities. Proven ability to analyze operations and corporate goals, then initiate solutions and changes that improve competitive performance. Relentless in the pursuit of quality-driven, cost-effective manufacturing. Extensive international travel. Multilingual in English, German, French.

Keep your narrative paragraph concise and to the point, and use it only to add key information that will strengthen the qualifications you've already established.

Never write anything that resembles the following two paragraphs. Not only are they long-winded, but they are jam-packed with clichés. Employers and recruiters are tired of hearing how "dynamic," "success-driven," "self-motivated," "results-oriented," or "people-oriented" someone is, or how they have a "take-charge personality" or "hands-on management style," or what an "expansive thinker" they are. Resume reviewers often snicker when they see these statements. Lacking credibility, they call them fluff or hype and often stop reading.

Dynamic, results-oriented, business-savvy professional who has demonstrated exceptional skills in collaborating with key stakeholders, correlating business and technology concepts, quickly identifying needs for new business processes, and transforming requirements into enterprise growth and profitability. Diverse background includes extensive knowledge of technology development, business process development, the Internet, and their seamless integration. A success-driven leader with expertise in building winning teams, generating fresh ideas, and applying cross-functional business process reengineering to help the enterprise achieve its goals. An expansive thinker with an outstanding record of achievement in implementing new business concepts, delivering innovative business solutions, and building strategic partnerships. An entrepreneurial leader with a high energy level who focuses on superior results and leads in a rapidly changing, fast-growth environment.

Insightful, analytical, and people-oriented executive with a track record of success. A creative and persistent problem solver who thrives on challenges, excels under pressure, and continuously exceeds goals. Bright, energetic, and self-motivated team player who possesses outstanding interpersonal and communication skills with a take-charge personality and hands-on management style. A demanding and empowering leader and motivator, an organized and thorough planner, and a strong negotiator who deals effectively with all levels of an organization. Accustomed to fast-pace environments and multiple projects. Understands competing agendas and meets deadlines while providing value-added advice to senior management, enabling the attainment of strategic and tactical goals.

Tips for Composing the Narrative Paragraph

Following are almost 100 descriptive statements and phrases pertaining to responsibilities, accomplishments, and strengths to consider using in your narrative paragraph. They're organized into two groups—Especially Effective for Managers, and More Appropriate for Individual Contributors. Some of these remarks will also be appropriate to use in your resume's experience section. Needless to say, modify a remark as necessary so that it best expresses your individual situation or experience.

You'll note that a good number of these remarks refer to increasing revenues, decreasing costs, and increasing profits. This is because these are the goals of all businesses, and more people work for a business than they do for any other kind of organization. If necessary, modify a remark so that it will pertain to the types of employers you've worked for.

Especially Effective for Managers

An innovative and energetic leader, skilled communicator / team builder, and adept negotiator. Proven ability to analyze businesses (operations) (markets) and growth opportunities, then introduce strategic and tactical solutions that improve competitive performance while increasing sales (revenues) (market share) (profits) (stockholder value).

Accomplished (expert) at organizational repositioning and development of strategic initiatives (solutions) that improve (competitive performance) (sales) (revenues) (margins) (market share) (profits) (shareholder value).

An accomplished corporate strategist and change agent who transforms missions and goals into workable business plans and bottom-line results (establishes goals, then reengineers organizations and business processes to achieve bottom-line results).

Repeated successes in diverse industries, including (name the industries).

Provided the vision, leadership, and innovation (technical direction) that (state the accomplishment).

An impeccable blend of credentials embracing (state your functional strengths).

Demonstrated leadership ability to develop and implement solutions that improve competitive performance (sales) (revenues) (margins) (profits) (output) (manufacturing capability).

A decisive and persuasive leader who establishes priorities, translates business strategies into quantifiable goals, and motivates personnel to perform at maximum levels.

An accomplished organizational leader and problem solver with the proven ability to develop and implement strategic and tactical plans that result in increased efficiencies and reduced costs while achieving operational objectives within budget constraints.

A proven strategist and change agent, relentless (tireless) in the pursuit of quality products (quality services) (efficient business processes) and corporate (organizational) growth.

A proven strategist and change agent, recognized for an uncompromising regard for quality products (quality services) (efficient business processes) and corporate (organizational) growth.

Achieves record results in flat markets.

Provided strategic and tactical leadership in achieving performance goals in an organization facing major (human resources) (business process) (equipment) (technology) (financial) issues.

Leveraged (operational) (sales) (marketing) (financial) (manufacturing) (engineering) (IT) strengths (background) to outperform the competition.

Leveraged resources and grew underfunded start-up into (an operating entity) (a thriving enterprise).

Reversed a competitive disadvantage to (then state the accomplishment).

Expert at identifying and capturing business in high-growth market segments.

Proven ability to deliver sustained sales / earnings growth and increased shareholder value through strategic and tactical planning and implementation.

A record of success at delivering sustained sales / earnings growth and increases in shareholder value.

Accomplished at managing diverse groups, people, and situations.

Identified top performers and promoted several employees to positions of increased responsibility.

Established accountability standards and encouraged risk taking and innovation among staff.

Refocused (restructured) (then name the function).

Revamped and expanded (name the function).

Expanded distribution activities and developed targeted marketing strategies.

Advanced rapidly throughout organizations, gaining increased autonomy and decision-making authority.

Implemented effective tools for measuring cost, productivity, and process efficiencies.

Achieved new benchmark standards using best practice models and continuous process improvements.

An exceptional mentor and motivator who maximizes staff performance through fostering a supportive and empowering management style.

An outstanding communicator who fosters a culture of team building with high employee involvement and motivation.

An outstanding manager and coach who fosters an environment of empowerment and high employee morale (involvement).

An energetic leader who communicates a compelling vision organization-wide and whose (enthusiasm) (commitment) (drive) motivates (departments) (staff) (personnel) to perform at levels that exceed established goals.

A visionary leader and communicator who aligns departments and personnel organization-wide plus motivates staff to work in unison (to achieve a common goal) (to exceed established goals).

Maintains open communications throughout an organization plus fosters an environment that motivates personnel to work in unison toward achieving a common goal (to exceed established goals).

An accomplished executive who aligns work groups and departments, resulting in outstanding communications and increased (productivity) (operating efficiencies).

Applies strong communications, mentoring / leadership skills, with the ability to create a stable and productive work environment that fosters teamwork and performance excellence.

Communicates effectively with people across diverse departments, cultures, and professions.

An accomplished leader with the proven ability to align staff and departments as well as motivate personnel company-wide.

Expert at communicating a common goal throughout an organization as well as instituting a team approach, resulting in unified and motivated personnel and enhanced performance.

Improves employee productivity through enhanced morale.

Expert at human resources development, motivation, and management, with an emphasis on team building and staff empowerment to achieve a common goal.

Combines outstanding planning, leadership, team-building, and communication skills with the proven ability to manage and motivate personnel to perform at levels that exceed established goals.

Exhibits an uncompromising regard for developing motivated and dedicated teams that deliver top-quality products and services, consistently exceeding goals.

A proven leader with the ability to motivate others to perform at higher levels of productivity.

Provides consistently enthusiastic leadership to promote departmental morale and harmony.

A history of building teams whose results surpass established goals and expectations.

A bottom-line producer with a track record of success at exceeding (standards) (quotas) (goals) (expectations).

Accomplished at initiating organizational change while maintaining employee morale.

An outstanding strategist and tactical implementer with exceptional communication and problem-solving skills.

Expert at motivating personnel through introducing a model leadership role.

A skilled communicator who eliminates cultural barriers and adapts to business protocols within a global environment.

Forged innovative partnerships through joint-development alliances.

Negotiated strategic partnerships with (cite prestigious organizations), establishing long-term growth alliances.

Proven ability to identify emerging trends and (consumer) (vertical market) demand.

An excellent strategist and tactical implementer with exceptional communication and problem-solving skills.

Built synergy, consensus, and buy-in (among staff) (organization-wide) (throughout department).

Successful at managing change with cross-functional teams.

A (state your title) with the bottom-line focus of a CEO.

Ousted entrenched suppliers (displaced the competition) (broke down competitive barriers) to (state the accomplishment).

Reversed a competitive disadvantage and delivered (state the accomplishment).

Strong leadership and supervisory skills.

These two statements are especially effective for financial executives:

A senior financial executive and accomplished strategic planner. Offers a record of success in a broad range of transactions with organizations undergoing rapid change and increasing competitive pressure.

Recognized for ability to use strong analytic, planning, and organizational skills in the development and implementation of innovative solutions to complex financial challenges and business problems.

When describing yourself in the narrative paragraph, you can refer to yourself in many different ways, such as: entrepreneur, executive, manager, supervisor, leader, innovator, critical thinker, analytical thinker, strategic thinker, corporate strategist, strategist, change agent, tactical implementer, decision maker, problem solver, mentor, coach, or motivator.

I'd like to make a special comment on the first entry that appeared:

An innovative and energetic leader, skilled communicator / team builder, and adept negotiator. Proven ability to analyze businesses (operations) (markets) and growth opportunities, then introduce strategic and tactical solutions that improve competitive performance while increasing sales (revenues) (market share) (profits) (stockholder value).

Because this statement incorporates so many important qualities that are always in demand, I recommend that you consider using it, or a portion or modification of it, as the building block of your narrative paragraph.

The significance of the first sentence is that virtually all organizations are attracted to people who are leaders and who are innovative, energetic, effective communicators, good team builders, and skilled negotiators. (Here "skilled negotiator" doesn't mean that you're adept at hammering out a contract; instead, it refers to the ability to get other people to see your point of view, support your ideas, and to want to work with you to achieve a common goal.) The second sentence shows that you're able to analyze and understand an organization and see opportunities for growth, then develop fresh ideas and implement them to make the organization more successful.

The ability to accomplish these things is relevant to a wide range of positions throughout a company, especially in the areas of general management, sales, marketing, operations, manufacturing, finance, and IT. All you need to do is to tailor this entry so that it speaks to your individual situation.

If you happen to work for an organization that's not a profit-driven business, you can modify the entry as follows:

An innovative and energetic leader, skilled communicator / team builder, and adept negotiator. Proven ability to analyze operations and growth opportunities, then introduce (strategic) (and tactical) solutions that improve performance and drive organizations to the next level of success.

More Appropriate for Individual Contributors

An outstanding communicator who works well with a wide variety of people.

An excellent communicator, both orally and in writing.

An excellent planner and organizer.

Outstanding communication and organizational skills.

Skilled at time management—completes projects on time, under budget, and according to quality standards.

Skilled at multitasking—consistently completes projects on time and according to quality standards.

Expert at juggling multiple tasks while performing quality work that adheres to schedules.

A high energy level—accomplished at multitasking.

Effective working under pressure, deadlines, and in fast-paced environments.

Flexible and adaptable to rapidly changing conditions.

Works well independently, without supervision.

Works well independently and as a group member.

Detail-oriented with excellent follow-through.

Highly motivated and goal-directed.

An outgoing and enthusiastic personality.

Well-organized, attentive to detail, excellent follow-through.

Relates well with a wide variety of people.

A skilled supervisor and motivator.

Computer proficient (state your computer skills).

A team player with a strong work ethic.

Excellent team-building skills.

Dependable and reliable.

A self-starter who anticipates problems and prevents them from occurring.

A self-starter who analyzes problems and develops effective solutions.

Exploited core competencies that resulted in (state the achievement).

The proven ability to analyze problem areas and formulate effective solutions.

Accomplished at synthesizing large amounts of information into concise reports.

Proven ability to transform complex concepts into understandable, cost-effective ideas and solutions.

Consistently cited for (state the skills or strengths).

Repeatedly recognized for (state the skills or strengths).

Continuously cited by supervisors for outstanding performance.

Successfully completes projects under time-critical conditions.

Played critical (significant) (pivotal) (lead) role in (describe the activity or accomplishment).

Served as key (critical) player in (describe the activity or accomplishment).

If you have an advanced degree that pertains to your field, conclude the narrative paragraph with this information. In the event that you hold an M.B.A. from one of the more prestigious programs—Harvard, Stanford, Wharton, Columbia, Chicago, Dartmouth, Kellogg—you might be tempted to list the name of the college. Don't. Many employers and recruiters consider this to be pretentious or arrogant. You'll gain points as well as show humility by writing "Top-school MBA" versus "Harvard MBA."

There's a closing remark I'd like to make about the narrative paragraph. As already explained, employers and recruiters are so tired of reading glowing statements about job hunters' abilities that many don't even read these paragraphs. To ensure that yours will be read, always precede it with the bulleted statements regarding your accomplishments. This will establish your capability and give you credibility, which will prompt people not only to read your narrative paragraph but to take it seriously.

Testimonials

A touch that will be extremely powerful and immediately catch a reader's eye is to include in your introductory section testimonials from people you've worked with. Their words of praise will give you instant credibility and distinguish your resume from all the others.

Reflect on the successes you've had throughout your career, as well as the different people with whom you've worked, and see who would be willing to vouch for your expertise. A testimonial will have the greatest impact if it comes from a current or former board member, manager, or customer.

Here's how an outstanding manufacturing manager in the automobile-parts industry used testimonials to showcase his capability.

Depending on the number and strength of your testimonials, it may or may not even be necessary to include accomplishments and the narrative paragraph. Larry Roder's testimonials were so strong that he omitted these entries and went right to the experience section.

Final Comments

I want to make a few final comments about the introductory section.

If you happen to have certain liabilities in your background, such as job hopping, periods of unemployment, or a history of unrelated

Larry L. Roder
1409 Williams Drive
Columbus, NE 68601

Tel: (512) 869-8899
Tel: (512) 869-8799

MANUFACTURING MANAGEMENT

**Start-Up Operations • Product Launch • Productivity Improvement • Cost Reduction
JIT • Kanban • SQC • Kaizen • Cellular Manufacturing • Focused Factory • CFM • TQM**

"Larry has been labeled by associates as 'The Wizard' for his uncanny knack for finding cost savings that add up to millions of dollars for his employer."

— George Barlos, General Motors Company
Senior Engineering Manager (retired)

"Larry Roder is one of the two best Program / Project Launch Managers in the Automotive Systems Industry."

— Ralph C. Blazek, Ford Motor Company
Corporate Product Design Engineering

"I would characterize Larry as empowered, detail-oriented, and outstanding at crisis management. His people skills are evident, and I consider him to be the consummate professional."

— Thomas W. Dycio, Ford Motor Company
Corporate Worldwide Purchasing

EXPERIENCE

positions or decreases in responsibility, this powerful beginning will help to offset these shortcomings. Readers will immediately be impressed with your background and will be less concerned about these negative factors when they learn about them upon reading your experience section.

The introductory section can be especially effective if you're pursuing a career change or are reentering the work force after an extended absence. In these two situations, your most recent work experience will seldom provide the information that will make people want to interview you. As soon as they read about your employment activities for the past few years, they'll most likely set your resume aside.

The introductory section is your opportunity to instantly showcase factors in your background that will demonstrate your qualifications for the position you're seeking. They can include education you've recently completed, a part-time job, a volunteer position, community work, a hobby, or personal strengths.

The three resumes that follow show three different formats, each geared to the unique situation of the job seeker.

Gail Marks decided to change careers after having been in the mental health field for almost 20 years. She wanted to become an event planner/coordinator and capitalize on her 7 years of experience in that line of work. Although her experience had been only on a volunteer basis, she knew that if she composed a resume that highlighted her successes in the events area, employers would see her as an accomplished events professional and not as a provider of mental health services. She therefore designed her resume (see p. 39) using the recommended introductory section.

Gail Marks
3613 Countryplace Blvd.
Sarasota, FL 34231

(941) 957-3384
GM3654@aol.com

EVENT PLANNER / COORDINATOR

Fund-raisers • Corporate Meetings • Weddings • Bar Mitzvahs • Private Parties

- Planned and coordinated over 25 events during past 7 years for numerous organizations, individuals, and charities, including The Ringling Museum of Art, Cerebral Palsy, United Way, and Heart Association.
- Created themes, negotiated for and secured sites, plus arranged for publicity, invitations, decorations, catering, and master of ceremonies / entertainment.
- Managed budgets ranging to $50,000 and supervised up to 25 volunteers per event.
- Performed these activities on a volunteer basis while working part-time at Manatee Memorial Hospital.

Recognized for outstanding planning and organizational strengths with a flair for creating the right ambience to ensure event success. Consistently complete projects on time and within budget.

ADDITIONAL EXPERIENCE

Manatee Memorial Hospital, Bradenton, FL. 1994 - present

Social Services Coordinator (Part-time)

- Perform case management for child and adolescent units, with duties including biopsychosocial assessments as well as individual, group, and family therapy for inpatients. Also collaborate with the patient, family, physician, and treatment team to carry out multi-disciplinary treatment plan.
- Teach and train rational emotive therapy to nurses and technicians.
- Facilitate groups on Rational Recovery and International Association of Clear Thinking, both for inpatients and outpatients.
- Perform discharge planning and community resource referrals.
- Serve as Quality Assurance Facilitator, responsible for identifying problem areas, instituting remedies, and monitoring progress.
- Perform marketing activities through giving seminars plus performing community education on stress management, depression, AIDS, and anxiety.
- Member of Multi-Disciplinary Committee, responsible for creation and implementation of behavioral health programs.

Hamot Institute for Behavioral Health, Erie, PA. 1984 - 1994

Manager - Adult and Geriatric Inpatient Social Service Department, 1990 - 1994

- Supervised 5 social workers.
- Assisted Director in hiring, training, scheduling, and evaluating personnel as well as in developing and implementing programmatic objectives, JCAHO standards, and policies and procedures to ensure high-quality patient care.
- Created and implemented behavioral health programs for chronic patients and for higher functioning cognitive patients.
- Participated in the budgeting process as well as in cost-containment activities; directed and monitored quality assurance programs; performed planned actions to promote quality delivery of services.
- Performed case management, including individual, group, and family therapy as well as cognitive behavioral therapy at the acute and subacute patient levels. Also coordinated community resources and education.
- As Facilitator of Top Quality Management, received intensive training in the program and also trained staff in techniques to improve problem solving.
- Served as Quality Assurance Facilitator.

In the event that you want to change careers but don't have directly related experience as Gail Marks did, your background won't be strong enough to use the dramatic four-part introductory section. In this case, use the standard heading where your name, address, and other contact information appear in the center of the page; then begin your resume by stating your job objective, followed by a Qualifications section that contains your related experience and strengths. Alexa Brookline, a school teacher who wanted to sell art supplies, used that format. Her resume appears on page 41.

If you're reentering the work force after a lengthy absence, you'll be able to use the four-part introductory section.

Toni Porter had a superb background as an acupuncturist but hadn't worked in five years because she had been caring for an ill relative. She knew that if her resume prominently showed that her last position ended five years ago, many people would not consider her.

She began her resume (see p. 42) with a convincing introductory section that immediately conveyed her capability as an acupuncturist.

Using the guidelines given here, you'll immediately gain readers' attention by *showing* them how good you are; your competition will only be *telling* readers how good they are. You'll distinguish yourself from the other job hunters, and your resume will be read, generating the interviews you want.

RESUME MECHANICS

Perfecting Your Resume

Don't expect to write your resume in one sitting. It will take a series of drafts before you're fully satisfied with what you've said. As you're working on each version, ask yourself the following questions to make sure you're presenting the best possible picture of your capability:

Does my resume convincingly convey my ability to perform the kind of work I'm seeking?

Does it accurately convey my most important responsibilities, activities, and accomplishments?

Are the statements short, crisp, and to the point?

Are there any negatives in my background that I need to remove or minimize?

For each piece of information you're offering, ask yourself:

What does this say about me?

What does this not say about me that it should?

What does this imply?

ALEXA BROOKLINE
48 Adella Ave.
West Newton, MA 02465
(617) 969-5023
Alexab@msn.com

OBJECTIVE

Sales Representative for an established and growing manufacturer or distributor of art supplies.

QUALIFICATIONS

- Extensive knowledge of arts supplies.
- An experienced negotiator with excellent communication skills and an outgoing and convincing personality.
- Set up Art Department for a middle school—specified equipment and supplies, designed layout of art room, selected and negotiated pricing with vendors, and coordinated contract preparation with bookkeeper.
- Knowledgeable of water colors, finger paints, oils, acrylics, colored pencils and chalks, crayons, charcoal, clay, plasteline, modeling tools, paint brushes, kilns, glazes, easels, canvasses, and paper.

EXPERIENCE

The Lincoln School, Brookline, MA. 1998 - Present

Art Teacher and **American History Teacher**

- Established Art Department, with key activities including specifying and purchasing equipment and supplies plus designing layout of art room.
- Teach eighth-grade American History course.
- Plan curriculum for both Art and American History, establish daily objectives, determine length and sequencing of topics, select teaching materials, and instruct students.
- Design, administer, and grade tests.
- Write progress reports on each student.
- Enforce rules for classroom conduct.

The Pierce School, Brookline, MA. 1994 - 1998

American History Teacher

- Planned and taught American History course to eighth-grade students.
- Performed testing, wrote student evaluations, and supervised extracurricular and fund-raising activities.

Boston Public Library, Boston, MA. 1991 - 1994

Library Assistant

- Coordinated Saturday Afternoon Children's Hour.
- Visited elementary schools to read stories to students.
- Prepared materials for children's programs and assisted Youth Librarian in acquisition of new books.

EDUCATION

M.Ed., Social Studies, University of Massachusetts. 1991
B.A., Art Education, University of Massachusetts. 1989

Toni Porter
2100 Woodburn Corners
Plano, TX 75075

(972) 867-3841
toniporter@aol.com

ACUPUNCTURIST

- 8 years' experience practicing acupuncture and electro-acupuncture.
- Expert at taking comprehensive medical / mental-health history, then developing effective treatment plan.
- Prescribe herbal remedies as necessary.
- Offer serene, warm nature that puts clients at ease and elicits trust.
- Discuss life-style changes with clients necessary for improving their health.
- Communicate information in an easy and confident way, empowering clients and motivating them to want to learn about their health options.
- Active License.

EDUCATION

Diploma, Acupuncture and Herbology, Florida Institute of Traditional Chinese Medicine, St. Petersburg, FL. 1990. No. AP534

Diploma, Massage Therapy, Florida School of Massage, Gainesville, FL. 1987. No. MA8106

Numerous workshops in Neuromuscular Therapy (St. John Levels 1 & 2), Shiatsu (Level 1), Connective Tissue Massage, Qi Gong, Kung Fu, and T'ai Chi Chuan.

EXPERIENCE

Private Practice, Plano, TX. 1990 - 1998

- Performed acupuncture, electro-acupuncture, Chinese herbology, massage rehabilitation, postural integration, neuromuscular therapy, and micro-current therapy.
  - Utilized acupuncture to balance the body as well as electro-acupuncture for clients who were needle-phobic.
  - Practiced Chinese herbology to help restore healthy balance naturally, with no side effects.
  - Performed massage rehabilitation and body work to help release pains, restrictions, and blockages that affect people on both the physical and psychological levels.
  - Practiced movement therapy through ancient art of T'ai Chi Chuan (taijiquan) and Chi Kung (qi gong), which incorporated slow rhythmic movements with deep breathing techniques to integrate mind, body, and spirit.

Sarasota School of Massage, Sarasota, FL. 1988 - 1990
Director, Professional Health Services Clinic

- Managed this outpatient clinic.
- Hired and supervised staff.
- Instructed massage therapy and connective tissue therapy.
- Developed and implemented marketing programs to generate continuous flow of new clients.
- Purchased equipment and supplies, plus performed inventory control.

Health Matters Neuromuscular Clinic, Sarasota, FL. 1987

- Practiced massage therapy with provisional license.

- Don't include salary information. Your income could be too high or too low and end up costing you interviews.

- Don't list aptitude scores and psychological tests results, even if they are high. Many employers and recruiters consider it pretentious to state high scores on a resume. In addition, many are skeptical of testing due to its varying degrees of accuracy. If a company is a proponent of testing, a session will be arranged for you.

- Don't state the reason why you left any of your employers, even if a company went out of business.

- Don't include your photograph on your resume or enclose one when mailing the document. An exception is if you're in one of those rare fields where an outstanding appearance is actually a job requirement, such as in modeling or the entertainment business.

- Don't state on your resume "Unavailable for travel" or "Unavailable for relocation," regardless of how set you are on these issues. You don't want to preclude yourself from being interviewed before you know how much travel is involved or where the position is located. It's possible that once a company has met you and decided it wants to hire you, you may be able to make changes in the position if the travel requirement is objectionable or if relocation is necessary. There's also the possibility that the company could be so interested in you that it would offer you a different job where travel or relocation wouldn't be required. Remember, the goal of your resume is to generate as many interviews as possible. Don't make any statements that could close doors.

- Don't state the date you prepared your resume. There's no reason to advertise how long you've been looking for a job, especially if it's been for an extended period of time.

- Don't write at the top of the first page "Resume" or "Resume of (Your Name)." Employers and recruiters will recognize the document immediately.

- Don't use the statement "References furnished on request." All employers know that references are available by asking for them.

Rewrite your resume as many times as necessary so that it will be as polished and as convincing as possible. Once you're satisfied with what you've written, get feedback from someone you currently work with or have worked with in the past. Your resume may not read to others the way you think it does. Additionally, the input from other people can be invaluable. Since they've seen you perform on the job, they might think of important things to say that you omitted.

While you might be tempted to show your resume to your spouse, significant other, or a close friend, their assessment of what you've written won't be as valuable as that from someone with whom you have a professional relationship.

Be sure to check for spelling, grammar, and punctuation. Your computer's spell check isn't 100 percent reliable. You may have written "there" instead of "their," "your" instead of "you're," or "lead" instead of "led." Spell check won't pick up these kinds of errors.

Resume Length

Writing a resume presents a unique challenge: You want the document to be as brief as possible yet not at the expense of omitting important information.

The ideal length is one or two pages; the latter is usually necessary for individuals with 10 or more years' experience. Your resume should never be longer than three pages, unless you have an extensive list of publishing, speaking, or performance credits.

If you're having difficulty reducing the length to two or three pages, concentrate on the last 10 to 15 years and summarize your earlier experience.

As far as page breaks are concerned, it isn't important to end page 1 by fully describing your experience with a company, then beginning page 2 with a discussion on another company. It's perfectly acceptable to begin the second page with statements pertaining to the last company you discussed on the first page.

Your resume isn't an artistic submission. It's a presentation of your professional capability. Never make the mistake of deleting important information or using small type just so you can complete your discussion of a company on the same page you began it.

Appearance

It's essential that the appearance of your resume be as impressive as its content.

Use a conservative font, such as Times Roman, Helvetica, Arial, Garamond, or Tahoma. A more creative or exciting font will be appropriate only if you work in an artistic field.

When using Times Roman, the size should be 10 or 11 point. Anything smaller will make the reader squint, and a larger size will look juvenile. For Arial and Helvetica, use 9.5 or 10 point; for Garamond 10.5 to 12 point; and Tahoma 9 to 10 point.

If you're short on space, use Arial 9.5. It will allow for more characters per line than the other fonts will in the above sizes.

Be sure there's ample "white space" throughout your resume so that the document is inviting to read. When a resume is cluttered and looks like a wall of words, it's often rejected. Use Joel Gregory's resume, or any of the after resumes in Part II, as an example of the look to emulate for line spacing. Set the top and bottom margins at no less than .5 and the left and right margins at no less than .7.

The appearance of your resume will be enhanced by the judicious use of bold type. Put the section headings, names of your employers, and your titles in bold. Don't use bold type for any words to make them more prominent. This will cheapen your resume's appearance.

Never use lowercase italics, underlining, shadows, or graphics. Many computer scanners can't read hard copy that's been set this way (italics in capital letters are intelligible, however). Although the vast majority of prospective employers and recruiters don't use scanners, there's no reason to do anything that could jeopardize interviews. Besides, if you want to highlight something, the best way to do it is to discuss it in your introductory section.

If you use slash marks, make sure there's a space between the mark and the letters next to it. Computer scanners can't read letters when they touch a mark.

Use full justification to achieve a polished look, and don't put a decorative border on your resume unless you're in an artistic or highly creative field.

If your resume is longer than one page, place your name and the page number in the header of each additional page.

When you're ready to print your resume, use 24-pound bond stock, selecting either off-white, ivory, or light gray. While a textured linen might be more attractive, the high-speed mail equipment at the post office will lift some of the laser print off the page. This won't happen with bond stock.

If your resume is two or more pages, attach the pages with a paper clip, not a staple.

You'll need to decide whether to use a No. 10 envelope or the 9" by 12" size if you'll be mailing your resume. While the latter is more expensive, it enables you to avoid folding the documents, which is considered to be more tasteful by some people. Additionally, you'll avoid the problem of computer scanners not being able to read text by the fold line. For mass mailings to recruiters and prospective employers, which could require mailing hundreds or even thousands of pieces, you might want to use a No. 10 envelope due to the cost factor. When contacting a select number of individuals, however, especially key executives, the larger envelope is preferable.

The Generic Resume

Some people have a resume that's so industry-specific it deters employers in other industries from wanting to meet them. The problem is that their resume contains so much information regarding products, services, customers, and/or business processes that are unrelated to any other industry that employers in a different field feel they would have difficulty making a transition to their company.

Take a good look at your resume and see if it casts you in such a light. If it does, you might want to create a second resume, a generic one, where you would delete all the industry-specific words so that your background would appeal to a wide range of organizations.

Two resumes for Peter Jensen, an accomplished sales executive in the medical device field, follow. The first resume (see p. 46), which contains many industry-specific words (underlined for your convenience), is the one he would use for contacting employers in his own industry. The second resume (see p. 47) omits the medical-related words so as not to typecast him as a medical salesperson.

Peter R. Jensen
3912 Morrowick Road
Charlotte, NC 28226
Tel: (704) 541-9234

Cell: (704) 607-4193
E-mail: Peterjensen@home.com

SALES / SALES MANAGEMENT / MARKETING EXECUTIVE—_Medical Devices_

• **Account Development & Management**	• **New Product Development**
• **Territory Management**	• **Sales & Technical Training Programs**
• **New Market Development**	• **Physician / Nurse Education**
• **Turnaround Management**	• **Marketing Material Development**

- 18 years' progressively responsible experience at Alliance Industries:
    - Won multiple national awards for quota achievement, innovation, and sales / marketing excellence.
    - Earned company-wide reputation for exceeding quota every year (achieving up to 153% of annual goal), converting competitive accounts, increasing business at existing accounts, turning around troubled accounts, penetrating new markets, and strengthening field sales organizations.
    - Grew highly competitive, 52-OR Presbyterian Hospital (Charlotte, NC) account from annual sales of $130,000 to $1.8 million, capturing 95% of the business.
- Created numerous sales and marketing tools still in use today, some 12 years after their inception.
- Accomplished at developing new products and programs, then conducting domestic and international launches.

An innovative and energetic leader, skilled communicator / team builder, and adept sales representative, sales trainer, and sales manager. Recognized for ability to identify problem areas and growth opportunities, then create the necessary tools and mobilize the required resources to propel sales organizations to the next level of success. Accomplished at selling in fast-paced, rapidly changing markets plus developing long-term relationships with customers built on trust and exceptional service. A driven sales executive and marketer, tireless in the pursuit of quota achievement, quality business processes, expertly trained personnel, and corporate growth.

EXPERIENCE

Alliance Industries, Inc., New York, NY. 1983 - 2002

Leading manufacturer and distributor of surgical supplies, with 2002 revenues in excess of $250 million.

Senior Account Representative, Charlotte, NC. 1997 - 2002

Responsible for sales in Charlotte territory. Activities included: providing technical support to surgeons and nurses in the operating room, creating and conducting educational programs for medical personnel, serving as corporate liaison for Integrated Delivery Network (IDN), developing and making financial presentations to hospitals' senior management, managing teams of sales management and sales reps during key competitive conversions, implementing value-added programs at hospitals, plus assisting in development of sales representatives.

- Exceeded quota every quarter, achieving as high as 201% in all products, 518% in suture, 206% in advanced technology, and 171% in mechanical.
- Grew territory revenues in 9 quarters from $1.9 million to $3.7 million.
- Converted $1.5 million in suture and endo-mechanical products at Presbyterian Hospital—the first large suture conversion in the area, opening up numerous opportunities in other territories.
- Organized and managed 5-8 person rotating conversion team at Presbyterian Hospital, including sales reps, sales managers, suture reps, and suture support reps from Mid-Atlantic Division.
- Won multiple awards, including Chairman's Council, President's Award, Winner's Circle, and special recognition for achieving over 100% of goal in every product category in 2001 and 2002.

Key Account Specialist, Charlotte, NC. 1995 - 1997

Responsible for resolving problems at troubled accounts and growing business in sales region consisting of half of North Carolina and almost all of South Carolina; region included 7 sales reps, 1 suture rep, and regional sales manager.

- Evaluated individual hospital situation, then developed strategic plan for generating business, including coordinating activities among company, hospital, and local sales team.

Peter R. Jensen
3912 Morrowick Road
Charlotte, NC 28226
Tel: (704) 541-9234

Cell: (704) 607-4193
E-mail: Peterjensen@home.com

SALES / SALES MANAGEMENT / MARKETING EXECUTIVE

• **Account Development & Management**	• **New Product Development**
• **Territory Management**	• **Sales & Technical Training Programs**
• **New Market Development**	• **Marketing Material Development**

- 18 years' progressively responsible sales and marketing experience:
  - Won multiple national awards for quota achievement, innovation, and sales / marketing excellence.
  - Earned company-wide reputation for exceeding quota every year (achieving up to 153% of annual goal), converting competitive accounts, increasing business at existing accounts, turning around troubled accounts, penetrating new markets, and strengthening field sales organizations.
  - Grew highly competitive account from annual sales of $130,000 to $1.8 million, capturing 95% of the business.
- Created numerous sales and marketing tools still in use today, some 12 years after their inception.
- Accomplished at developing new products and programs, then conducting domestic and international launches.

An innovative and energetic leader, skilled communicator / team builder, and adept sales representative, sales trainer, and sales manager. Recognized for ability to identify problem areas and growth opportunities, then create the necessary tools and mobilize the required resources to propel sales organizations to the next level of success. Accomplished at selling in fast-paced, rapidly changing markets plus developing long-term relationships with customers built on trust and exceptional service. A driven sales executive and marketer, tireless in the pursuit of quota achievement, quality business processes, expertly trained personnel, and corporate growth.

EXPERIENCE

Alliance Industries, Inc., New York, NY. 1983 - 2002

Leading manufacturer and distributor, with 2002 revenues in excess of $250 million.

Senior Account Representative, Charlotte, NC. 1997 - 2002

Responsible for sales in Charlotte territory. Activities included: providing technical support and conducting educational programs for users, developing and making financial presentations to senior management, managing teams of sales management and sales reps during key competitive conversions, implementing value-added programs at accounts, plus assisting in development of sales representatives.

- Exceeded quota every quarter, achieving as high as 201% in all products and up to 518% in individual products.
- Grew territory revenues in 9 quarters from $1.9 million to $3.7 million.
- Converted $1.5 million in key products at major customer—the first large conversion in the area, opening up numerous opportunities in other territories.
- Organized and managed 5-8 person team serving key account, with members including sales reps, sales managers, and product specialists from Mid-Atlantic Division.
- Won multiple awards, including Chairman's Council, President's Award, Winner's Circle, and special recognition for achieving over 100% of goal in every product category in 2001 and 2002.

Key Account Specialist, Charlotte, NC. 1995 - 1997

Responsible for resolving problems at troubled accounts and growing business in sales region consisting of half of North Carolina and almost all of South Carolina; region included 7 sales reps, 1 product specialist, and regional sales manager.

- Evaluated individual account situation, then developed strategic plan for generating business, including coordinating activities among company, the account, and local sales team.
- Focused activities on prestigious account where all business except for proprietary products had been lost to the competition. Developed and implemented value-added programs that resulted in immediate successes and laid the foundation for future conversions.

The Functional Resume

As explained earlier, the style of resume we've been discussing is called the chronological. You should be aware that there's another style, the *functional*.

A functional resume first discusses work experience according to job function, not by individual employer, then it presents the employment history followed by the education section. Using the secondary sections is optional, just as in the chronological resume.

The goal of a functional resume is threefold: first, to enable job hunters to immediately highlight certain parts of their background; second, if necessary, to conceal a history of unrelated or less responsible positions; and third, in the instance when someone has job hopped or has had periods of unemployment, to make such a powerful initial impression on readers that when they do learn about any job hopping or periods of unemployment, they will be less concerned about these liabilities.

There are two very serious problems with this resume, and because of them, you shouldn't use it. First, this type of presentation has been utilized for decades as a device to cover up liabilities in a background, and many people are aware of this, especially recruiters; so as soon as they see this format, they set the resume aside. Second, because of the way information is organized, readers can't tell when or where someone's accomplishments occurred.

The primary benefit offered by the functional resume—being able to instantly highlight key background information—is provided by the introductory section that you now know how to write.

As part of the resume-writing process, you'll be getting feedback from others on your resume. If anyone suggests using the functional approach, you now know why not to.

So that you'll be familiar with this format, the resume on pages 49–50 shows what Joel Gregory's background would look like using the functional approach.

The Electronic Resume and the Text Resume

When you cut and paste your resume and transmit it as part of an e-mail message, you create what's known as an *electronic resume*. This document loses all formatting. An example appears on pages 51–52. Whatever was bold becomes regular type; underlining, italics, centering, and justification disappear; and your resume will be transmitted in the font you've designated for e-mailing.

When you save your resume as a text document, the formatting is also lost. (Internet postings and print ads frequently request that resumes be sent as text documents.)

In the event that you want to highlight certain words in either of these resumes, use CAPITAL LETTERS.

While the handsome appearance you worked so hard to create no longer exists, don't be concerned. These two resumes are about content and nothing else. The software that will be used to read them will do its job, and resume reviewers will be protected against viruses.

When you e-mail your resume as an attachment, all of the formatting will be maintained. However, some people won't open up the document for fear of a virus.

Peter Jensen's generic resume set up as an electronic or text document appears on pages 51–52.

Joel H. Gregory
376 Rosemarie Lane
Georgetown, MA 01833
Tel: (508) 352-3806
Fax: (508) 352-7210
JHGregory17@aol.com

Results-oriented sales executive with over 10 years' experience in a broad range of sales and sales management positions for manufacturers and distributors of industrial products. Proven leader and problem solver with strong communication and team-building skills. An expansive thinker capable of quickly grasping changing business dynamics and successfully driving change throughout an organization. A strong hands-on leader and sales trainer who consistently exceeds revenue and profit goals.

- P&L
- Strategic Planning
- Sales Channels
- Vertical Sales
- National Accounts
- Turnarounds
- Sales Training
- Project Management

SALES MANAGEMENT

- Directed 2 separate divisions for $185 million manufacturer / distributor of high-performance composite coatings and specialty chemicals, generating gross margin of 60-70%. Oversaw 80 independent distributors and 4 levels of internal personnel, including 2 product managers, 3 regional managers, 7 sales managers, and 20 sales representatives.
    - Restructured both divisions and established separate sales organizations for each one.
    - Rigorously analyzed sales organizations and markets, then instituted sweeping changes that reversed 9 years of flat and / or declining sales and grew revenues 100% in 4 years, dwarfing industry growth rate, plus expanding profit from 8% to 20%.
    - Upgraded sales management and sales personnel; implemented time and territory management programs; automated sales organizations; added new distributors and service partners; established OEM sales channel that contributed 65-75% gross-margin sales.
    - Grew sales in United Kingdom and Ireland 52% while on 18-month special assignment. Repaired damaged distributor relationships; hired new sales managers; performed extensive training of sales force; personally called on end users.
    - Member of Strategic Planning Team. Personally established template for sales / marketing plan that was instituted globally.
    - Initiated domestic product line extension program.
    - Present new and existing products to groups of up to 200 personnel, plus give presentations to prospective distributors and key accounts.
    - Organize and conduct annual North American Sales Meeting and Global Managers' Meeting.
- Reversed 3 years of declining sales for $7.5 million manufacturer and distributor of premium-priced, high-performance electrical maintenance products, anchoring and drilling equipment, and specialty chemicals.
    - Delivered revenues of $10 million, 33% ahead of previous year.
    - Won "District Manager of the Year" once and "District Manager of the Month" 11 times.

SALES TRAINING

- Devised and implemented personalized training programs for field personnel, plus conducted advanced training seminars for developing managers at corporate headquarters.
- Selected by top management to teach sales rep training seminars at corporate level.
- Expanded collegiate recruiting program.
- Created and instituted modular training programs;
- Only Zone Manager to successfully train and promote 2 District Managers in Boston and New York City districts.
- Recruited, hired, and trained 2 individuals who won "Sales Rep of the Year" and 3 out of 4 first-year inductees into company's "Hall of Fame."
- Trained third-place finisher for "New Sales Rep of the Year" developed and promoted 2 Field Trainers.

MEMBERSHIPS

Industrial Distributors Association
American Supply & Machinery Manufacturers Association
Member, Young Executive Forum
American Management Association

EDUCATION

Executive M.B.A. Program, University of New Hampshire, Durham, NH. 2002
B.S., Marketing, Boston University, Boston, MA. 1990

Peter R. Jensen
3912 Morrowick Road
Charlotte, NC 28226   Cell: (704) 607-4193 Tel: (704) 541-9234 E-mail: Peterjensen@home.com

SALES / SALES MANAGEMENT / MARKETING EXECUTIVE
o   Account Development & Management o   New Product Development
o   Territory Management o   Sales & Technical Training Programs
o   New Market Development o   Marketing Material Development
· 18-years' progressively responsible sales and marketing experience:
- Won multiple national awards for quota achievement, innovation, and sales / marketing excellence.
- Earned company-wide reputation for exceeding quota every year (achieving up to 153% of annual goal), converting competitive accounts, increasing business at existing accounts, turning around troubled accounts, penetrating new markets, and strengthening field sales organizations.
- Grew highly competitive account from annual sales of $130,000 to $1.8 million, capturing 95% of the business.
· Created numerous sales and marketing tools still in use today, some 12 years after their inception.
· Accomplished at developing new products and programs, then conducting domestic and international launches.
An innovative and energetic leader, skilled communicator / team builder, and adept sales representative, sales trainer, and sales manager. Recognized for ability to identify problem areas and growth opportunities, then create the necessary tools and mobilize the required resources to propel sales organizations to the next level of success. Accomplished at selling in fast-paced, rapidly changing markets plus developing long-term relationships with customers built on trust and exceptional service. A driven sales executive and marketer, tireless in the pursuit of quota achievement, quality business processes, expertly trained personnel, and corporate growth.

EXPERIENCE
Alliance Industries, Inc., New York, NY. 1983 - 2002
Leading manufacturer and distributor, with 2002 revenues in excess of $250 million.
Senior Account Representative, Charlotte, NC. 1997 - 2002
Responsible for sales in Charlotte territory. Activities included: providing technical support and conducting educational programs for users, developing and making financial presentations to senior management, managing teams of sales management and sales reps during key competitive conversions, implementing value-added programs at accounts, plus assisting in development of sales representatives.
· Exceeded quota every quarter, achieving as high as 201% in all products and up to 518% in individual products.
· Grew territory revenues in 9 quarters from $1.9 million to $3.7 million.
· Converted $1.5 million in key products at major customer-the first large conversion in the area, opening up numerous opportunities in other territories.
· Organized and managed 5-8 person team serving key account, with members including sales reps, sales managers, and product specialists from Mid-Atlantic Division.
· Won multiple awards, including Chairman's Council, President's Award, Winner's Circle, and special recognition for achieving over 100% of goal in every product category in 2001 and 2002.
Key Account Specialist, Charlotte, NC. 1995 - 1997

Responsible for resolving problems at troubled accounts and growing business in sales region consisting of half of North Carolina and almost all of South Carolina; region included 7 sales reps, 1 product specialist, and regional sales manager.

· Evaluated individual account situation, then developed strategic plan for generating business, including coordinating activities among company, the account, and local sales team.

· Focused activities on prestigious account where all business except for proprietary products had been lost to the competition. Developed and implemented value-added programs that resulted in immediate successes and laid the foundation for future conversions.

Concluding Words

A resume is an extremely subjective document. While everyone agrees that its primary goal is to paint an exciting picture of a job hunter's strengths, accomplishments, and capability, there's disagreement on the most effective way to do this. For example, when it comes to fonts, some people don't like Times Roman and prefer Ariel. Others dislike Ariel and believe that Garamond is best. There are also people who feel that in order for a resume to be effective, it must be one page in length. Others state that if people can express their experience and successes on only one page, they haven't done much in their career. There's even a book on the market today that advocates a five-page resume! The arguments go on and on, addressing other matters such as the proper way to compose the heading, how much information should appear in the introductory section, whether or not an objective should be included, the use of left-hand or full justification, what the correct amount of white space is, the value of providing personal information, and even where dates of employment should be placed.

The bottom line is that no matter how you prepare your resume, there will be something in it that someone could take issue with, only because of a personal preference. By writing your resume according to the guidelines of *The Resume Makeover*, however, you'll make a compelling impression on the greatest number of people possible and generate more interviews than you would through presenting your background any other way.

You should also understand that your resume isn't a magic wand that you can wave across the employment landscape to produce interviews at will. It's your primary job-search tool, but, still, only a tool.

Because an effective resume is an accomplishments-focused document, you won't have much success with certain job-search strategies if your resume doesn't contain a good number of accomplishments. These strategies include contacting recruiters, writing to prospective employers on an unsolicited basis, and answering Internet postings and classified ads. Here, your background simply won't compete with the other submissions that are packed with achievements. What you'll need to do is to concentrate your job-search efforts on networking, where you would meet with prospective employers through an introduction arranged by a mutual acquaintance.

Networking provides two key benefits: (1) you'll have little competition, if any, from other job hunters, and (2) you'll have immediate credibility due to the favorable remarks being made about you by the people who are sponsoring you. This credibility will often offset the lack of accomplishments in your resume. In fact, many employers will place more value on what your networking contact is saying about you than they will on the details of your work background. It is for these two reasons that employment experts agree that networking accounts for approximately 75 percent of all job changes.

If you do have a resume with a wealth of achievements, you'll be able to utilize the above-mentioned strategies. But you should also spend a good deal of time networking due to the results the approach traditionally brings.

Your resume will play a key role in the networking process. Whenever you're speaking with someone about your interest in setting up interviews, be sure that the person has a copy of your background. Nothing will make it easier for a networking contact to represent you than having this document to refer to since it showcases your successes. The result will be more interviews quicker.

If posting your resume on career Web sites will be part of your plan for generating interviews, you should expect to receive replies from people representing organizations known as retail-outplacement, career-management, and career-marketing firms. These individuals aggressively monitor employment sites in an effort to drum up business. They'll try to convince you of their expertise in resume writing and job hunting, then offer to rewrite your resume for a fee ranging from a few hundred dollars to as much as $1000 or conduct a job-search campaign for anywhere from several thousand dollars to $20,000. They'll also assure you that their fee will be reimbursed by your next employer.

I know many outstanding people in the career-services field, but not one of them advertises or prospects for business, or hires a sales force to do the prospecting for them. These proven producers have all the clients they need through referrals from their current and former clients due to the exceptional results they provide.

Be extremely wary when you're approached by people who saw your resume on a career Web site and now want to sell you a career service.

3

Writing High-Impact Cover Letters

When you send people your resume, whether it's through regular mail, overnight mail, e-mail, or a fax, it's important to include a one-page cover letter. This letter must be carefully written so that it's just as convincing a document as your resume. The reason for this is that the only purpose of a cover letter is to provide information about yourself that will make people want to *read* your resume.

Gone are the days when a cover letter was a formality, where it sufficed to offer a few sentences explaining that you were enclosing your resume because you wanted to set up an interview. The cover letter has evolved to the point where, today, it's a key component of a job search, and in order to be effective it must include important facts about your background, most notably your accomplishments. Many people will judge your qualifications as much on this letter as they will on your resume. If properly prepared, your cover letter will play an active role in developing interviews. If poorly prepared, it can cost you interviews, with prospective employers and recruiters simply filing your letter and resume away. In other words, your cover letter can't make you, but it can easily break you.

You may need a cover letter for as many as five different situations: (1) contacting prospective employers on an unsolicited basis, (2) writing to a prospective employer on an unsolicited basis but with a referral from a mutual acquaintance, (3) approaching recruiting firms, (4) answering Internet postings and/or classified advertisements, and (5) contacting venture capital firms.

In addition to these letters, there's another type of correspondence for generating interviews: the networking letter. This is where you write to someone not for the purpose of setting up an interview but, instead, to *elicit their help* in arranging interviews. Depending on how well you know the person, you may or may not include a resume with your letter.

You can seek this networking assistance under four different conditions: (1) when you have an ongoing relationship with someone; (2) when you have met someone, let's say, only once or twice; (3) when you don't know the person you want to talk to but have been referred to him or her by a mutual acquaintance; and (4) when you know of someone who is very influential (this could be a businessperson, community or religious leader, politician, physician, attorney, etc.) who has a wide range of contacts and you need to approach the person cold, without an introduction.

There's one final letter you'll want to have at your disposal, the one you'll write to the key individuals you met at an interview. Some people refer to this letter as a follow-up or thank-you letter, but it's purpose goes far beyond expressing appreciation for the interview.

Let's discuss each of these letters in detail.

Contacting Prospective Employers on an Unsolicited Basis

When writing to organizations that could possibly employ you, write by name and title to the person who has the authority to hire you, not to someone in the Human Resources Department. The people who work in this department are primarily responsible for the screening and administrative portions of the staffing process. They don't determine who should receive an offer (unless someone is applying for a position in their department). As in any other endeavor, it's best to deal directly with the ultimate decision maker.

There's one instance, however, when it's preferable to write to an HR representative. This is when someone is seeking an administrative or support-type position that could exist in a number of different departments throughout the organization. An HR representative will know exactly where an opening is and be able to forward the resume to the appropriate manager.

One caveat about trying to develop interviews through writing to the person who could hire you: If you feel that your background is so strong that this individual might be threatened by your successes and view you as competition for his or her job, then write to the person at the next level up. For example, a regional sales manager with a very powerful background would be better off writing to the vice president of sales than to the national sales manager.

To get the names and titles of the managers to write to, either call prospective employers on the phone or visit your local library. The reference librarian will show you the directories that list companies and the names of their key executives.

Here's how to write a cover letter for contacting prospective employers on an unsolicited basis.

The first paragraph is an introductory one. Give a brief overview of your background by explaining the type of position you hold and your key strengths. Then explain that you're writing to set up an interview and are enclosing your resume for this purpose.

The second part of your letter is the most important one. It contains the information that will prompt people to read your resume. Here, you state your most significant accomplishments so that you'll immediately convey your capability and the value you'll bring to your next employer. Look to the introductory section of your resume for the accomplishments to discuss. Just as in your resume, these are the hooks to get people's attention and interest. Be sure to reword the statements, though, so they don't appear verbatim.

You may then want to add one or two paragraphs to round out your background and further your qualifications. Topics to discuss include personal qualities and/or professional skills that have enabled you to excel at your work. What's especially effective is to mention a recent industry trend, along with the challenges or problems it's presenting, then explain how you're managing the situation to maximize your performance. Omit discussion about your earnings or compensation goals.

Your letter can conclude in a variety of ways depending on whether or not you plan on taking any follow-up action. Different possibilities for closing the letter will be discussed a little later in this chapter.

A sample cover letter follows on page 58.

If you're not accustomed to writing a letter with bullets, the format shown might seem strange to you. I strongly recommend it, however. Without the bullets, the accomplishments will be buried in the text, and the letter will have much less impact.

If you happen to be knowledgeable about the organization you're writing to, especially its products, services, recent successes, or future plans, say something to this effect. This will make an extremely favorable impression on the reader and give you a leg up on the competition. Here's how John Bellows would have begun his letter to Sigfreid Heinz at Illinois Protection Services had he had certain information about the company:

November 16, 2002

Mr. Sigfreid Heinz
VP - Operations
Illinois Protection Services, Inc.
2 North Riverside Plaza
Chicago, IL 60606

Dear Mr. Heinz:

I'm aware that you're considering installing a state-of-the-art IR system in your plants as well as utilizing canine patrols. I'm an accomplished security manager with over 15 years' experience in the field coupled with an extensive background in both of these areas. At the present time I'm seeking a new opportunity and challenge and would like to meet with you to discuss how my background could play a key role in your security program. My resume is enclosed for your review. Select highlights include:

John A. Bellows
530 Frazier Court
Wheaton, IL 60187
(630) 665-3975
Jab17@msn.com

November 16, 2002

Mr. Sigfreid Heinz
VP - Operations
Illinois Protection Services, Inc.
2 North Riverside Plaza
Chicago, IL 60606

Dear Mr. Heinz:

As an accomplished security manager, I have over 15 years' experience in the field, with employers consisting of both corporations and security services, namely Motorola, American Express, and Burns / Pinkerton. Key strengths include multiple-site responsibility, program development and implementation, executive protection, loss prevention, crisis management, guard services, investigations, and logistics. At the present time I'm exploring career opportunities on a confidential basis and would like to meet with you to discuss how my background could play a key role in your growth and future plans. My resume is enclosed for your review. Select highlights include:

- Created and instituted programs that reduced monthly incidents 83% from 278 violations per month to 48.
- Initiated and introduced programs that provided 100% safety to executive personnel, with zero incidents to report.
- Revamped daily procedures, plus revised bid processes for new equipment and services, resulting in 15% annual reductions in operating costs.
- Planned and administered budgets ranging to $2.2 million, with the responsibility for 15 administrative, manufacturing, warehousing, and sales facilities totaling over 3.2 million square feet and housing 10,700 employees.

Employers recognize me for my comprehensive knowledge of state-of-the-art security procedures and equipment. I am also known for my ability to build and lead dedicated teams of personnel.

I am eager to meet with you and look forward to your reply. Thank you in advance for reviewing my background.

Sincerely,

John A. Bellows

Writing to a Prospective Employer on an Unsolicited Basis When Referred by a Mutual Acquaintance

If you're fortunate enough to have a referral to a prospective employer, nothing could be more powerful. This introduction will give you instant credibility and carry just as much weight, if not more, than any of your accomplishments. When referred to someone, you're immediately a known quantity versus being one of dozens or possibly hundreds of job hunters trying to set up an interview. For this reason, always begin your cover letter by explaining that you're writing at the suggestion of a mutual acquaintance.

Here's how John Bellows would have begun his letter had he been referred to Sigfreid Heinz at Illinois Protection Services:

November 16, 2002

Mr. Sigfreid Heinz
VP - Operations
Illinois Protection Services, Inc.
2 North Riverside Plaza
Chicago, IL 60606

Dear Mr. Heinz:

Paulette Hastings suggested I contact you. I'm an accomplished security manager with over 15 years' experience in the field. Employers have consisted of both corporations and security services, namely Motorola, American Express, and Burns / Pinkerton. My key strengths include multiple-site responsibility, program development and implementation, executive protection, loss prevention, crisis management, guard services, investigations, and logistics. At the present time I''m seeking a new opportunity and challenge and would like to meet with you to discuss how my background could play a key role in your security program. My resume is enclosed for your review. Select highlights include:

Beginnings and Endings

Many people know exactly what they want to say in their cover letter but have difficulty deciding how to begin and close the letter. Here are some suggestions. The different ways to begin the letter are underlined for your convenience.

Beginnings

As a graduating student with a B.S. - Marketing degree from Boston University, enclosed is my resume for consideration for an entry-level position in your Marketing Department.

I'm an accomplished quality inspector at International Bearings, Inc. Supervisors repeatedly praise me for both my speed and accuracy.

During the past seven years, I have progressed from sales representative to key account manager to district sales trainer. I take great pride in my ability to establish outstanding relationships with customers that are built on trust and mutual respect and that result in record sales. I'm equally proud of my communication and training skills, which enable me to develop high-performing sales representatives and account managers.

Recruited by the Bank of America as a senior customer service representative, I have a history of accomplishment in selling life insurance, fixed and variable annuities, and mutual funds to both new and existing customers. I'm equally proud of my success in resolving the numerous problems that customers encounter, especially with their checking accounts, savings accounts, IRAs, and government savings bonds.

With 10 years' experience in corporate real estate, I have a record of success in purchasing, leasing, and managing office space, including disposing of properties and subleasing surplus space. I'm currently responsible for over 3 million square feet.

Throughout my career as a finance and insurance manager in the auto industry, I developed excellent relationships with lenders to ensure the maximum acceptance of loan applications, especially risky ones. I also compiled an enviable record of selling add-ons.

Some job hunters believe that a strong attention-getting device is to begin their letter by asking a question, such as:

Are you in need of a strong quality control engineer?

Is your company's growth rate less than you would like it to be?

Does your company embrace the principle of continuous improvement?

Are you having trouble finding the ideal candidate for the Controller position currently posted on your Web site?

This is actually a much weaker way to start than by immediately conveying your responsibilities and key strengths. Don't begin your letter with a question.

Endings

There are numerous ways to close your letter, with the main variable being whether or not you plan to follow up with a phone call:

I appreciate your time and consideration and look forward to meeting (speaking with) you. Thank you in advance for reviewing my background.

Thank you for your time and consideration, and I look forward to speaking with (meeting) you.

I appreciate (Thank you for) your time in reviewing my qualifications (credentials) (background), and I look forward to meeting (speaking with) you.

I would welcome the opportunity to meet with you in person and will follow up next week.

I would welcome an interview and look forward to hearing from you.

I am eager to meet with you and look forward to your reply.

I am eager to meet with you and will call your office next week to discuss the appropriate next step.

I am eager to meet with you to discuss your current needs and future plans and how my background could play a role in helping to attain your growth goals.

Let me plan on following up with you shortly (next week) to discuss the appropriate next step. Thank you in advance for reviewing my credentials (qualifications) (background).

Thank you for reviewing my background (credentials) (qualifications). I will phone you next week to follow up, and I look forward to meeting you.

Thank you in advance for reviewing my background (credentials) (qualifications). I appreciate your confidentiality and look forward to your reply.

Thank you in advance for reviewing my background (credentials) (qualifications). I look forward to your reply and a personal meeting where we can exchange information regarding my background and goals and your company and its future plans.

If you have a need for an individual with my capability, I would be delighted to interview with you. Thank you in advance for reviewing my background (credentials) (qualifications).

Increasing the Odds of an Interview

Research has shown that speaking with the person to whom you've written can increase the likelihood of an interview.

Depending on the number of letters you'll be mailing and the chances of reaching someone on the telephone, consider concluding your letter with

Thank you in advance for reviewing my background. I will call you next week to discuss the appropriate next step.

Methods of Contacting Potential Employers

Several options are available for sending people your cover letter and resume: regular and overnight mail, faxing, and e-mail.

Despite the ease and popularity of using the Internet, when it comes to contacting prospective employers on an unsolicited basis, it's best to send them a letter. A letter is a much more personal document. Also, your e-mail could get deleted because the recipient didn't recognize your screen name. When many people check their electronic mail, they immediately delete the "junk." Your correspondence could be put in this category by mistake.

Contacting Recruiters

Your letter to recruiters will be the same as the one you write to prospective employers, with the exception of the statements that are underlined in the example that appears on page 62.

The Question of Salary

There's no hard-and-fast rule as to whether or not you should discuss your compensation level with recruiters. Many job hunters do, while a large number do not. I recommend that you include this information. A recruiter may specialize in your field and therefore have several positions to discuss with you, either now or in the future. Knowing what your compensation level is will save both of you time.

You need not be specific when discussing your income. A brief statement like Leonard Watkins made in the fourth paragraph of his letter will suffice.

E-Mailing Recruiters

Recruiters are inundated with cover letters and resumes. Some prefer to receive e-mail while others prefer hard copy. If you opt for the electronic means, conclude your e-mail message by stating that your resume is being sent as both a cut-and-paste document and an attachment. Some recruiters will read only the cut-and-paste version because they don't want to risk a virus. Others are confident in their anti-virus software and will read an attachment, where the formatting remains in tact. Give recruiters a choice.

Leonard R. Watkins
29061 Hamden Lane
Huntington Beach, CA 92646
(714) 593-3972
Lenwat@socal.rr.com

January 4, 2003

Mr. Thomas L. Bradbury
Costello & Bradbury Executive Search Consultants
1727 State St.
Santa Barbara, CA 93101

Dear Mr. Bradbury:

I'm an accomplished corporate tax manager with 15 years of experience and a history of success working for companies in manufacturing, financial services, and information technology. Key strengths include tax minimization, state and federal compliance, planning and research, acquisitions, and audits. At the present time I'm exploring career opportunities on a confidential basis <u>and would like to apprise you of my background.</u> My resume is enclosed for your review. Key highlights include:

- Directed the Tax Department for Sebastian Technology, a manufacturer with 15 subsidiary companies totaling $200 million in annual sales.
- Started up and managed U.S. Ventures' Tax Department, responsible for 70 companies in 20 states. Played an instrumental role in restructuring the organization as well as in its IPO.
- Identified numerous opportunities for tax refunds at all employers, realizing rebates as large as $1 million.

I take great pride in my strategic planning strengths, which have enabled me to make significant contributions to organizations undergoing rapid change and increasing competitive pressures. I'm equally proud of my ability to use strong analytical, planning, and organizational skills in the development and implementation of innovative solutions to complex tax challenges and business problems. I hold a Master of Accountancy and am a CPA with Big 5 experience.

You should be aware that my salary and bonus have been in the $100,000-$135,000 range the past few years. This does not include stock options and benefits.

<u>Please contact me at your convenience if you need any additional information. Otherwise, I look forward to hearing from you when my background is appropriate for a client need.</u>

Thank you in advance for reviewing my credentials.

Sincerely,

Leonard R. Watkins

If you happen to have a Web site, post your cover letter and resume on it; then provide e-mail recipients with a link to your URL so they can click right on.

This Web resume/cover letter approach provides several advantages. First, the transmission is fast while providing higher quality print than faxing. Second, you maintain the formatting that's automatically lost when pasting your cover letter and resume into an e-mail message. Third, recipients don't have to download your materials, eliminating concern about a virus.

It won't be worth your while to follow up with recruiters after sending them your resume. If your background is appropriate for a client's need, you'll be contacted immediately since you represent a potential fee of 15 to 30 percent of your first year's compensation. Recruiters will also place your resume in their database and contact you in the future when they're working on an assignment that requires your experience.

Answering Internet Postings and Classified Ads

Responding to ads posted on the Internet or that appear in the classified section of newspapers and trade publications requires a completely different cover letter.

Here, you begin the letter by referencing the announcement, then presenting your qualifications according to the requirements that have been listed. If an ad asks for any experience that doesn't appear in your resume, and you have performed this work, be sure to discuss these activities in your letter.

When you describe your background, always look to the bulleted statements that appear in the introduction to your resume, rewording them, of course, so they don't appear verbatim.

In the event that there's a specific reason why you'd like to work for a certain organization, discuss this in your cover letter, so long as your reason has to do with career advancement or the company's growth record or prospects for expansion. Topics could include the company's products, services, recent successes, or future plans. Never state that you're interested in joining an organization because of, for example, its location or elegant offices. Additionally, if there's something special in your background that would advance your candidacy with a particular company, be sure to discuss this.

Many ads ask applicants to furnish their salary history or the level of compensation they're seeking. Whether or not you should provide this information depends on a number of factors:

First of all, you don't want to be evaluated on financial matters before you've had the opportunity to speak with a prospective employer or recruiter and discuss your qualifications. If your salary is low, your capability could be suspect and you might be ruled out. If your earnings are high, you could be rejected because you wouldn't fit into the salary range that's been established for the position. However, if you have the opportunity to first speak with a recruiter or prospective employer, you can counter any objection that's made about your compensation level.

For example, if your salary is low, you can explain that you're working for an organization that has a low pay scale but offers an outstanding benefits package. If your salary is high, you can state that you have flexibility concerning compensation and that there are other factors that are equally important to you. In addition, you might demonstrate during the conversation that you have certain talents that the company wasn't expecting but would be willing to compensate you for.

Other factors to consider are how strong your qualifications are for the position under consideration and how large a response you think the company will receive. The stronger you suspect the competition will be, the more pressing it will be to provide the compensation information requested, since the company might initially contact only those applicants who offered this information. However, if your qualifications are exceptional, and your background is in great demand but difficult to find, companies will be more inclined to contact you even though you didn't comply with their request.

A final factor to consider is how high or low your salary is. The further away it is from what could be considered the norm for the position you're applying for, the more of a barrier it will be.

Weigh all these factors when you see an employment opportunity that interests you, then use your best judgment in deciding how to treat the request for salary information.

If you decide not to discuss salary, conclude your letter by stating, "I would be pleased to discuss compensation during a personal conversation." Here, you're acknowledging the company's request and not being rude by ignoring it.

The only time it's essential to discuss your earnings is when an ad states "Refusal to provide salary history will result in disqualification." You will see this statement very rarely.

When answering ads and Internet postings, follow the instructions being given for submission. If no specific instructions are offered and you'll be e-mailing, state at the end of your cover letter "My resume follows as both a cut-and-paste document and an attachment."

A template for answering ads and Internet postings is shown on page 65. An ad that appeared in the *Wall Street Journal* for a Customer Service Manager and the cover letter that was prepared in response are provided on pages 66 and 67.

Cover Letters for Networking

It bears repeating that networking accounts for approximately 75 percent of all job changes. Because of the overwhelming success of this strategy, it should play a key role in your search campaign.

When networking, you approach people for information, not for a job interview. This is because the likelihood is that any individual you contact will not have a position for you, but he or she may very well know of someone who could hire you or know of people who could lead you in the right direction. The more people you speak with, the larger your network of contacts will become and the quicker you'll find your new position.

Your Name
Street Address
City, State Zip Code
Telephone Number
E-mail Address

Date

Name and Title of Person (if available)
Name of Company (if available)
Street Address (if available)
City, State Zip Code (if available)
(E-mail address)
(Fax number)

Dear (name of person):   (if blind box ad, write, ''Dear Sir or Madam'')

I read with great interest your advertisement for a (name of position) that appeared (on the Internet) in the (date) issue of the (name of newspaper or trade magazine). I have the background and qualifications you're seeking and would like to set up an interview to discuss this opportunity. My resume is enclosed for your review. (My resume follows as both a cut-and-paste document and an attachment.)

Important factors in my experience include:

-
- State important things about your work experience, strengths, and educational background
- that address the requirements listed in the ad.
-

My resume will amplify on these successes as well as discuss other significant parts of my background.

I look forward to a personal meeting where we can discuss my background and goals and how they relate to your current needs and future plans.

Thank you in advance for reviewing my credentials.

Sincerely,

Your Name

CUSTOMER SERVICE MANAGER

Excellent growth opportunity with a Long Island, NY-based nationwide distributor of medically related CNC electro-mechanical equipment. We seek a technically strong manager to achieve our goal of providing the highest customer satisfaction in the industry.

Candidate must have a proven record of innovative solutions for technically oriented customer after-sales service. Attributes required are vision, integrity, creativity, team-building strengths and in-depth knowledge of the customer service function. You will direct a department consisting of technical telephone support, field service, and in-shop repair personnel and will report to the Director of Operations. Candidates must possess a BA/BS, preferably in engineering, as well as 5+ years' management experience in this capacity.

If you are equally customer and profit-driven, with strong analytical, communication, and leadership skills, e-mail or mail your resume and salary history to:

Customer Service
34 East Main St. PMB 235
Smithtown, NY 11787
or ldc0713612001@yahoo.com

Following are the four networking letters you can write. While each one has a different tone, the letters have three things in common: You state the type of position you're interested in; you tell the recipient that you'd like to return the favor you're asking for; and you close the letter by stating that you'll be following up with a phone call. In two of the letters, you also enclose your resume.

Writing to Someone with Whom You Have an Ongoing Relationship

This letter is the least formal of the four and far less formal than the cover letters you would write to prospective employers and recruiters (see p. 68). This is also one of the networking letters that states you're enclosing your resume. Not only will this document provide your networking contacts with a complete understanding of your background, it will also enable them to send your resume to others.

The purpose of this letter is to show how markedly different the tone can be from other letters we've discussed. Since it's unlikely that the last company you worked for was just sold, here's how to begin your letter in a way that would be appropriate for your situation.

Dear Steve:

As you know, I'm a manufacturing manager at American Sprinkler. While things are going well, I would be interested in talking to other companies, especially if I could increase my level of responsibility and join a company that has greater prospects for growth. I'm hoping you'll have some ideas for me, either people to talk to who could hire me or who could arrange introductions for me elsewhere.

So that you're up to date on my background . . .

Peter R. Fleming
459 Tamarack Avenue
San Carlos, CA 94070
Tel: 650-595-4025
E-mail: pf19511956@yahoo.com

March 22, 2003

Customer Service
34 East Main St. PMB 235
Smithtown, NY 11787

Dear Sir or Madam:

I read with great interest your advertisement for a Customer Service Manager that appeared in the March 18th issue of *The Wall Street Journal*. I have the experience and qualifications you're seeking and would like to set up an interview to discuss this opportunity. My resume is enclosed for your review.

Important factors in my background include:

- 8 years' experience managing customer service departments, with activities including telephone support, field service, and in-shop repair.
- Developed and implemented processes that reduced call-waiting time 50%, increased the number of daily service calls 20%, and improved customer satisfaction 35%.
- I'm recognized as an outstanding leader, communicator, and team builder.
- My educational background includes a B.S.M.E.

My resume will amplify on these successes as well as discuss other significant parts of my background.

I would be delighted to discuss compensation during a personal conversation.

I look forward to speaking with you, where we can discuss my background and goals and how they relate to your current needs and future plans.

Thank you in advance for reviewing my credentials.

Sincerely,

Peter R. Fleming

Thomas J. D'Orsey
105 N. Stafford Street
Arlington, VA 22203
703-516-4518
Tjdorsey@metronets.com

October 22, 2002

Mr. Steven H. Bigelow
1735 Spruce St.
Arlington, VA 22203

Dear Steve:

A few months ago, I never would have imagined that I would be writing you this kind of letter. I just got the shock of my life: Baxter has sold my division, and the company that bought us isn't going to be keeping any of the management team. That means I'm looking for a job! I'm hoping you'll have some ideas for me, either people to talk to who could hire me or who could arrange introductions for me elsewhere.

So that you're up to date on my background, I have 10 years' experience in the manufacture of electromechanical products, the last three years in management. With a B.S.I.E., my successes include laying out plants, starting up new operations, as well as improving existing production processes. I'm experienced in KanBan, Kaizen, JIT, QS and ISO, cellular manufacturing, lean manufacturing, and demand flow. I have worked in union and non-union plants as well as in high-volume, intermittent-run, and job shop environments. My resume is enclosed so you'll have all the facts about my background, especially my achievements in reducing cycle times, costs, and inventories, while improving quality and productivity. Colleagues recognize me as an outstanding manufacturing manager, and that's the type of position I'm after.

I'll give you a call next week to follow up, Steve. Any suggestions you might have would be great. Of course, if there's anything I can do to return the favor, either now or in the future, just let me know.

Very truly yours,

Thomas J. D'Orsey

Writing to Someone You've Met Only Briefly

This letter requires a more formal tone. Your resume is also omitted because you don't want to do anything that might lead the recipient to believe that you're trying to set up a job interview with them versus elicit their assistance. Unfortunately, networking has been misused and abused over the years, and some people might be suspicious about your true intention if you enclosed your resume. Many job hunters have used their interest in getting introductions as a guise, when they were really trying to develop a job interview with the person to whom they were writing. The letter on page 70 is an example of how to write to someone when you've met them just one or two times.

Writing to Someone You Don't Know but Have Been Referred To

When you have the luxury of being referred to someone, begin your correspondence by stating the name of the person who suggested you write the letter. This will give you immediate credibility and ensure that your letter will be read. Then proceed along the lines of the first networking letter, including enclosing your resume. A letter demonstrating how Thomas D'Orsey would have altered his letter had he been referred to Livingston Otis by Steven Bigelow follows on page 71.

Writing to a Prospective Networking Contact You've Never Met and without a Referral

Of the four networking letters, this has the least likelihood of generating interviews. The letter does produce results, though, and its salient feature is that it enables you to approach any individual of your choice. For example, you might know of someone in your industry or community who is extremely well connected and who would be in a position to arrange introductions for you if you could establish a relationship with them. This letter is your entrée.

When writing the letter, your tone must be much more businesslike, and you never include your resume. If you were to do so, you'd probably lose all credibility, with the recipient believing that you're really looking for a job at his or her company. For this reason, provide less information about yourself, especially your successes. If you've struck an empathetic ear, the recipient will respond to your request, regardless of your achievements. An example of such a letter appears on page 72.

Contacting Venture Capital Firms

Contacting venture capital firms is only appropriate for senior-level executives. These companies have equity positions in a number of start-up and emerging businesses, and it's possible that at the time you contact them they could have a need for someone with your background.

The letter you would write would be almost identical to the one used for contacting prospective employers, with the exception of one change in the introductory paragraph. An example of the letter, with that change underlined, is shown on page 73.

Holly Reppert
2372 Vallejo St.
San Francisco, CA 94123
(941) 921-4063
Holrep@aol.com

February 21, 2003

Ms. Barbara Strax
2531 Baker St.
San Francisco, CA 94123

Dear Barbara:

We met a couple of weekends ago at Alice and Tom's party, where we talked about the upcoming walk-a-thon. I really enjoyed our conversation and look forward to seeing you at the event.

I hope you don't think this is presumptuous of me, but I've recently begun a job search and would like to acquaint you with my background, hoping you might know of people who would be interested in talking to me. Alice had mentioned to me that you know a large number of people in the area.

To summarize my experience, I've been in outside sales for 15 years, most recently selling software to businesses but before that selling insurance and office equipment. I have an outstanding track record in opening new accounts as well as penetrating new markets. In fact, I've been one of the top-producing sales reps at Diamondback for several years now. Colleagues recognize me as an outstanding closer as well as someone who is skilled at developing new business through the consultative approach. I have always found it easy and fun to generate leads, then develop business through showing people the value that my products and services would bring to their companies. I see myself as a career B2B sales rep/account manager; I'm not interested in running a sales organization.

I would be most appreciative if you could share with me any ideas you might have regarding companies and/or individuals for me to talk to. Needless to say, if there is any way I can return the favor, please do not hesitate to ask. I will give you a call next week to follow up. Thank you in advance.

Sincerely,

Holly Reppert

Thomas J. D'Orsey
105 N. Stafford Street
Arlington, VA 22203
703-516-4518
Tjdorsey@metronets.com

August 17, 2002

Livingston Otis
325 Elm Street
Arlington, VA 22203

Dear Livingston:

Steve Bigelow suggested I write to you. I've been with American Sprinkler for four years now, and I'm a manufacturing manager there. While things are going well, I would be interested in talking to other companies, especially if I could increase my level of responsibility and join a company that has greater prospects for growth. Steve thought you might have some ideas for me, either people to talk to who could hire me or who could arrange introductions for me elsewhere.

Briefly, I have 10 years' experience in the manufacture of electromechanical products, the last three years being in management. With a B.S.I.E., my background includes laying out plants, starting up new operations, as well as improving existing production processes. I'm experienced in KanBan, Kaizen, JIT, QS and ISO, cellular manufacturing, lean manufacturing, and demand flow. I have worked in union and non-union plants as well as in high-volume, intermittent-run, and job shop environments. My resume is enclosed so you'll have all the facts about my background, especially my successes in reducing cycle times, costs, and inventories, while enhancing quality and productivity. Colleagues recognize me as an outstanding manufacturing manager, and that is the type of position I'm seeking.

Let me thank you in advance for your anticipated help, Livingston. If there's anything I can do to return the favor, either now or in the future, please let me know. I'll give you a call in a few days to follow up.

Sincerely,

Thomas J. D'Orsey

Gregory W. Handler
1205 West 20th Avenue
Spokane, WA 99203
(509) 747-3739
g.handler@attbi.com

January 5, 2003

MaryJo Aronovici
VP-Finance
Washington Engineered Products, Inc.
North 4407 Division St.
Northtown Office Bldg., Suite #900
Spokane, WA 99207

Dear Ms. Aronovici:

With eight years' experience as a division controller then corporate controller, I have compiled a record of success at high-tech manufacturers, service organizations, and retailers. Key contributions have included delivering reductions in costs and increases in operating efficiencies. I'm currently seeking a new opportunity and challenge and am writing to ask for your assistance in my search. Due to the position you hold at Washington Engineered Products, I imagine that you know a large number of people in the area.

The first step in a carefully planned job search requires obtaining information. This is where I'm hoping you will be able to help me. I'm seeking the names of individuals at other companies. These people might have positions for me, but if not, they might be able to suggest other individuals for me to contact. Career experts estimate that 75% of the job openings are never made public, and that the key to uncovering these opportunities is to elicit information from as many people as possible.

I realize you're busy, Ms. Aronovici, but I would appreciate it if you would give me just a few minutes of your time. I'll call you next Tuesday, and hopefully you will have been able to jot down names of people that came to mind. If there's any way I can return the favor to express my appreciation, please do not hesitate to ask.

Thank you in advance.

Sincerely,

Gregory W. Handler

Lawrence R. Danforth
10 Bevelander Place
West Sayville, NY 11796
Tel: (631) 567-4697
LRD@aol.com

February 25, 2003

Mr. James Sykes
Managing Partner
Everest Associates
370 Lexington Avenue
New York, NY 10017

Dear Mr. Sykes:

Heading up companies' sales and marketing initiatives for the past 10 years, I have amassed a record of achievement in the composite chemicals and coatings industry, most recently with International Chemicals & Coatings. Key strengths include P&L management, strategic planning, turnarounds, start-ups, new market development, and e-commerce. At the present time I'm seeking a new opportunity and challenge and would like to meet with you <u>to discuss how my background could be of value to one of the companies in your investment portfolio</u>. My resume is enclosed for your review. Select highlights include:

- Delivered sales of $302 million in 2002, which was 21% ahead of the 2001 level and at a growth rate 73% higher than the industry norm.
- Led a team to profitability for the first time in the organization's 5-year history, while generating the largest divisional profit increase in 4 years.
- Grew the eastern region's sales over 200%, from $20 million in 1996 to $61 million in 2000, while producing the fastest dollar volume growth in the country. Concurrently, increased the region's contribution to national sales from 26% to 32%.

Many of my accomplishments resulted from building dedicated and motivated teams that supported me in my mission. I have the proven ability to recognize and attract top talent as well as create an environment where people work with commitment to achieve established goals.

In short, I combine outstanding human relations skills with the management knowledge, resourcefulness, and drive that are required to propel an organization to the next level of success and profitability.

Thank you in advance for reviewing my background. I appreciate your confidentiality and look forward to your reply.

Sincerely,

Lawrence R. Danforth

The Follow-Up or Thank-You Letter

While this isn't actually a cover letter, it's an important letter to write to prospective employers.

After you've been interviewed by an organization, follow up by writing a letter to each of the key people you met. This letter has several purposes.

First of all, it's both courteous and good job-search etiquette to express your appreciation for the meeting. Always begin the letter with this sentiment.

Second, the letter enables you to convey your understanding of the company's key needs and your ability to fill them. This will reinforce your capability and advance your candidacy.

Third, the letter is an excellent opportunity to express your interest in joining the organization. Just as you want a potential employer to be enthusiastic about hiring you, employers want applicants to be enthusiastic about working for them. Don't be concerned that stating your interest in joining the organization will result in a lower salary offer. It won't. Besides, a company's initial offer is negotiable.

Fourth, you can present an important piece of information that you may have omitted during the interview.

Fifth, you can discuss a point that you think may require clarification or clear up a misconception you believe the interviewer may have about something the two of you discussed.

An example of a follow-up letter is provided.

Ronald F. Owsley
213 Maplewood Dr.
Cedar Falls, IA 50613
(319) 266-6294
RFO17@aol.com

February 23, 2003

Ms. Arlene Magee
Executive Vice President
The Thompson Companies, Inc.
400 Locust St.
Des Moines, IA 50309

Dear Arlene:

It was a great pleasure meeting with you yesterday, and I want to thank you for the time you gave me. Our conversation was as informative as it was enjoyable.

There's no doubt about the success Thompson will have in the years to come. With your rapidly expanding customer base and continuous product innovation, you will be one of the key players in the industry, in both domestic and international markets. I would certainly enjoy being a member of the team.

You mentioned that several HR functions were of critical importance to you, and I would like to summarize my successes in these areas:

Recruitment. This is one of my greatest strengths. I have established the function for start-up companies plus completely revamped it for established organizations. New programs that I have instituted have reduced recruitment costs up to 73% and decreased hiring cycles as much as 60%. Staffing responsibilities have ranged from the executive level to temporary workers.

Training. I have saved companies large sums of money through bringing training in-house versus outsourced. Management programs that I have developed have improved the quality of service delivery, morale, and job satisfaction, resulting in turnover dropping from as high as 65% to 20%.

Compensation & Benefits. My contributions in this area have been extensive. Healthcare plan costs have been reduced as much as 20% with no reduction in extent of benefits or increase in cost to employees. I have also changed 401k retirement plan providers, decreasing costs as much as 85%. As far as compensation is concerned, I have implemented pay-for-performance programs, where salary increases, bonuses, and long-term incentive awards were linked to results. I have also introduced stock option programs as an incentive for all employees, not just executives, plus developed global and country-specific sales incentive plans that resulted in significantly higher revenues and profits.

Union Avoidance. Key successes in this area include identifying and thwarting a local Teamsters' attempt to organize drivers as well as detecting and eliminating the IBEW's attempt to organize assembly workers.

As you can see, I am a true HR generalist, with both breadth and depth of experience. Top management has always praised me on my ability to understand corporate needs and goals, then develop and implement HR programs and processes that facilitate the attainment of those goals. I feel confident that I could make major contributions to Thompson and play a vital role in driving the company to an industry-leading position.

I look forward to speaking with you in the near future. Again, thank you for the meeting yesterday.

Sincerely,

Ronald F. Owsley

II

FIXING THE 50 COMMON PROBLEMS IN WRITING RESUMES AND COVER LETTERS

Problems with Presenting Work Experience in Resumes

Problem 1: Omitting an Introductory Section

Alexander has a superb background, but her resume lacks the key component necessary for generating the maximum number of interviews: a powerful introductory section. By omitting this section, Alexander is asking people to wade through two pages of information without knowing anything about her capability. A number of readers will balk and turn to the next resume.

Joyce Alexander

1080 Beacon St.
Brookline, Massachusetts 02116
Tel: (617) 262-3806
E-mail: jalexander@hotmail.com

PROFESSIONAL EXPERIENCE

The Saltonstall Performing Arts Centre, Boston, Massachusetts. November 1996 - Present
Executive Director
P&L responsibility for all artistic and administrative functions at this 1,700-seat performing arts hall. Responsible for planning and directing all functions, including strategic planning, operations, programming, fund-raising, and outreach. Serve over 300,000 patrons annually with over 250 events per year. Annual budget in excess of $8 million.

- Operate facility at 96% of earned income, versus industry average of 55%.

- Increased operating reserve more than 70% and grew capital reserve 200%.

- Expanded programming direction and developed new patrons from more diverse demographics, yielding 8% increase in ticket revenues.

- Implemented innovative marketing programs that increased event attendance up to 400%.

- Redesigned institutional image and logo in all marketing materials, media exposures, and brochures.

- Achieved numerous goals of "Vision 2015," the long-range plan to position the hall for the future. Accomplishments included expanding educational and outreach component, securing additional funding, and implementing an architectural / engineering survey.

- Initiated Boston Hall Corporate Circle, plus expanded grants program to generate 10-fold increase in acquisitions from public and private sources.

- Achieved "First Place" designation in highly competitive Boston Cultural Institutions Program and received $617,000 grant.

- Conceived of, created, and instituted comprehensive education and outreach program to serve Boston and develop new audiences.

- Initiated measures to improve patron satisfaction and maximize revenues from box office and food and beverage services.

- Created and implemented training programs for both staff and volunteers to ensure finest service possible.

- Designed and implemented major anniversary season with numerous special programs, including 30-minute televised documentary on the facility. Program was aired nationally.

- Completed comprehensive architectural and engineering evaluation addressing major renovation, expansion, and facility addition.

- Directed extensive training as well as internship program in all phases of operations.

The problem is solved in the makeover by the addition of the introductory section. Alexander's impeccable qualifications are thereby established at the outset. Her compelling discussion ensures maximum readership.

Joyce Alexander
1080 Beacon St.
Brookline, MA 02116

(617) 262-3806
jalexander@hotmail.com

PERFORMING-ARTS-HALL MANAGEMENT

- **P&L Responsibility**
- **Strategic Planning**
- **Programming**

- **Operations**
- **Fiscal Management**
- **Fund-raising**

- Operated facilities at up to 96% of earned income versus industry average of 55%, while expanding operating reserve more than 70% and capital reserve up to 200%.
- Introduced initiatives that increased ticket revenues up to 8% and event attendance to 400%.
- Conceived of, planned, and instituted events that were covered by international media; also created an anniversary season that was covered by national television.

A distinguished career in developing and managing all facets of performing-arts centers, with a history of success at increasing revenues and attendance as well as booking world-class artists from diverse genres. Well-traveled and knowledgeable of different cultures. Conversant in Russian, Spanish, and French.

EXPERIENCE

The Saltonstall Performing Arts Centre, Boston, MA. 1996 - Present
Executive Director

P&L responsibility for all artistic and administrative functions at this 1,700-seat performing arts hall. Responsible for planning and directing all functions, including strategic planning, operations, programming, fund-raising, and outreach. Serve over 300,000 patrons annually with over 250 events per year. Annual budget in excess of $8 million.

- Operate facility at 96% of earned income, versus industry average of 55%.
- Increased operating reserve more than 70% and grew capital reserve 200%.
- Expanded programming direction and developed new patrons from more diverse demographics, yielding 8% increase in ticket revenues.
- Implemented innovative marketing programs that increased event attendance up to 400%.
- Redesigned institutional image and logo in all marketing materials, media exposures, and brochures.
- Achieved numerous goals of "Vision 2015," the long-range plan to position the hall for the future. Accomplishments included expanding educational and outreach component, securing additional funding, and implementing an architectural / engineering survey.
- Initiated Boston Hall Corporate Circle, plus expanded grants program to generate 10-fold increase in acquisitions from public and private sources.
- Achieved "First Place" designation in highly competitive Boston Cultural Institutions Program and received $617,000 grant.
- Conceived of, created, and instituted comprehensive education and outreach program to serve Boston and develop new audiences.
- Initiated measures to improve patron satisfaction and maximize revenues from box office and food and beverage services.
- Created and implemented training programs for both staff and volunteers to ensure finest service possible.
- Designed and implemented major anniversary season with numerous special programs, including 30-minute televised documentary on the facility. Program was aired nationally.

Problem 2: Writing Too Lengthy an Introductory Section

Because the introduction is so long, many people won't bother to read it. As a result, they won't read the rest of the resume either.

BARRY J. TOMLINSON
120 East 75th Street
(212) 717-2377
New York, NY 10021
bjtomlinson@hotmail.com

SUMMARY

A highly qualified and results-driven top management executive bringing extensive experience in planning and implementing domestic and international business development directives as well as experience in complete fiscal control. Establish strategic direction through innovative business planning and development strategies, boosting profit margins and securing competitive market positions.

High-caliber presentation, negotiation, and closing skills demonstrated through domestic and international experience developing businesses and coordinating major mergers and acquisitions. A catalyst for change, transformation, and performance improvement, utilizing bilingual and bicultural capabilities to expand business opportunities and drive revenue increases. Passion for building company growth, facilitating new product development, and executing market penetration as demonstrated by proven, consistent track record of delivering positive bottom-line results.

AREAS OF EXPERTISE

P&L Management
Domestic and International Business Formation / Expansion
Acquisition and Divestiture Implementation
Strategic Planning and Launch
Resource Planning and Management Development
Total Quality Management
Marketing and Sales Strategy
New Product Development
International and Domestic Legislation
Compensation and Benefits Administration
General Cost Accounting
Legal Administration
Financial Analysis and Planning
Commercial and Investment Banking

PROFESSIONAL HIGHLIGHTS

- Instrumental in structuring, negotiating, and forming corporations, partnerships, and joint ventures.
- Planned, negotiated, and implemented complex acquisitions and divestitures.
- Provided vision and direction to reposition a company to capitalize on technology and market demand.
- Launched aggressive infrastructure redesign to streamline financial areas.
- Served on corporate boards and partnership steering committees.
- Formulated and implemented Total Quality Management and zero injury programs.
- Designed and implemented company-wide 401(k) plan.
- Integrated innovative marketing techniques into fast-paced environment, increasing market share and profit.

The rewritten introductory section in the makeover takes up half the space of the original one, yet it says far more, describing Tomlinson's achievements in detail. Resume reviewers immediately understand the value Tomlinson brings to organizations and are eager to read his resume.

Barry J. Tomlinson
120 East 75th Street
New York, NY 10021

(212) 717-2377
bjtomlinson@hotmail.com

Director of International Sales / Business Development / Finance

- P&L
- Strategic Planning
- Start-ups
- Turnarounds
- Corporate Finance

- New Business Development
- New Market Entry
- Mergers
- Acquisitions
- International Experience

- Started up international sales function for chemicals company and generated $500 million in revenues, while completing over $200 million in acquisition financing; then ran sales at 5 companies, achieving record levels—grew market share of one company 60% while increasing profits 200%; opened new territories at second company, expanding profit margin 500%; turned around third company, reversing $5 million loss and generating profit, leading to sale of company for over $20 million; grew market share 60% at fourth company while increasing profit margin 315%.

- Started up division for another chemicals company to enter Latin American markets—delivered 25% EBITDA in less than 2 years; formed new companies, plus made acquisitions ranging in value from $15 million to $140 million. Concurrently, refinanced parent's $225 million credit facility, saving $7 million a year in interest charges.

- Increased an oil company's annual revenues 32% to $175 million level, while growing earnings 70% to $8 million.

An entrepreneurial leader, skilled communicator / team builder, and adept negotiator with broad strengths in sales, finance, and business development. Proven ability to analyze businesses, operations, markets, and growth opportunities, then introduce strategic and tactical solutions that improve competitive performance while increasing sales, market share, and profits. A driven corporate strategist and change agent, tireless in the pursuit of quality business processes and maximum growth. MBA, BS-Industrial Engineering.

EXPERIENCE

International ChemEx, Inc., New York, NY. 1995 - 2003
Multibillion-dollar, global chemical company.
Director of International Sales & Business Development - ChemEx of Latin America (6 years)
Director of Finance - ChemEx, Inc., (2½ years)

Planned and directed international sales activities, conducting business in the U.S., Belgium, Mexico, Argentina, Venezuela, the Dominican Republic, Surinam, and Jamaica, in addition to holding financial responsibility as CFO for accounting, tax, and IT. Served as primary interface with financial institutions, insurance companies, auditors, and outside attorneys, as well as with board members and shareholders. Reported to President and CEO of ChemEx, Inc.

- Played key role in starting up Latin American Division and made major contributions in areas of sales, corporate development, financial management, cost savings, business planning, and organizational development.

- Negotiated and acquired numerous entities in the U.S., plus recommended and implemented penetration of Latin American market, beginning with Mexico. Closed stock and asset transactions ranging in value from $15 million to $140 million.

- Negotiated and acquired several companies in Mexico, growing business from zero to approximately 450,000 tons of chemical grade products, capturing 15% market share over 2-year period and selling over 1 million tons of products. Expansion generated approximately $30 million in new business in less than 2 years, with approximately 25% EBITDA.

- Prepared 5-year strategic plan for business development in Mexico.

Problem 3: Using a Typical Introductory Section

This type of introduction is used as extensively as any other. It consumes one to two inches of space and begins with a paragraph that describes the person's strengths, then lists their key job functions. While this introduction is preferable to one that takes up an entire page, its weakness is that readers have no idea how well someone has performed on the job and therefore have no incentive to continue reading.

SANFORD N. JOSEPHSON
44 Ramblewood Court
Charlotte, North Carolina 28226
snjosephson@carolina.rr.com

Tel: 704.544.6391

Fax: 704.544.3349

CAREER SUMMARY

High-performance manager with 15+ years of experience managing high-volume, fast-paced, multi-site business operations. Leader in the conceptualization, development, and implementation of processes and applications that improve efficiencies and productivity. Consistently deliver strong and sustainable operating results. Rapidly promoted through the ranks. Offer a broad-based, multifunctional background.

- **Strategic Planning**
- **Operations**
- **Supply Chain Management**
- **Logistics**
- **Risk Management**
- **Customer Service**

EXPERIENCE

North Carolina Security Group, Charlotte, North Carolina. 12/87 - present

$200+ million manufacturer with over 10,000 products.

Director of Logistics, 1991 - present

Broad-based responsibilities, including strategic planning, operations at fulfillment centers with national coverage, as well as customer service and support at both corporate and 3 manufacturing facilities nationwide. Coordinate all modes of transportation on worldwide basis. Member, E-business Council. Manage 75 personnel and report to VP - Operations.

- Rigorously analyzed operations, then made sweeping changes organization-wide, including implementing lean manufacturing techniques through Kaizen events, that dramatically improved efficiencies and profits:
  - Reduced cycle time 50% and operating costs 67% through developing and implementing B2B Extranet application and workflow optimization process.
  - Slashed inventories $2.1 million, or 23%, while increasing annual turns from 6 to 19 through revamping inventory control processes.
  - Improved on-time delivery from 75% to 96+% through designing and deploying new computer program. Also developed and implemented 24-hour, direct-fulfillment programs for 6 major brands.
- Developed strategies to further reduce inventories and increase turns, focusing on visibility, forecasting collaboration, and demand planning.
- Designed distribution center to improve efficiencies, costs, and service-level performance.
- Maintained same-day order processing through designing web-based real-time measurements of order backlog.
- Led teams that integrated 4 acquisitions into operations, adding $131 million to sales and decreasing operating costs 75% while improving productivity, efficiency, and customer satisfaction.

The rewritten introduction in the makeover contains Josephson's most impressive accomplishments, which convey his capability. Employers and recruiters are impressed by the results he has achieved and want to learn more about his work experience.

Sanford N. Josephson
44 Ramblewood Court
Charlotte, NC 28226
Tel: (704) 544-6391

Fax: (704) 544-3349
snjosephson@carolina.rr.com

LOGISTICS / SUPPLY CHAIN MANAGEMENT

- **Strategic Planning**
- **Operations**
- **Risk Management**
- **Customer Service**

- Designed new distribution center, revamped multi-site operations at existing facility, and introduced solutions that slashed cycle time 50%, operating costs 67%, and inventories 23%, while increasing annual turns from 6 to 19 and on-time delivery from 75% to over 96%.
- Created direct-fulfillment programs with national coverage that enabled 24-hour shipment of 3300 products from 1950 SKUs.
- Established outstanding relationships with customers that played key role in 5-year, 57% increase in sales despite mature market.
- Led business integration strategies that reduced operating costs 75% while improving productivity, efficiency, and customer satisfaction.
- Developed strategy for third-party logistics outsourcing that achieved operating savings of up to 70% while improving efficiencies.

An innovative and energetic leader, skilled communicator / team builder, and adept negotiator. Accomplished at analyzing operations and growth opportunities, then introducing strategic and tactical solutions that improve competitive performance while increasing revenues and decreasing costs. Recognized for broad strengths in policy and procedure development, project management, multi-site management, conceptualization and design of new business processes and applications, development of quick-ship programs, as well as development and management of customer base. Six Sigma-trained.

EXPERIENCE

North Carolina Security Group, Charlotte, NC. 1987 - present
$200+ million manufacturer with over 10,000 products.

Director of Logistics, 1991 - Present
Broad-based responsibilities, including strategic planning, operations at fulfillment centers with national coverage, as well as customer service and support at both corporate and 3 manufacturing facilities nationwide. Coordinate all modes of transportation on worldwide basis. Member, E-business Council. Oversee 75 personnel and report to VP - Operations.

- Rigorously analyzed operations, then made sweeping changes organization-wide, including implementing lean manufacturing techniques through Kaizen events, that dramatically improved efficiencies and profits:
  - Reduced cycle time 50% and operating costs 67% through developing and implementing B2B Extranet application and workflow optimization process.
  - Slashed inventories $2.1 million, or 23%, while increasing annual turns from 6 to 19 through revamping inventory control processes.
  - Improved on-time delivery from 75% to 96+% through designing and deploying new computer program. Also developed and implemented 24-hour, direct-fulfillment programs for 6 major brands.

Problem 4: Stating Responsibilities, Not Accomplishments

By discussing only his responsibilities, Michaelson gives no indication of the contributions he has made to his employers, therefore providing no reason to contact him for an interview.

Howard E. Michaelson
5134 161ˢᵗ Street West
Rosemount, MN 55068
Home Telephone: (952) 953-4969
E-mail Address: Hem@aol.com

Summary:

Experienced financial professional and CPA with both private and public accounting experience with organizations in the manufacturing, retailing, and service sectors.

Experience:

Division Controller, Midwest Metals, Minneapolis, MN. 1999 to Present
- Provide accurate and quality information for the control of business decision making directed at adding value to the company.
- Advise and guide management team on proper internal control systems. Responsible for 4 manufacturing facilities' financial statement reporting requirements, with annual sales in excess of $50 million.
- Direct the preparation and presentation of facility operating budgets. Advise and assist functional managers in the development of departmental budgets.
- Analyze variances between budget performance, standard cost, and actual cost results in order to properly identify corrective action.

Controller, The Houston House, Houston, TX. 1995 to 1999
Responsible for opening this 297-room hotel, with duties including accounting, financial reporting, and cost control.

Controller, Remington Corporation, Waco, TX. 1994 to 1995
- Responsible for the development, implementation, and operation of an effective accounting system with internal controls.
- Advised and made recommendations to the President concerning company objectives, policies, and plans.
- Accountable for financial statement compilation and reporting for a $30 million corporation.

Staff Accountant, International Furniture, Belton, TX. 1992 to 1994
- Managed Accounts Receivable, Accounts Payable, and Cost Accounting functions.
- Established controls for capital project management.
- Maintained bill of materials and product structure costs.

Staff Accountant, Waco Community Hospital, 1990 to 1992
- Assisted in monthly close as well as in preparation of financial statements.
- Prepared monthly account reconciliations, cost-accounting statements, and monthly analyses of general ledger accounts.

Accountant, Ries and Ficarra, P.A., Waco, TX. 1988 to 1990
- Assisted in audits as well as in preparation of personal and corporate tax returns.

Michaelson's accomplishments now appear in the makeover, and they convey the value he has brought to his employers, prompting readers to want to interview him.

Howard E. Michaelson
5134 161st Street West
Rosemount, MN 55068

Tel: (952) 953-4969
E-mail: Hem@aol.com

FINANCIAL MANAGEMENT—Public & Private Sectors

Controllership • Multi-plant Manufacturing • Service Organizations • Start-up Operations

- Established and managed Accounting Department for new upscale hotel, ultimately controlling bad debts to .15% of sales while decreasing food costs 19% and energy costs 20%.
- Increased $50 million metals fabricator's cash flow 50% while reducing bad debt 75%, property insurance premiums 8%, and health insurance costs 40%.

A skilled financial professional and CPA with experience in metals manufacturing, the hospitality and healthcare industries, consumer goods manufacturing, furniture retailing, and public accounting. A record of success at analyzing operations, then instituting systems, procedures, and controls that improve operating efficiencies while reducing costs. An outstanding negotiator, communicator, and team builder.

EXPERIENCE

Midwest Metals, Minneapolis, MN. 1999 - Present

$50 million metals fabricator with 4 production facilities.

Division Controller

Provide accurate and quality information for the control of business decision making directed at adding value to the company. Advise and guide management team on proper internal control systems. Responsible for manufacturing facilities' financial statement reporting requirements. Direct the preparation and presentation of facility operating budgets. Advise and assist functional managers in the development of departmental budgets. Analyze variances between budget performance, standard cost, and actual cost results in order to properly identify corrective action.

- Instituted credit policy that reduced bad debt 75%.
- Increased cash flow 50% by reducing aging of receivables.
- Decreased property insurance premiums 8%.
- Reduced health-insurance premiums 40% through implementing self-insured program. Also instituted disability coverage and 401-K plan.

The Houston House, Houston, TX. 1995 - 1999

297-room luxury hotel.

Controller

Responsible for opening hotel, with duties including accounting, financial reporting, and cost control.

- Established Accounting Department, including all systems and controls for monitoring / controlling costs and preparing documents for financial reporting.
- Controlled bad debts to .15% of sales.
- Negotiated $50,000 reduction in county property tax assessment.
- Reduced food costs 19% while maintaining quality level, plus decreased energy consumption 20%.

Remington Corporation, Waco, TX. 1994 - 1995

$30 million manufacturer of consumer paper products.

Controller

Responsible for the development, implementation, and operation of an effective accounting system with internal controls as well as financial statement compilation and reporting.

Problem 5: Stating Accomplishments Only in General Terms

This resume summarizes Patzner's accomplishments but fails to say how much he improved operations at his employers. Readers therefore have no idea of his capability and the value he represents. The resume gives no incentive to bring Patzner in for an interview.

---

25 Maple Street
Norwalk, CT 06851
(203) 750-1133
RJPatzner@msn.com

Robert J. Patzner

EXPERIENCE

New England Stainless Steels and Special Metals, Norwalk, CT. 1991 - Present
$50+ million precision strip and foil manufacturer of stainless and specialty steels.

Quality & Engineering Manager - Strip Mill & Aerodyne Service Groups, 1999 - present
Responsible for Quality, Metallurgical, and Plant Engineering groups for 2 divisions. Oversee 16 personnel through Supervisors of Metallurgy, Quality Engineering, and Plant Engineering. Report to General Manager.

- Implemented processes that resulted in cost savings, faster production, and fewer errors.
- Responsible for all capital project expenditures.
- Revised management system to attain ISO 9001 certification.
- Attained NADCAP approval for testing facilities in 2002.

Production Supervisor - Strip Mill Rolling & Annealing, 1996 - 1999
Responsible for manufacturing operations for cold reduction and continuous bright annealing. Oversaw 50 hourly and 5 salaried employees. Reported to General Manager.

- Introduced initiatives that improved on-time performance and reduced order-entry / processing time as well as unplanned absences of employees.

Quality Supervisor - Strip Mill, 1991 - 1996
Responsible for all Quality and Metallurgical groups in $50 million division. Managed staff of 8 and reported to General Manager.

- Improved Quality System to achieve ISO 9002 registration in 1995.
- Attained Rolls Royce aircraft approval for numerous products.
- Maintained nuclear, medical, and automotive customer approvals.
- Worked with Metallurgy Group to implement computerized standard processes.
- Instrumental in full implementation of shop floor control systems.

General Spring, Hartford, CT. 1987 - 1991
Precision stamping and spring manufacturer serving numerous markets.

Product Engineering Manager, 1991

- Led group of 5 responsible for developing new products and tooling, performing field service support, developing new manufacturing processes, and troubleshooting to support $40 million product line.

Quality / Process Engineer, 1987 - 1991

- Managed all shop floor activities in stamping and heat-treating areas.
- Coordinated Ford Q-1 effort.

The rewritten resume details Patzner's accomplishments, which show him to be extremely talented in his field. Readers now have every reason to want to interview him.

Robert J. Patzner
25 Maple Street
Norwalk, CT 06851

(203) 750-1133
RJPatzner@msn.com

MANUFACTURING & QUALITY MANAGEMENT

- Developed and implemented numerous manufacturing and quality processes that dramatically improved operations:
  - Reduced cycle time as much as 70% while eliminating 50% of existing errors.
  - Increased plant throughput as much as 25%.
  - Improved on-time performance 14%.
  - Slashed order-entry / processing time 66%.

An innovative and energetic manufacturing / quality manager, skilled communicator / team builder, and adept negotiator. A history of achievement at analyzing operations and growth opportunities, then introducing solutions that significantly improve manufacturing performance.

EXPERIENCE

New England Stainless Steels and Special Metals, Norwalk, CT. 1991 - Present

$50+ million precision strip and foil manufacturer of stainless and specialty steels.

Quality & Engineering Manager - Strip Mill & Aerodyne Service Groups, 1999 - Present

Responsible for Quality, Metallurgical, and Plant Engineering groups for 2 divisions. Oversee 16 personnel through Supervisors of Metallurgy, Quality Engineering, and Plant Engineering. Report to General Manager.

- Instituted lean manufacturing teams that improved sales-quotation and order-entry processes, resulting in 70% reduction in cycle time and eliminating 50% of existing errors.
- Led 2 separate Kaizen initiatives, with plant relayout resulting in 25% increase in throughput; implemented Kan Ban system in Roll Grinding area, eliminating tooling stock outs.
- Responsible for continuous improvement initiative that delivered savings of $100,000 a year.
- Coordinate and develop all capital project expenditures, including rolling mill upgrades averaging $500,000 per project.
- Revised management system to attain ISO 9001certification.
- Attained NADCAP approval for testing facilities in 2002.

Production Supervisor - Strip Mill Rolling & Annealing, 1996 - 1999

Responsible for all manufacturing operations for cold reduction and continuous bright annealing. Oversaw 50 hourly and 5 salaried employees. Reported to General Manager.

- Improved on-time performance from average of 72% to 82% through adjusting work-in-process inventories to achieve a pull system.
- Conducted Kaizen improvement sessions with Sales organization, resulting in reducing order-entry / processing from an average of 3.5 days to 1.2 days.
- Implemented team approach to manufacturing.
- Reduced unplanned absences of employees from average of 5 days to 2, working in conjunction with HR Department.

Quality Supervisor - Strip Mill, 1991 - 1996

Responsible for all Quality and Metallurgical groups in $50 million division. Managed staff of 8 and reported to General Manager.

- Restructured Quality System to achieve ISO 9002 registration in 1995.
- Attained Rolls Royce aircraft approval for numerous products.
- Maintained nuclear, medical, and automotive customer approvals.
- Worked with Metallurgy Group to implement computerized standard processes.
- Instrumental in full implementation of shop floor control systems.

General Spring, Hartford, CT. 1987 - 1991

Precision stamping and spring manufacturer serving numerous markets.

Product Engineering Manager, 1991

Problems with Presenting Work Experience in Resumes

89

Problem 6: Placing Most Important Accomplishments at End of Discussion of Experiences

This resume exemplifies how some job hunters try to intrigue readers by telling a story that gradually builds to a climax, culminating with their most exciting achievements (underlined for your convenience). By taking this approach, successes are buried in a resume and are often not read. Additionally, many reviewers get bored after reading four or five statements that don't say anything particularly noteworthy, so they set the resume aside.

Peter Brewster
49 Wetherill Lane
Head-of-the-Harbor, NY 11780
Tel: (631) 862-2839
E-mail: pbrewster@aol.com

CAREER SUMMARY

Accomplished consumer products marketing strategist with B2C and B2B experience and a record of success in increasing sales, market share, and profits. Expert in strategic planning, start-ups, P&L management, brand management, market segmentation, product launch, advertising and promotions, and e-commerce. International experience. MBA - Marketing.

PROFESSIONAL EXPERIENCE

THE NATURAL MARKET, Westbury, NY.   1999 - 2003
Specialty retailer of natural foods.

VP - Marketing
- Hired by VC firm to be member of 3-person executive start-up team, with complete responsibility for marketing.
- Wrote and implemented strategic marketing plan, then hired and led creative teams that set new natural-foods industry standards for marketing, advertising, promotions, and merchandising by adding a hip, sophisticated edge to an arena dominated by a more "crunchy granola" identifier.
- Directed production of graphics work for Internet, direct mail, brochures, signage, private label, and club card promotions, plus managed advertising for print, radio, and the Web.
- Delivered first-year sales of $10 million, achieving 127% of goal, then grew business at 35% CAGR.

CONTINENTAL SPECIALTIES, New York, NY.   1990 - 1998
Privately owned importer of specialty foods, wines, and beers.

Marketing Manager, 1996 - 1998
P&L responsibility for sales, marketing, and business development nationwide. Managed $2.3 million budget and oversaw 2 Field Managers and 2 Brand Managers. Reported to VP - Marketing.
- Hired 4-person team, attracting key talent from leading competitors.
- Developed and implemented strategic sales and marketing plans for brand portfolio, with accounts including wholesalers, chain retailers, and independents.
- Performed market segmentation, including consumer, channel, and geographic, to maximize profits and minimize cannibalization. Activities included environmental analysis, target analysis and selection, brand positioning / strategy, and execution / allocation of resources.
- Conducted U.S. launch of flagship cheese brand, designed to compete against market leaders, with 3-year breakeven goal.
- Gained publicity for brands through placing products in motion picture films and securing media articles.
- Directed all advertising and promotional programs as well as development of marketing collateral, packaging, merchandise, and point-of-sale materials.
- Directed launch and administration of brand web sites.
- Planned and oversaw all activities for trade shows, conventions, general sales meetings, and kickoff meetings with customers. Personally addressed up to 1000 attendees.
- Grew sales from $1.6 million in 1996 to $2.8 million in 1998, while expanding gross margin 27%.
- Planned and conducted numerous launches, achieving 100,000 cases of a French wine in 3 years and 75,000 cases of a German beer in 1 year.
- Increased sales of an Italian wine 50% a year, repositioned a non-alcoholic wine, attaining 15% annual increases, and repositioned a French wine, generating 23% annual increases.

By presenting accomplishments at the beginning of a discussion (again, under-lined), the resume immediately gains reviewers' attention, prompting them to read it in its entirety.

Peter Brewster
49 Wetherill Lane
Head-of-the-Harbor, NY 11780

(631) 862-2839
pbrewster@aol.com

SENIOR MARKETING EXECUTIVE—B2B / B2C

- **P&L**
- **Strategic Planning**
- **Start-ups**
- **Brand Management**
- **Market Segmentation**
- **Product Launch**
- **Advertising**
- **Promotions**
- **E-commerce**
- **International Experience**

- Started up natural-foods retail business and delivered first-year sales of $10 million, achieving 127% of goal, then grew business at 35% CAGR. Utilized e-commerce, direct mail, brochures, as well as print and radio advertising.
- Grew annual revenues of importer of specialty foods, wine, and beer from $1.6 million to $2.8 million in 2 years, while expanding gross margin 27%; launched new wine products, surpassing wholesale distribution goals and attaining growth rates as high as 50% a year.
- Repositioned key wine brand, generating 20% increase in gross margin.

An accomplished consumer products marketing strategist with B2C and B2B experience and a record of success at increasing sales, market share, and profits. MBA - Marketing.

EXPERIENCE

The Natural Market, Westbury, NY. 1999 - 2003

Specialty retailer of natural foods.

VP - Marketing

- Hired by VC firm to be member of 3-person executive start-up team, with complete responsibility for marketing.
- Delivered first-year sales of $10 million, achieving 127% of goal, then grew business at 35% CAGR.
  - Wrote and implemented strategic marketing plan, then hired and led creative teams that set new natural-foods industry standards for marketing, advertising, promotions, and merchandising by adding a hip, sophisticated edge to an arena dominated by a more "crunchy granola" identifier.
  - Directed production of graphics work for Internet, direct mail, brochures, signage, private label, and club card promotions, plus managed advertising for print, radio, and the Web.

Continental Specialties, New York, NY. 1990 - 1998

Privately owned importer of specialty foods, wines, and beers.

Marketing Manager, 1996 - 1998

P&L responsibility for sales, marketing, and business development nationwide. Managed $2.3 million budget and oversaw 2 Field Managers and 2 Brand Mangers. Reported to VP - Marketing.

- Hired 4-person team, attracting key talent from leading competitors.
- Grew sales from $1.6 million in 1996 to $2.8 million in 1998, while expanding gross margin 27%.
- Planned and conducted numerous launches, achieving 100,000 cases of a French wine in 3 years and 75,000 cases of a German beer in 1 year.
- Increased sales of an Italian wine 50% a year, plus repositioned a non-alcoholic wine, attaining 15% annual increases, and repositioned a French wine, generating 23% annual increases.
- Achieved successes through multiple marketing initiatives:
  - Developed and implemented strategic sales and marketing plans for brand portfolios, with accounts including wholesalers, chain retailers, and independents.
  - Performed market segmentation, including consumer, channel, and geographic, to maximize profits and minimize cannibalization. Activities included environmental analysis, target analysis and selection, brand positioning / strategy, and execution / allocation of resources.
  - Conducted U.S. launch of flagship cheese brand, designed to compete against market leaders, with 3-year breakeven goal.

Problem 7: Presenting Work Experience in Chronological Order

Because Ladd begins this resume by discussing his early experience, he sends the wrong message about his capability and value. Recruiters and employers want to know what he can do today to improve and grow organizations, not what he did when he began his career over 15 years ago.

ANDREW J. LADD

13 Holly Lane
East Hills, New York 11577
516.625.3812
ajl17@aol.com

EXPERIENCE

North Shore Home Furnishings, Roslyn, New York. 12/'85 to 10/'87
Sales Associate at this retailer of home furnishings.

- #1 Sales Associate out of 6 on the floor.
- Won numerous awards and prizes for exceeding quota.

Decorama, Garden City, New York. 11/'87 to 12/'93
Assistant Sales Manager at this home furnishings retailer with annual sales of over $1 million.

- Recruited by owner.
- #1 sales producer, consistently exceeding quota.
- Interviewed potential Sales Associates plus trained and managed new hires.
- Assisted Sales Manager with merchandising, displays, advertising, special promotions, and inventory control.

Hempstead Home Furnishings & Furniture, Hempstead, New York. 01/'94 to 12/'98
Sales Manager at this retailer of home furnishings and furniture with annual sales of $3 million.

- Grew sales 25% per year over 5-year period.
- Introduced incentive program to motivate sales force.
- Created and instituted multi-media advertising campaign, utilizing print, radio, and television.
- Promoted store throughout local area through participating in community activities.
- Worked closely with owner in upgrading merchandise and expanding profit margins.
- Accompanied owner on buying trips and at trade shows.

Miracle Mile Furniture Center, Manhasset, New York. 01/'99 to 12/'02
General Manager of this $5 million furniture retailer.

P&L responsibility for all operations, including sales, purchasing, merchandising, inventory control, advertising and promotion, and administration. Oversaw 25 full- and part-time employees and reported to owner.

- Completely revamped store, growing sales 30% while increasing profits 70% over 4-year period.
- Upgraded furniture line, focusing on higher-margin merchandise, plus modernized showroom.
- Secured new vendors, personally negotiating all contracts.
- Hired and trained new sales team.

EDUCATION

B.A., Marketing, Long Island University, 1985.

By beginning with his most recent successes, Ladd establishes himself as an accomplished retail executive with expertise in all the key areas of running a business.

Andrew J. Ladd
13 Holly Lane
East Hills, NY 11577

(516) 625-3812
aj17@aol.com

RETAIL EXECUTIVE—FURNITURE & HOME FURNISHINGS

- **P&L**
- **Strategic Planning**
- **Reengineering**
- **Sales**

- **Advertising**
- **Promotion**
- **Merchandising**
- **Buying**

- Repeated successes at increasing sales, margins, and profits, growing profits as much as 70% in 4 years while boosting sales 30%.
- Accomplished at upgrading lines, instituting highly successful advertising and promotional programs, plus developing high-performance sales teams.
- An expert negotiator who sources and signs new vendors at extremely favorable pricing and terms.

EXPERIENCE

Miracle Mile Furniture Center, Manhasset, NY. 1999 - 2002

General Manager of this $5 million furniture retailer.

P&L responsibility for all operations, including sales, purchasing, merchandising, inventory control, advertising and promotion, and administration. Oversaw 25 full- and part-time employees; reported to owner.

- Completely revamped store, growing sales 30% while increasing profits 70% over 4-year period.
- Upgraded furniture line, focusing on higher-margin merchandise, plus modernized showroom.
- Secured new vendors, personally negotiating all contracts.
- Hired and trained new sales team.

Hempstead Home Furnishings & Furniture, Hempstead, NY. 1994 - 1998

Sales Manager at this retailer of home furnishings and furniture with annual sales of $3 million.

- Grew sales 25% per year over 5-year period.
- Introduced incentive program to motivate sales force.
- Created and instituted multi-media advertising campaign, utilizing print, radio, and television.
- Promoted store throughout local area through participating in community activities.
- Worked closely with owner in upgrading merchandise and expanding profit margins.
- Accompanied owner on buying trips and at trade shows.

Decorama, Garden City, NY. 1987 - 1993

Assistant Sales Manager at this home furnishings retailer with annual sales of over $1 million.

- Recruited by owner.
- #1 sales producer, consistently exceeding quota.
- Interviewed potential Sales Associates plus trained and managed new hires.
- Assisted Sales Manager with merchandising, displays, advertising, special promotions, and inventory control.

North Shore Home Furnishings, Roslyn, NY. 1985 - 1987

Sales Associate at this retailer of home furnishings.

- #1 Sales Associate out of 6 on the floor.
- Won numerous awards and prizes for exceeding quota.

Problem 8: Providing Only Job Titles, with No Discussion of Activities

In this resume, Richardson is relying on his job titles to convey his responsibilities and on the names of the prestigious clubs that employed him to express his expertise in his field. What recruiters and prospective employers want to know, however, is what his specific contributions were. Richardson gives no information in this area, which will cause some people to believe that his performance was subpar.

OLIVER S. RICHARDSON

900 Sunridge Drive • Sarasota, FL 34234 • 941-351-5092 • Olrich@aol.com

OBJECTIVE

P&L responsibility for managing all operations at an upscale country club.

WORK EXPERIENCE

Palm Aire Country Club, Sarasota, FL.   1997 - 2002
General Manager of this 1,000-member club with 2 18-hole golf courses.

Tierra del Sol, Aruba, Dutch West Indies.   1991 - 1996
General Manger of this 600-home, master-planned community with 18-hole Robert Trent Jones golf course plus hotel facilities, fitness center, and clubhouse.

Wykagyl Country Club, Bronxville, NY.   1988 - 1991
General Manager of this 600-member, nonresidential club.

Siwanoy Country Club, Bronxville, NY.   1985 - 1988
General Manager of this 700-member club located in the town that at the time had the highest per capita income in the United States.

Palm Beach Polo & Country Club, Palm Beach, FL.   1978 - 1984
Assistant General Manager / General Manager of this 1650-acre resort with 2 golf courses, 4 restaurants, 11 polo fields, stadium, 24 tennis courts, and hotel facilities.

Cat Cay Club, The Bahamas.   1975 - 1978
Assistant General Manager of this affluent 700-member club with 84-slip marina facility, hotel, and tennis.

Holiday Inns, Various Locations.   1970 - 1975
Held increasing responsible positions, starting as Management Trainee, then progressing through the ranks to General Manager of 300-room hotel in Florida.

EDUCATION / TRAINING / MEMBERSHIP

B.S., Business Administration, University of Sydney, Sydney, Australia.
Food & Beverage Hotel, Zurich, Switzerland.
Club Managers' Association of America.
20-year member, C.M.A.A.

The makeover details Richardson's responsibilities and many successes, depicting him as outstanding in his field.

Oliver S. Richardson
900 Sunridge Drive
Sarasota, FL 34234

(941) 351-5092
Olrich@aol.com

COUNTRY CLUB MANAGEMENT

P&L • Start-ups • Turnarounds • Membership Expansion • Program Development • Renovations

- Extensive experience managing prestigious clubs and resorts in the U.S. and Caribbean, with members including a President of the United States, several congressmen, and numerous CEOs of Fortune 500 companies.
- Expert at planning and managing capital and operating budgets, plus working effectively with committees and Board of Governors.
- Achieved profitability for first time at one club, plus reversed another's $330,000 annual loss, delivering $100,000 profit within 18 months.
- Expanded a third club's membership from 100 to 1100 within 3 years, plus grew facility usage at a fourth club 40%, particularly the dining room, grill, and bar.
- Hosted numerous events, including L.P.G.A. Classic, Rolex World Cup Polo Matches, and celebrity golf and tennis tournaments.

EXPERIENCE

Palm Aire Country Club, Sarasota, FL. 1997 - 2002

1,000-member club with 2 18-hole golf courses.

General Manager

- Rigorously analyzed operations, then instituted cost-reduction and revenue-enhancement programs that achieved first profit in club's history.
- Assessed members' needs, then developed and implemented programs that increased club's usage 40%, particularly in the dining room, grill, and bar.
- Hired new chef and revamped all food and beverage operations.
- Planned and organized first 4-day member-guest tournament that attracted participants from across the United States.

Tierra del Sol, Aruba, Dutch West Indies. 1991 - 1996

600-home, master-planned community with 18-hole Robert Trent Jones golf course plus hotel facilities, fitness center, and clubhouse.

General Manger

- Recruited by owners to start up and manage club, responsible for planning and administering $5 million budget.
- Designed kitchen, bar, and pro shop; created menu and wine list; planned and arranged for live entertainment.
- Recruited and hired 160 employees, including 10 managers.
- Established all operating systems, procedures, and controls; developed and implemented training programs for all personnel.
- Achieved immediate success, meeting all milestones; subsequently transferred by owners to Curacao to organize new golf club, with activities including writing pro forma, soliciting bids, and planning tennis courts, clubhouse, and membership-development strategy.

Problem 9: Providing Only Job Functions, with No Discussion of Activities

Jaworsky is assuming in this resume that by stating his job functions people will understand what he did and therefore be able to make a determination regarding his capability. As in the previous resume, prospective employers and recruiters want to know exactly what someone's contributions were before they'll agree to set up an interview.

Leopold S. Jaworsky

29 Fernview Road
Parsippany, NJ 07054

973-292-4491 Phone
973-539-8023 Fax
973-723-9810 Cell
Leo_S_Jwrsky@msn.com

Objective	A challenging position in property management.
Experience	NEW JERSEY PROPERTIES, INC., Morristown, NJ. January 2001 - June 2002 **Director of Operations** Property Management Coordinator of Sales & Leasing Teams Information Technology Development
	BRANDON AGENCY, Morristown, NJ. August 1996 - January 2001 **Operations Supervisor - Real Estate Development / Property Manager** Property Management Commercial Sales & Leasing Asset Allocation
	U.S. ARMY, Fort Benning, GA and Fort Jackson, SC. July 1983 - July 1996 **Drill Sergeant** Drill Instructor, 2nd Division Infantry, Staff Sergeant (E-6)
	IRVINGTON BOARD OF EDUCATION, Irvington, NJ. September 1980 - May 1983 **Teacher** First male kindergarten educator in state of New Jersey Procurement and development of computer training
Education	1975 - 1977 Ocean County Community College, Toms River, NJ.
	1977 - 1980 Monmouth University, West Long Branch, NJ. B.S., Education Graduated Kappa Delta Pi, National Educational Honor Society Certified Reading Specialist United States Army, Drill Instructor
Interests	Computers, Technology, Sports, Music

The rewritten resume clearly sets forth Jaworsky's responsibilities and successes, offering the information that's necessary for people to want to interview him.

Leopold S. Jaworsky
29 Fernview Road
Parsippany, NJ 07054
Tel: (973) 292-4491
Cell: (973) 723-9810

Fax: (973) 539-8023
Leo_S_Jwrsky@msn.com

PROPERTY MANAGEMENT EXECUTIVE

- Repeated successes at managing commercial, industrial, office, residential, condominium, and townhouse properties, with total monthly rental income averaging as much as $750,000.
- Supervised staffs of up to 10.
- Consistently #1 revenue producer, leasing as much as $2 million in space within 1 year's time.

EXPERIENCE

New Jersey Properties, Inc., Morristown, NJ. 2001 - 2002

Director of Operations at this development company whose properties included commercial, industrial, office, residential, condominiums, and townhouses.

Responsible for property management, coordination of sales and leasing teams, and IT development. Oversaw staff of 10 and reported to owners.

Property Management

- Responsible for all tenant / owner relations for approximately 1000 apartment units, 50 retail stores, and dozens of commercial, industrial, and office properties generating average monthly rental income of $750,000. Activities included lease negotiations, lease origination, rent collection, dispute resolution, addendum preparation, and coordination of tenant fit up.
- Analyzed and evaluated current and future projects.
- Organized and supervised interoffice meetings to coordinate all business activities, including strategy planning, infrastructure reorganization, staff alignment, assignment, and evaluation.
- Revamped interoffice processes, information distribution, and infrastructure within 1-year period to increase efficiency of operations.

Coordinator of Sales & Leasing Teams

- Coordinated and disseminated information, including scheduling, follow-up, and sales- and leasing-related matters to approximately 5 in-house sales personnel.
- Evaluated and improved sales procedures on regular basis, plus trained new sales personnel.
- Redesigned sales literature and brochures to improve marketability of projects.
- Conducted partner and staff meetings to discuss procedures and assignments. Made recommendations to improve efficiency of operations, plus advised owners on all human resource issues regarding 50 employees.
- Showed properties to prospective owners and tenants, then negotiated and closed leases and sales. #1 producer out of 6, leasing over $2 million of space the first 12 months.

Information Technology Development

- Specified and established company's first IT initiative, with activities including design, procurement, and installation of hardware and software, including telephony, internet, and intranet designs.
- Trained staff in operations and maintenance.

Brandon Agency, Morristown, NJ. 1996 - 2001

Operations Supervisor - Real Estate Development and **Property Manager** at this developer of commercial / industrial / office properties.

Responsible for property management, commercial sales and leasing, and asset allocation.

Problem 10: Offering Too Much Information on Employers, Responsibilities, and Activities Performed

Due to containing so much extraneous information, Rixe's resume is boring to read. The voluminous information also makes Rixe appear to be a very detail-oriented and uninspiring individual.

Stephen M. Rixe

19 Washington St., Landing, New Jersey 07850
973.691.4887
smrixe@optonline.net

QUALIFICATIONS SUMMARY

Growth-oriented sales and marketing executive with proven accomplishments in formulating marketing strategies, restructuring organizations, improving customer relations, and developing system sales strategies for diverse marketplaces. Able to conceive of, develop, and implement strategies that are responsive to customer market needs.

PROFESSIONAL EXPERIENCE

1991 - 2002, U.S. NARROW FABRICS, INC., New York, New York.

Leading <u>65-year-old</u> manufacturer of woven narrow fabrics, with 3 separate divisions generating annual revenues of up to $190 million and serving diverse base of accounts in the U.S., Canada, Mexico, the U.K., and Europe. <u>Company operates plants in Clinton, South Carolina; Dalton, Georgia; and Greenville, South Carolina.</u>

National Sales Manager

Complete responsibility for sales, channel strategies, <u>sales analysis and forecasting, pricing, customer service, advertising, and special promotions.</u> Oversaw up to 70 personnel, including 5 regional sales managers and 63 direct and independent sales representatives. Responsible for sales to chain accounts, warehouse clubs, drug stores, dollar stores, supermarkets, specialty companies (<u>Crate and Barrel, William Sonoma, Toys R Us</u>), home improvement stores (<u>Lowe's</u>), as well as to distributors of notions, crafts, floral products, and paper products. Reported to COO <u>who in turn reported to CEO.</u>

- Grew annual sales from $33 million to $58 million, a 76% gain, exceeding industry growth rate of 38% <u>during same period.</u>
- Expanded business with existing customer base, plus tripled supermarket business through introducing new sales strategy, landing leading national accounts, including Safeway, Albertson's, and Publix.
- Led company into drug store market and warehouse clubs, the latter including BJ's and Costco.
- Hired reps specializing in targeted markets, resulting in adding numerous new accounts <u>in home improvement, warehouse club, supermarket, and specialty sectors.</u>
- <u>Upgraded sales force through effective training and motivational programs, working in the field with both company sales personnel and independent reps.</u> Developed and implemented sales training programs <u>on products as well as on effective lead-development, presentation, and closing skills. Trained personnel individually as well as in groups.</u>
- <u>Formulated and set standards of performance for sales personnel.</u>
- <u>Planned and conducted regional and national sales meetings with both customers and sales staff.</u>
- <u>Planned participation at national conferences and trade shows.</u>
- <u>Developed pricing models.</u>
- <u>Created business forecasting models.</u>
- <u>Generated market share studies, sales budgets, and customer / product rationalization initiatives, with emphasis on profit maximization.</u>
- Identified new markets to penetrate, <u>including e-commerce, Home Shopping Network, and quilting market.</u>
- <u>Worked with retail accounts in development of effective displays and fixtures for different product lines.</u>
- <u>Interfaced with production personnel to coordinate sales planning with manufacturing capabilities and product distribution.</u>
- <u>Monitored Customer Service Department regarding quality of service provided to incoming callers.</u>
- <u>Rewrote outbound telemarketing script.</u>

Having deleted the unimportant information in the makeover, the resume now has pace and the accomplishments have impact. Rixe is depicted as a dynamic, aggressive sales leader.

Stephen M. Rixe
19 Washington St.
Landing, NJ 07850

(973) 691-4887
smrixe@optonline.net

SENIOR SALES MANAGEMENT EXECUTIVE—Consumer Goods

Strategic Planning • Mass Merchandise / Drug Store / Supermarket Channels

- Drove textile manufacturer's sales from $33 million to $58 million, delivering 76% gain versus industry growth rate of only 38%—landed leading accounts, including Safeway, Albertson's, Publix, BJ's, Costco.
- Maintained $25 million domestic textile manufacturer's sales level despite severe industry downturn, adding key accounts, including Wal-Mart and Famous Footwear, while increasing sales up to 75% with existing customer base.
- Doubled customer base in 3 years for $300+ million footwear wholesaler / importer, opening up new accounts, including Sears, T.J. Maxx, Ross Department Stores, and Q.V.C; earlier during tenure, grew divisional sales from $3 million to $45 million while tripling customer base, selling to K mart, Target, Wal-Mart, Payless, and Meijers.

EXPERIENCE

U.S. Narrow Fabrics, Inc., New York, NY. 1991 - 2002

Leading 3-plant manufacturer of woven narrow fabrics, with annual revenues of up to $190 million and serving diverse base of accounts in the U.S., Canada, Mexico, the U.K., and Europe.

National Sales Manager

Complete responsibility for all sales activities, overseeing up to 70 personnel, including 5 regional sales managers and 63 direct and independent sales representatives. Responsible for sales to chain accounts, warehouse clubs, drug stores, dollar stores, supermarkets, specialty companies, home improvement stores, as well as to distributors of notions, crafts, floral products, and paper products. Reported to COO.

- Grew annual sales from $33 million to $58 million, achieving a 76% gain and exceeding industry growth rate of only 38%.
- Expanded business with existing customer base, plus tripled supermarket business through introducing new sales strategy, landing leading national accounts, including Safeway, Albertson's, and Publix.
- Led company into drug store market and warehouse clubs, the latter including BJ's and Costco.
- Redirected sales strategy through identifying new markets to penetrate, developing and implementing targeted sales programs, and providing comprehensive training to sales organization.

Fairview Textiles, Inc., Quincy, MA. 1985 - 1991

$25 million international manufacturer and distributor of textile products specializing in proprietary moisture management fabric systems developed for medical, sporting goods, active wear, and footwear industries.

International / Domestic Sales and Marketing Manager

Responsible for developing and implementing strategic sales plan. Oversaw 15 domestic and international sales reps covering 250 accounts, plus planned and administered $300,000 annual advertising budget. Reported to President.

- Revamped strategic sales plan, resulting in maintaining company's domestic sales level during severe downturn in domestic footwear industry, while growing international sales 10%.
- Opened numerous new accounts, including Wal-Mart and Famous Footwear, plus expanded business up to 75% with key accounts, including New Balance, Timberland, Eagle Creek, and Brown Shoe.
- Tripled non-footwear sales to $1.25 million level within 2 years through entering medical and sporting goods industries.

Pagoda Trading Company, Division of Brown Group, St. Louis, MO. 1983 - 1985

Leading $300+ million wholesaler / importer of footwear.

National Account Executive

- Doubled customer base in 3 years, generating $13 million in annual sales and $2.3 million in gross profits.

Problem 11: Providing a Narrative Discussion That Summarizes an Entire Career

Some job hunters begin their resume with a lengthy narrative discussion that summarizes their entire work background, similar to telling a story about their career. Many employers and recruiters find these discussions time-consuming and boring and don't read the resumes. When searching for qualified applicants, people don't want to be given stories. They want to read facts, especially about successes.

Barry M. Robertson

20 Oxbow Road
Wellesley, MA 02181

Telephone: (781) 237-9331
E-mail: Brobertson@aol.com

PROFILE

Mr. Robertson has been involved in Management for the past 23 years in a variety of mid- to large-size organizations. As a business professional he specializes in managing organizations to develop programs that enhance performance, increase revenue, and reduce operating costs. He has demonstrated strong business, entrepreneurial, analytical, organizational, and communication skills throughout his career progression. His educational background includes a B.A. from the College of the Holy Cross and an M.A. from Assumption College. He has also completed numerous courses and seminars in Management and Business Administration.

EXPERIENCE SUMMARY

Mr. Robertson is currently the District Vice President and General Manager of HR Services Corporation, a Washington, DC-based payroll / human resources services vendor. He holds P&L responsibility for numerous functions in a northeastern district. They include sales, customer service, software installation, data center production, facilities management, and finance. He is also responsible for a $15 million sales quota. His territory includes Massachusetts and Connecticut, and he has offices in both Wellesley, Massachusetts, and Stamford, Connecticut. To date, he has boosted annual revenues 44% while reducing costs 25%.

Earlier with the company, Mr. Robertson was the District Vice President for Services in Columbia, Maryland. He had P&L responsibility for customer service, software installation, data center production, facilities management, and finance in a territory generating $7 million in annual revenues. The territory included Southeast Pennsylvania, Maryland, the District of Columbia, and Northern Virginia. He successfully turned around operations, reversing a 15% loss on sales and generating a 10% profit on sales.

Prior to joining HR Services Corporation, Mr. Robertson was Director of Operations for Innovation Management Systems in Westboro, Massachusetts, a software development firm. He was responsible for managing the data center and an annual data center budget of $1 million. He was also directly responsible for the voice / data telecommunications network and all of the facility operations at Innovation Management. Mr. Robertson made dramatic changes in operations, and in the first 3 months saved the company $50,000.

Previously, Mr. Robertson was a Senor Account Manager with The Farnsworth Group's Information Consulting practice in the Boston Office. He was responsible for managing the efforts of consultants assigned to major Boston-based clients as well as acting as the client interface on designated projects. His contributions included developing new clients as well as increasing the number of engagements with existing clients.

The narrative discussion has been replaced with bulleted accomplishments that begin with action verbs. Robertson's resume is now easy to read, with his successes jumping off the page.

Barry M. Robertson
20 Oxbow Road
Wellesley, MA 02181

Tel: (781) 237-9331
E-mail: Brobertson@aol.com

SALES & OPERATIONS MANAGEMENT

- **Profit & Loss Responsibility**
- **Turnaround Management**
- **Process Improvement**
- **Productivity Enhancement**
- **Organizational Reengineering**
- **Information Systems**

- Grew annual revenues of payroll / HR services company 44% to $15 million level while decreasing costs 25%; concurrently, increased productivity 40% with no increase in operating expenses. Earlier, turned around district losing 15% on sales and delivered 10% profit.
- Reengineered operations of $1 million CAD / CAM software developer, saving $50,000 the first 3 months.

An accomplished corporate strategist and change agent, skilled at analyzing operations, services, markets, and growth opportunities, then developing and implementing initiatives and processes that increase revenues, productivity, and profits.

EXPERIENCE

HR Services Corporation, Washington, DC. 1991 - Present

$50 million company providing payroll and human resource services.

District Vice President / General Manager, Wellesley, MA. 1996 - Present

P&L responsibility for Sales, Customer Service, Software Installation, Data Center Production, Facilities Management, and Finances for $15 million Massachusetts / Connecticut territory. Manage 2 separate offices (Wellesley and Stamford, Connecticut) and oversee approximately 50 personnel, including 3 District Managers. Report to Eastern Regional Vice President.

- Rigorously analyzed operations, then restructured all departments to establish platform for sustained growth in revenues and profits.
- Boosted annual revenues 44% to $15 million level while reducing costs 25%.
- Improved business systems and processes, resulting in 40% increase in throughput with zero escalation in operating expenses.
- Reduced headcount in Stamford office and implemented virtual office space and remote connectivity for 90% of personnel, saving $100,000 a year.
- Upgraded IBM ES9000 / 210 to IBM Multiprise 2003 / 215 and 3 Xerox 9790 printers to 4635's.
- Member, President's Club.

District Vice President - Services, Columbia, MD. 1991 - 1996

P&L responsibility for $7 million territory consisting of Southeast Pennsylvania, Maryland, the District of Columbia, and Northern Virginia. Oversaw 25 personnel, including 2 District Managers. Reported to District Vice President / General Manager.

- Turned around district losing 15% on sales and delivered 10% profit.
- Brought budget back in line with plan by controlling expenses, primarily reducing freight, equipment, supplies, and labor approximately 20%.
- Improved operating efficiencies through upgrading computer systems.
- Restructured and improved efficiencies of Billing Department and Customer Service Department.
- Conducted customer satisfaction survey that resulted in "role model," the highest rating.
- Installed new business system, with immediate success resulting in corporate-wide installation.

Problems with Presenting Work Experience in Resumes

Problem 12: A History of Job-Hopping

Readers quickly learn that Canatella has had four jobs in four years, a red flag in most people's eyes. The fact that she left the school system to teach from home will also cause some resume reviewers to believe that her job-hopping caught up with her, and she had trouble getting offers after her short stint at Alta Vista Elementary School.

Camille Canatella

2916 9th St. Ct. West
Bradenton, FL 34205
941.747.2839
Camille.Canatella@cs.com

OBJECTIVE

Elementary Education Teacher, with a preference for grades 1-3.

WORK EXPERIENCE

Canatella Family Child Care Home, Bradenton, FL. 2002 - Present
Owner / Operator of this registered home daycare affiliated with Project Child Care.

- Founded home daycare and teach 8 students ranging in age from 1 to 5.
- Design preschool curriculum and prepare lesson plans, with subjects including speaking skills / pronunciation, letters, colors, shapes, crafts, music, dance, math, science, and animals.
- Utilize teaching tools, including tapes, books, flash cards, and counting devices.
- Conduct wide range of activities, including Show & Tell and Story Time.
- Interact with children's parents on daily basis, apprising them of progress being made and any special problems or situations requiring attention.
- Answer questions from parents regarding children's behavior, motivation, and required discipline.

Alta Vista Elementary School, Sarasota, FL. 2001 - 2002
Teacher, 2nd Grade Regular Education

- Prepared and gave weekly lesson plans based on children's needs, interests, and developmental skills. Topics included day and night, transportation, reptiles, birds, science, and places around the world, utilizing activity areas for optimum learning.
- Wrote and produced a historical play for school's 40th anniversary. Trained students in their parts and coordinated costuming and presentations.
- Selected to be Presenter and Facilitator at Core Knowledge Conference, Miami, Florida.
- Served on numerous committees: Core Knowledge, Science Fair (Chair), Grade, and Hospitality.

TLC School, Sarasota, FL. 2000 - 2001
Pre-K Teacher

- Designed curriculum and taught children about wide variety of subjects.
- Gave hands-on art activity; determined themes for weekly bulletin board and constructed board; developed appropriate learning centers for active learning; created activity-based math and reading skills; performed student evaluations; held parent conferences.
- Featured on local television news show for outstanding teaching skills.

Sarasota County School Board, Sarasota, FL. 1999 - 2000
Substitute Teacher, Grades 1-3

EDUCATION

B.S., Elementary Education, Florida State University, 1998.

The introductory section in the makeover portrays Canatella as an exceptional teacher who is extremely enthusiastic about her work. This initial favorable impression will offset the job-hopping that will surface upon reading her resume. Most employers will be so impressed by Canatella's introductory remarks that they will give her the benefit of the doubt and will look to the interview for learning why she changed jobs so often.

Camille Canatella
2916 9th St. Ct. West
Bradenton, FL 34205

(941) 747-2839
Camille.Canatella@cs.com

ELEMENTARY EDUCATION TEACHER

- Featured on local television news show for outstanding classroom skills.
- Cited by supervisors for ability to create classroom environment conducive to learning.
- Adore children—patient and understanding; an excellent disciplinarian as required.

EXPERIENCE

Canatella Family Child Care Home, Bradenton, FL. 2002 - Present

Owner / Operator of this registered home daycare affiliated with Project Child Care.

- Founded home daycare and teach 8 students ranging in age from 1 to 5.
- Design preschool curriculum and prepare lesson plans, with subjects including speaking skills / pronunciation, letters, colors, shapes, crafts, music, dance, math, science, and animals.
- Utilize teaching tools, including tapes, books, flash cards, and counting devices.
- Conduct wide range of activities, including Show & Tell and Story Time.
- Interact with children's parents on daily basis, apprising them of progress being made and any special problems or situations requiring attention.
- Answer questions from parents regarding children's behavior, motivation, and required discipline.

Alta Vista Elementary School, Sarasota, FL. 2001 - 2002

Teacher, 2nd Grade Regular Education

- Prepared and gave weekly lesson plans based on children's needs, interests, and developmental skills. Topics included day and night, transportation, reptiles, birds, science, and places around the world, utilizing activity areas for optimum learning.
- Wrote and produced a historical play for school's 40th anniversary. Trained students in their parts and coordinated costuming and presentations.
- Selected to be Presenter and Facilitator at Core Knowledge Conference, Miami, Florida.
- Served on numerous committees: Core Knowledge, Science Fair (Chair), Grade, and Hospitality.

TLC School, Sarasota, FL. 2000 - 2001

Pre-K Teacher

- Designed curriculum and taught children about wide variety of subjects.
- Gave hands-on art activity; determined themes for weekly bulletin board and constructed board; developed appropriate learning centers for active learning; created activity-based math and reading skills; performed student evaluations; held parent conferences.
- Featured on local television news show for outstanding teaching skills.

Sarasota County School Board, Sarasota, FL. 1999 - 2000
Substitute Teacher, Grades 1-3

EDUCATION

B.S., Elementary Education, Florida State University, 1998.

Problem 13: Numerous Periods of Unemployment

A quick scan of this resume reveals five jobs with at least a year of unemployment between each one, a liability that causes concern about Merriweather's stability and capability. Many employers will automatically reject her as a candidate.

ROSALIND MERRIWEATHER

7102 Arcturas Drive • Sarasota, Florida 34243 • (941) 351-2839

QUALIFICATION SUMMARY:

Extensive broad-range nursing experience leading to excellent knowledge base in various phases of the profession. Task and detail-oriented; able to carry out multifaceted responsibilities in an efficient and effective manner. Strong communication and interpersonal skills; able to interface and easily establish rapport with physicians, patients, and families. Skilled in the orientation of new personnel and supervision of health care units.

EXPERIENCE:

Sarasota Memorial Hospital, Sarasota, FL. May 1999 - December 2002
Charge RN - Emergency Room and Ambulatory Health Care Clinics

- As sole ER nurse, performed triage, full nursing assessment, and all nursing care.
- Administered all medications, including IV therapy such as T.P.A., streptokinase, and emergency drips.
- Responsible for respiratory therapy, patient admissions, patient education, and discharge planning.
- Oriented new ER physicians and RNs on policies of ER / AHC.

Venice Hospital, Venice, FL. March 1994 - October 1997
Charge RN - Medical Ward, 12:00-8:00 shift

- Cared for 30-35 acute medical patients, including giving medications, IV therapy, and respiratory treatments.
- Responsible for patient education; updated nursing care plans; performed admissions, chart audits, and patient discharge planning.
- Supervised 2 nursing assistants.

Manatee Memorial Hospital, Bradenton, FL. May 1989 - December 1992
Hospital Night Supervisor

- The only supervisor at this 500+ bed hospital on 12:00-8:00 shift.
- Scheduled and supervised over 50 RNs, LPNs, and NAs.
- Provided staff education, counseling, guidance, and problem solving to include all staffing problems on night tour.

Tampa General Hospital, Tampa, FL. February 1984 - November 1987
Staff Nurse - Orthopedics and Ophthalmology wards

- Cared for 30-40 surgical patients, including patient education, dressing changes, medications (PO, IV, IM), starting IVs, admissions, discharges, chart audits, traction, and respiratory therapy.
- Supervised 2 NAs.
- Assisted Head Nurse with staff scheduling and staff counseling, guidance, and education.

HCA L.W. Blake Hospital, Bradenton, FL. August 1979 - October 1982
Registered Nurse - Emergency Care Center

- Assisted physicians during various procedures and followed through with orders and protocol.

EDUCATION:

B.S., Nursing, University of Bridgeport, Bridgeport, CT. 1978

The introductory section in the makeover immediately establishes Merriweather's capability, ensuring that her resume will be read in its entirety.

Rosalind Merriweather
7102 Arcturas Drive
Sarasota, Florida 34243

(941) 351-2839

REGISTERED NURSE

- Broad nursing experience, including the ER, orthopedics ward, and ophthalmology ward.
- Provided care for up to 40 patients; supervised over 50 nurses and aides on night shift at 500+ bed hospital.
- Consistently cited by Directors of Nursing for outstanding supervisory skills, assistance to physicians, and patient care.
- B.S., Nursing.

EXPERIENCE

Sarasota Memorial Hospital, Sarasota, FL. 1999 - 2002

Charge RN - Emergency Room and Ambulatory Health Care Clinics

- As sole ER nurse, performed triage, full nursing assessment, and all nursing care.
- Administered all medications, including IV therapy such as T.P.A., streptokinase, and emergency drips.
- Responsible for respiratory therapy, patient admissions, patient education, and discharge planning.
- Oriented new ER physicians and RNs on policies of ER / AHC.

Venice Hospital, Venice, FL. 1994 - 1997

Charge RN - Medical Ward, 12:00-8:00 shift

- Cared for 30-35 acute medical patients, including giving medications, IV therapy, and respiratory treatments.
- Responsible for patient education; updated nursing care plans; performed admissions, chart audits, and patient discharge planning.
- Supervised 2 nursing assistants.

Manatee Memorial Hospital, Bradenton, FL. 1989 - 1992

Hospital Night Supervisor

- The only supervisor at this 500+ bed hospital on 12:00-8:00 shift.
- Scheduled and supervised over 50 RNs, LPNs, and NAs.
- Provided staff education, counseling, guidance, and problem solving to include all staffing problems on night tour.

Tampa General Hospital, Tampa, FL. 1984 - 1987

Staff Nurse - Orthopedics and Ophthalmology wards

- Cared for 30-40 surgical patients, including patient education, dressing changes, medications (PO, IV, IM), starting IVs, admissions, discharges, chart audits, traction, and respiratory therapy.
- Supervised 2 NAs.
- Assisted Head Nurse with staff scheduling and staff counseling, guidance, and education.

HCA L.W. Blake Hospital, Bradenton, FL. 1979 - 1982

Registered Nurse - Emergency Care Center

- Assisted physicians during various procedures and followed through with orders and protocol.

EDUCATION

B.S., Nursing, University of Bridgeport, Bridgeport, CT. 1978

Problem 14: Stating Reasons for Each Job Change

By explaining the reason behind each job change, Kraemer brings out the difficulty she has had in determining a clear career path. She presents herself as a high-risk hire who could decide once again that she wants to do something different. Her uncertainty will significantly reduce her number of interviews.

BARBARA KRAEMER
301 East 88th Street, 15C • New York, NY 10024 • Tel: (212) 369-7679 • E-mail: BarbKra@aol.com

EXPERIENCE

1999 - Present   **Doubleday,** New York, New York.
Associate Editor
- Perform line editing and copy editing on fiction and nonfiction manuscripts.
- Write copy for jackets, author bios, and marketing collateral material.
- Review manuscripts submitted by agents.
Reason for leaving: seeking more responsibility as an editor, either with a book publisher or magazine publisher.

1996 - 1998   **Universal Pictures,** New York, New York.
Story Analyst
- Evaluated book manuscripts to determine potential for feature film adaptation.
- Wrote analyses and synopses of literary properties.
- Developed contacts with book editors, scouts, and literary agents.
- Interacted on regular basis with Los Angeles executives.
- Recommended Elmore Leonard's "Out of Sight," which was made into a film.
Reason for leaving: to return to book editing.

1996 - 1996   **The Reader's Digest Association,** Pleasantville, New York.
Associate Editor
- Selected and edited popular fiction and nonfiction for long-running, global, condensed book series.
- Managed edit process from manuscript through rufs stage.
- Scouted New York publishing houses for literary properties.
- Wrote jacket blurbs, author bios, and other collateral material.
Key Accomplishment
- Discovered 2 emerging writers for fiction series.
Reason for leaving: to be more involved in the film business.

1995 - 1996   **MGM / United Artists,** New York, New York.
Assistant to Vice President
- Secured book manuscripts by developing relationships with literary agents and book editors.
- Attended story meetings.
- Wrote detailed synopses of literary properties.
- Read feature film scripts in development.
Reason for leaving: to edit books.

1994 - 1995   **Self Magazine,** New York, New York.
Researcher / Reporter
- Provided original reporting and research on feature articles for leading women's health and fitness magazine.
- Responsible for accuracy of features and columns.
- Veted articles with Legal Department.
- Acted as liaison among senior editors, copy editors, sources, and writers.
- Rewrote copy as required.
Reason for leaving: to be more involved with books.

When Kraemer deletes the reasons for changing jobs in the makeover resume, readers are now able to focus on Kraemer's capability and successes.

Barbara Kraemer
301 East 88th Street, 15C
New York, NY 10024

Tel: (212) 369-7679
E-mail: BarbKra@aol.com

EDITOR—FICTION & NONFICTION

Books & Book Series • Women's Magazines • Feature Film Development

- Repeated successes with leading publishers and movie studios, including Doubleday, The Reader's Digest, Universal Pictures, MGM / United Artists, and Self Magazine.
- Edited fiction and nonfiction, both books and magazines.
- Discovered 2 emerging writers for The Reader's Digest.
- Recommended "Out of Sight" to Universal Pictures, which was made into a film.

Highly talented editor covering popular fiction and nonfiction as well as women's health and fitness, fashion, and beauty. Excellent relationships with Manhattan publishing houses, book editors, scouts, and literary agents.

EXPERIENCE

Doubleday, New York, NY. 1999 - Present

Associate Editor

- Perform line editing and copy editing of fiction and nonfiction book manuscripts.
- Review manuscripts submitted by agents.
- Write copy for jackets, author bios, and marketing collateral material.

Universal Pictures, New York, NY. 1996 - 1998

Story Analyst

- Evaluated book manuscripts to determine potential for feature film adaptation.
- Wrote analyses and synopses of literary properties.
- Developed contacts with book editors, scouts, and literary agents.
- Interacted on regular basis with Los Angeles executives.
- Recommended Elmore Leonard's "Out of Sight," which was made into a film.

The Reader's Digest Association, Pleasantville, NY. 1996

Associate Editor

- Selected and edited popular fiction and nonfiction for long-running, global, condensed book series.
- Managed edit process from manuscript through rufs stage.
- Scouted New York publishing houses for literary properties.
- Wrote jacket blurbs, author bios, and other collateral material.

Key Accomplishment

- Discovered 2 emerging writers for fiction series.

MGM / United Artists, New York, NY. 1995 - 1996

Assistant to Vice President

- Secured book manuscripts by developing relationships with literary agents and book editors.
- Attended story meetings.
- Wrote detailed synopses of literary properties.
- Read feature film scripts in development.

Self Magazine, New York, NY. 1994 - 1995

Researcher / Reporter

- Provided original reporting and research on feature articles for leading women's health and fitness magazine.
- Responsible for accuracy of features and columns.
- Veted articles with Legal Department.
- Acted as liaison among senior editors, copy editors, sources, and writers.

Problem 15: Being Close to or Past Retirement Age

By discussing the specifics of his experience at each employer, as well as including the dates when he received his two degrees, Jankowski appears to be 62 years old.

Bruce E. Jankowski
2405 Pacific Ave.
San Francisco, CA 94123
Phone: (415) 921-4062
E-mail: bej17@msn.com

Profile

Dynamic senior-level executive with exceptional leadership, motivational, alliance-building, and communication skills. Extensive finance, marketing, sales, business development, IT, and corporate development experience.

Work Experience

OnLineDigitalSolutions, Inc., San Francisco, CA.   April '98 to November '02

A pioneer in providing fully hosted, outsourced web services platform to enable enterprise customers, including banks, telecommunications companies, and other major corporations, to deliver web-based business service applications and content to their small business customers. 2002E revenue: $6.7 million; 2001: $2.3 million; 2000: $7.2 million.

Chief Operating Officer, May '00 to November '02

P&L responsibility for all operations, including strategic planning, engineering and applications, IT, marketing, business development, and human resources. Oversaw up to 120 personnel through 6 VPs and Directors.

- Promoted to position to restructure and redirect company in response to investment community's 2000 reevaluation of high-technology businesses.
- Redirected strategic sales/marketing plan to target higher-margin channel partners and large corporations versus selling directly to small, lower-margin companies.
- Led financial and operational restructuring of company to align with new growth strategy and market conditions:
  - Slashed annual operating expenses from $24 million to $5.1 million while reducing cash burn from $1.3 million/month to $230,000/month.
  - Streamlined management layers and rationalized entire employee base, reducing headcount 70%.

Senior VP - Corporate Development & Strategic Alliances, January to May '00

- Planned, introduced, and led corporate development strategy:
  - Reviewed 36 transactions, completed due diligence on 14, completed 3 negotiations.
  - Structured 2 asset purchases and 1 combination.
- Played key role in formulating and executing financing strategy, including completion of Series D and E rounds of financing, generating $48 million.

VP - Strategic Alliances, January '98 to January '00

Hired and directed staff of 25 for functions of transaction services, business development, and channel marketing to expand growth strategy from direct marketing approach.

- Conceived of, pioneered, and implemented distribution, transaction, and sponsorship strategies that drove company to market-leading position for small business distribution networks.
- Developed 55 strategic partners through pioneering B2B syndication distribution strategy implemented across 62 branded leaders in every sub-sector of online business center space, with partners including Dell, AOL, American Express, Office Depot, Citibank, Wells Fargo, Lycos, IBM, AT&T, and Bank of America.
  - Generated professional service and license revenue for 1999 and 1Q 2000 of $6.4 million, or 480% of goal.
  - Drove overall margin from 19% to 34%.
  - Created dominant distribution and generated largest quarterly revenues in the space - as high as $3 million.
  - Delivered 30-40% of corporate revenues, 100% of gross margin (offsetting negative gross margin sources).
  - Sold 100% of available sponsorship and advertising inventory.
- Played critical role in development of branded leadership in space, resulting in consistent analyst recognition.
- Continuously exceeded goals for revenue, distribution channels, and registered usership over 6 quarters.

CSL Lighting Manufacturing Inc., Valencia, CA.   January '90 to December '97

$20 million designer, manufacturer, and distributor of high-end lighting and architectural products for hospitality industry.

VP & General Manager

Recruited by CEO and former client to join company, with mission of turning around virtually bankrupt organization, then selling company.

- Rigorously analyzed operations and growth opportunities, then developed and implemented strategic turnaround plan that delivered positive cash flow from operations in under 90 days and drove sales from $12 million a year to $20 million run rate while reversing $3.6 million annual loss and achieving breakeven. Successfully sold company to $400 million conglomerate in February 1999.
- Completely reengineered organization, including securing new financing and upgrading senior management team. Raised over $15 million in working capital through establishing new banking relationship and issuing private debt and equity. Restructured processes and procedures throughout company.
- Closed and/or sold non-performing operations in China and Morocco, plus relocated production from China, Thailand, and the Philippines to U.S.
- Reduced headcount from 115 to 45 while in 1 week's time increasing shipping as much as 25-35%.
- Eliminated 34% of SKUs, plus dramatically improved quality, reducing returned goods from 30% to 3% and defective merchandise from 20% to 1%.
- Replaced direct sales force with rep organization, saving over $950,000 a year; then worked closely with rep agencies to motivate personnel, replacing and appointing new agencies as required.
- Made strategic acquisition of lighting manufacturer.
- Restored company's reputation in marketplace, leading to successful sale of company.

Manufacturing & Financial Management Resources, Boca Raton, FL. January '85 - January '90

Consulting firm serving manufacturing clients in the optimization of production capability as well as corporate and business development, the latter including strategic planning, financial planning, corporate finance, organizational restructuring, business process development, mergers, acquisitions, joint ventures, and strategic alliances.

Senior Consultant

- Specialized in areas of manufacturing, financial planning, and corporate finance.

H. J. Meyers Inc., Boca Raton, FL. October '82 - December '84

Investment banking and brokerage firm.

VP - Corporate Finance/Director - Private Placements

- Managed over 20 public equity offerings totaling $250 million.
- Selected and closed over 30 private debt/equity placements totaling $22 million.
- Established and managed Private Placement Department.

First Florida Bank, Sarasota, FL. June '80 - August '82

Senior VP - Trust & Investment Services Group

- Directed merger of 3 separate trust departments into single entity totaling $900 million, with 60 employees.
- Established Trust Department for Sarasota County, personally delivering $170 million in assets in 5 years.
- Led mergers of 2 banks, with combined assets of $70 million, into First Florida Bank.

Sun Bank/Broward, N.A., Lauderdale-By-The-Sea and Palm Beach, FL. January '75 - May '79

VP & Regional Trust Manager, February '77 - May '79

- Established office and personally built trust assets to $25 million in 2½ years.

VP - New Business & Sales, Palm Beach County, January '75 - February '77

- Developed Sun's first comprehensive trust marketing plan, with many of its components still in use today.

Southeast Bank, Miami and Lauderdale-By-the Sea, June '65 - December '74

- Held progressively responsible trust positions culminating in Senior Trust Officer.

Education

MBA, Finance, University of Florida, 1964; B. S., Production Management, University of Florida, 1962.

In the revised resume, it's now impossible to tell how old Jankowski is. He deleted the dates of his degrees and summarized his banking experience, omitting the dates of employment.

Bruce E. Jankowski
2405 Pacific Ave.
San Francisco, CA 94123

(415) 921-4062
bej17@msn.com

SENIOR GENERAL MANAGEMENT EXECUTIVE—E-Commerce / Manufacturing

- **P&L**
- **Strategic Planning**
- **Organizational Restructuring**
- **Marketing & Sales**
- **Business and Corporate Development**
- **Finance**

- Instituted strategic growth strategy for Internet company that delivered largest quarterly revenues in the space while driving overall margin from 19% to 34% and generating professional service and license revenues at 480% of goal.
- Developed dominant distribution network in the space, forming partnerships with Dell, AOL, American Express, Office Depot, Citibank, Wells Fargo, Lycos, IBM, AT&T, and Bank of America.
- Tapped by Board to restructure company in response to 2000 devaluation of technology sector—introduced new sales / marketing strategy and reengineered company, slashing annual operating expenses 79% to $5.1 million and reducing cash burn 82% to $230,000 a month, ensuring viability and positioning company for sustained growth.
- Reengineered unprofitable $12 million lighting / architectural products manufacturer, leading to successful sale of company—generated positive cash flow from operations in less than 90 days, grew sales from $12 million a year to $20 million run rate, and transformed $3.6 million annual loss to breakeven.

An entrepreneurial executive with exceptional strategic planning, change management, crisis management, and turnaround strengths. A driven corporate strategist recognized for achievements in organizational repositioning, with extensive tactical experience in finance, marketing, sales, manufacturing, business development, IT, and corporate development. MBA, Finance; BS, Production Management.

EXPERIENCE

OnLineDigitalSolutions, Inc., San Francisco, CA. 1998 - 2002

A pioneer in providing fully hosted, outsourced web services platform to enable enterprise customers, including banks, telecommunications companies, and other major corporations, to deliver web-based business service applications and content to their small business customers. 2002E revenue: $6.7 million, 2001: $2.3 million, 2000: $7.2 million.

Chief Operating Officer, 2000 - 2002

P&L responsibility for all operations, including strategic planning, engineering and applications, IT, marketing, business development, and human resources. Oversaw up to 120 personnel through 6 VPs and Directors.

- Promoted to position to restructure and redirect company in response to investment community's 2000 reevaluation of high-technology businesses.
- Redirected strategic sales / marketing plan to target higher-margin channel partners and large corporations versus selling directly to small, lower-margin businesses.
- Led financial and operational restructuring of company to align with new growth strategy and market conditions:
  - Slashed annual operating expenses from $24 million to $5.1 million while reducing cash burn from $1.3 million / month to $230,000 / month.
  - Streamlined management layers and rationalized entire employee base, reducing headcount 70%.

Senior VP - Corporate Development & Strategic Alliances, 2000

- Planned, developed, and led corporate development strategy:
  - Reviewed 36 transactions, completed due diligence on 14, completed 3 negotiations.
  - Structured 2 asset purchases and 1 combination.
- Played key role in formulating and executing financing strategy, including completion of Series D and E rounds of financing generating $48 million.

VP - Strategic Alliances, 1998 - 2000

Hired and directed staff of 25 for functions of transaction services, business development, and channel marketing to expand growth strategy from direct marketing approach.

- Conceived of, pioneered, and implemented distribution, transaction, and sponsorship strategies that drove company to market-leading position for small business distribution networks.
- Developed 55 strategic partners through pioneering B2B syndication distribution strategy implemented across 62 branded leaders in every sub-sector of online business center space, with partners including Dell, AOL, American Express, Office Depot, Citibank, Wells Fargo, Lycos, IBM, AT&T, and Bank of America.
  - Generated professional service and license revenue for 1999 and 1Q 2000 of $6.4 million.

- Drove overall margin from 19% to 34%.
- Created dominant distribution and generated largest quarterly revenues in the space - as high as $3 million.
- Delivered 30-40% of corporate revenues, 100% of gross margin (offsetting negative gross margin sources).
- Sold 100% of available sponsorship and advertising inventory.
- Played critical role in development of branded leadership in space, resulting in consistent analyst recognition.
- Continuously exceeded goals for revenue, distribution channels, and registered usership over 6 quarters.

CSL Lighting Manufacturing Inc., Valencia, CA. 1990 - 1997

$20 million designer, manufacturer, and distributor of high-end lighting and architectural products for hospitality industry.

VP & General Manager

Recruited by CEO and former client to join company, with mission of turning around virtually bankrupt organization, then selling company.

- Rigorously analyzed operations and growth opportunities, then developed and implemented strategic turnaround plan that delivered positive cash flow from operations in under 9090 days and drove sales from $12 million a year to $20 million run rate while reversing $3.6 million annual loss and achieving breakeven. Successfully sold company to $400 million conglomerate in February 1999.
- Completely reengineered organization, including securing new financing and upgrading senior management team. Raised over $15 million in working capital through establishing new banking relationship and issuing private debt and equity. Restructured processes and procedures throughout company.
- Closed and / or sold non-performing operations in China and Morocco, plus relocated production from China, Thailand, and the Philippines to U.S.
- Reduced headcount from 115 to 45 while in 1 week's time increasing shipping as much as 25-35%.
- Eliminated 34% of SKUs, plus dramatically improved quality, reducing returned goods from 30% to 3% and defective merchandise from 20% to 1%.
- Replaced direct sales force with rep organization, saving over $950,000 a year; then worked closely with rep agencies to motivate personnel, replacing and appointing new agencies as required.
- Made strategic acquisition of lighting manufacturer.
- Restored company's reputation in marketplace, successful sale of company.

Manufacturing & Financial Management Resources, Boca Raton, FL. 1985 - 1990

Consulting firm serving manufacturing clients in the optimization of production capability as well as corporate and business development, the latter including strategic planning, financial planning, organizational restructuring, business process development, mergers, acquisitions, joint ventures, and strategic alliances.

Senior Consultant

- Specialized in areas of manufacturing, financial planning, and corporate finance.

H. J. Meyers Inc., Boca Raton, FL. 1982 - 1984

Investment banking and brokerage firm.

VP - Corporate Finance / Director - Private Placements

- Managed over 20 public equity offerings totaling $250 million.
- Selected and closed over 30 private debt / equity placements totaling $22 million.
- Established and managed Private Placement Department.

Earlier experience included progressively responsible trust positions in the banking industry, culminating with Senior VP - Trust & Investment Services Group, First Florida Bank. Previous employers included Sun Bank and Southeast Bank.

EDUCATION

MBA, Finance, University of Florida.
B. S., Production Management, University of Florida.

Problem 16: A History of Unrelated Positions

This resume depicts Tilson as an unstable individual who skips from one industry to another, with no career direction.

OWEN L. TILSON

600 Golden Gate Point, #6
Sarasota, FL 34236
941-957-4207
Owentat1@yahoo.com

WORK BACKGROUND

GULF SHORES INN, Siesta Key, FL. 1999 - Present
General Manager
- Hold P&L responsibility for this 132-room, limited-service property with 30 employees.
- Boosted average occupancy rate from 65% to 79% within 1 year while delivering record operating profit.
- Upgraded staff, implemented effective marketing and training programs, and conducted $200,000 refurbishment.

PALM MARINA, Miami Beach, FL. 1993 - 1998
General Manager
- Managed this full-service marina / boatyard with 500 slips, overseeing $3 million budget and 25 technicians, yard personnel, and office workers. P&L responsibility.
- Increased revenues 1000% in 5 years while delivering profits as high as 140% of goal.
- Upgraded technical and service staff, plus created and instituted innovative marketing programs, including developing and giving seminars to business groups and the public to increase customers and revenues.
- Trained personnel to provide outstanding service to customers.

NORTH COBB COUNTY BRANCH, JIM ROYER REALTY, INC., Atlanta, GA. 1982 - 1992
VP & Managing Broker
- Held P&L responsibility and expanded annual business from $4.5 million with 16 agents to over 50 agents generating approximately $100 million in sales.
- Achieved #1 ranking for sales units, dollar volume, and listings out of 5 branches.
- Continuously motivated and trained sales organization.
- Initially joined company as a salesman.

IMPOSTERS JEWELRY CO., Sarasota, FL. 1978 - 1981
Store Manager, 1979 - 1981.
- Raised gross margin 5 percentage points, increased net income 30%, and drove store's ranking from #31 out of 150 stores nationwide to #9. P&L responsibility.
- Restaffed store; continuously trained and motivated staff.
- Initially joined company as a salesman; set records for production.

EDUCATION

Pursued B.S., Marketing, University of West Florida, 1977 - 1979.

The new introductory section shows Tilson as an exceptional manager with a distinguished record of growing consumer businesses—both product and service—in vastly different industries. Anyone who owns a business serving the public and who needs a strong manager, trainer, and motivator would benefit from Tilson's expertise in the consumer marketplace.

Owen L. Tilson
600 Golden Gate Point, #6
Sarasota, FL 34236

(941) 957-4207
Owenta1@yahoo.com

GENERAL MANAGEMENT EXECUTIVE—CONSUMER BUSINESSES

P&L • Strategic Planning • Turnarounds • Marketing • Staff Training / Development / Motivation

Repeated successes in diverse consumer sectors, including hospitality industry, pleasure boating, real estate, and retailing.

- Delivered record operating profit at 132-room motel while increasing occupancy rate 21.5%.
- Grew marina's revenues 1000% in 5 years while exceeding profit goals up to 40%.
- Drove real estate firm's annual sales from $4.5 million to almost $100 million level, achieving #1 ranking in chain.
- Turned around retail jewelry business, increasing gross margin 5 points and operating profit 30%.

An accomplished manager of retail businesses, with a record of success at growing revenues and profits through developing and implementing innovative marketing programs as well as building outstanding teams of personnel who continuously exceed established goals. Recognized as an exceptional trainer and motivator.

EXPERIENCE

Gulf Shores Inn, Siesta Key, FL. 1999 - Present

132-room, limited service property with 30 employees.

General Manager

- Boosted average occupancy rate from 65% to 79% within 1 year while delivering record operating profit. P&L responsibility.
- Upgraded staff, implemented effective marketing programs, and conducted $200,000 refurbishment.

Palm Marina, Miami Beach, FL. 1993 - 1998

Full-service marina / boatyard with 500 slips.

General Manager

- Held P&L responsibility, overseeing $3 million budget and 25 technicians, yard personnel, and office workers.
- Increased revenues 1000% in 5 years while delivering profits as high as 140% of goal.
- Upgraded technical and service staff, plus created and instituted innovative marketing programs, including developing and giving seminars to business groups and the public to increase customers and revenues.

North Cobb County Branch, Jim Royer Realty, Inc., Atlanta, GA. 1982 - 1992

VP & Managing Broker, 1987 - 1992

- Held P&L responsibility and expanded annual business from $4.5 million with 16 agents to over 50 agents generating approximately $100 million in sales.
- Achieved #1 ranking for sales units, dollar volume, and listings out of 5 branches, 1980 and 1981.
- Initially joined company as a salesman.

Imposters Jewelry Co., Sarasota, FL. 1978 - 1981

Store Manager, 1979 - 1981

- Raised gross margin 5 percentage points, increased net income 30%, and drove underperforming store's ranking from #31 out of 150 stores nationwide to #9. P&L responsibility.
- Restaffed store and continuously trained and motivated sales personnel.
- Initially joined company as a salesman; set records for production.

Problem 17: Lacking the Experience a Position Traditionally Requires

This resume does nothing to bring forth Keyworth's qualifications to change careers and succeed as a salesperson, her new career choice.

Betsy Keyworth

4000 N. Lockwood Ridge Road
Sarasota, Florida 34234
(941) 351-4398

Objective:

Outside sales position with a company marketing products and/or services to healthcare facilities.

Experience:

Plymouth Manor, Bradenton, FL.   1999 to present
Director, Activity Department

- Plan and conduct educational, entertainment, and therapeutic programs for 200 residents at 3 multi-level retirement facilities, ensuring that federal and state guidelines are adhered to.
- Restructured 2 departments, including hiring and training new staff.
- Prepare and administer department budget; manage special projects and coordinate with other department managers; prepare monthly QA reports; and purchase required supplies and services.
- Provide inservice training to appropriate staff.
- Serve as liaison between residents and administration / department managers; represent residents at council meetings; and mediate grievances as required.
- Serve on task force to help residents transition from one level of service to another.
- Member of interdisciplinary care-plan team, responsible for participating in resident assessment and development of effective plans of care.
- Serve as Volunteer Coordinator, responsible for recruiting, hiring, and training volunteers.
- Perform public relations activities requiring networking throughout local community with civic and charitable organizations.
- Plan and conduct special events to market facility throughout Sarasota-Bradenton community.
- Attend meetings with Marketing Department to determine eligibility of new clients as well as coordinate move-ins.
- Conduct tours of facility to prospective clients and present features and benefits.

Accomplishments

- Improved department through upgrading staff.
- Manage deficiency-free department.
- Identified process to save facility $12,000 a year in administrative costs.
- Created Volunteer Handbook and developed new forms for department.
- Wrote grant for creating therapeutic multifunctional environment for dementia residents in an outdoor area.
- Selected by Administrator to conduct market research on baby boomers' expectations of a retirement center.
- Recognized throughout facility as an employee advocate. Planned and conducted an employee appreciation event.

Asbury Harbor, Sarasota, FL.   1996 to 1999
Assistant to Director of Activities

- Planned and conducted activities for residents in skilled-nursing facility.
- Assisted Director in wide variety of tasks.

After stating Keyworth's objective, the resume presents a "Qualifications" section that immediately establishes her sales aptitude and related successes, positioning her as qualified to perform outside sales.

Betsy Keyworth
4000 N. Lockwood Ridge Road
Sarasota, Florida 34234
(941) 351-4398

OBJECTIVE

Outside sales position with a company marketing products and / or services to healthcare facilities.

QUALIFICATIONS

- Extensive experience in the healthcare field, with employers including retirement homes, skilled nursing facilities, hospitals, and walk-in clinics.
- A record of success at networking throughout the community as well as conducting special events to market a retirement home to local population.
- Possess a persuasive personality with outstanding communication skills and the proven ability to work effectively with a wide variety of people.
- Goal-directed and self-motivated, with strong desire to prospect as well as increase business with existing accounts.
- Background includes purchasing supplies and services, affording an in-depth understanding of an outside salesperson's role.

EXPERIENCE

Plymouth Manor, Bradenton, FL. 1999 - present
Director, Activity Department

- Plan and conduct educational, entertainment, and therapeutic programs for 200 residents at 3 multi-level retirement facilities, ensuring that federal and state guidelines are adhered to.
- Restructured 2 departments, including hiring and training new staff.
- Prepare and administer department budget; manage special projects and coordinate with other department managers; prepare monthly QA reports; and purchase required supplies.
- Provide inservice training to appropriate staff.
- Serve as liaison between residents and administration / department managers; represent residents at council meetings; and mediate grievances as required.
- Serve on task force to help residents transition from one level of service to another.
- Member of interdisciplinary care-plan team, responsible for participating in resident assessment and development of effective plans of care.
- Serve as Volunteer Coordinator, responsible for recruiting, hiring, and training volunteers.
- Perform public relations activities requiring networking throughout local community with civic and charitable organizations.
- Plan and conduct special events to market facility throughout Sarasota-Bradenton community.
- Attend meetings with Marketing Department to determine eligibility of new clients as well as coordinate move-ins.
- Conduct tours of facility to prospective clients and present features and benefits.

Accomplishments

- Improved department through upgrading staff.
- Manage deficiency-free department.
- Identified process to save facility $12,000 a year in administrative costs.
- Created Volunteer Handbook and developed new forms for department.

Problem 18: Required Experience Appears in an Early Job

Because Waterman wants to be a private investigator, many readers will set this resume aside as soon as they see that her last two jobs have been in retailing.

HARRIET W. WATERMAN
2914 9th Street Court West
Bradenton, Florida 34205
Residence: (941) 747-9128 E-mail: Wwaterman@aol.com

OBJECTIVE

Private investigator with investigative-services firm.

WORK EXPERIENCE

PAYLESS SHOESOURCE, Tampa, Florida. 2001 - Present
<u>Area Training Supervisor</u> for this nationwide retailer of footwear.

- Assist District Supervisor in hiring and training store management trainees and store associates for 23 locations.
- Implement skill-development programs for new hires, plus conduct management skill workshops for continuous training of Store Managers.
- Communicate stores' merchandising needs to District Supervisor, improve displays and store layout, plus develop and conduct local promotions.

ETIENNE AIGNER, Orlando, Florida. 1999 - 2001
<u>Assistant Manager</u> at this upscale retailer of women's apparel.

- Hired, trained, scheduled, and supervised up to 10 sales associates.
- Managed all operations, including opening and closing store, sales, merchandising, displays, cash control, and inventory control.
- Trained associates individually as well as in group settings.
- Generated sales 10% above goal, plus set company record for achieving lowest personnel turnover.

BUSINESS CHECK, INC., Tampa, Florida. 1996 - 1998
<u>Independent Contractor</u>

- Contracted with marketing research firms across the country to evaluate operations of businesses, retail organizations, and apartment buildings.
- Assessed wide variety of factors, including appearance and attitude of employees, quality of services provided, prices offered, safety and cleanliness of facility, and decor.
- Prepared comprehensive reports on each assignment.

TAMPA SURVEILLANCE, Tampa, Florida. 1992 - 1995
<u>Private Investigator</u> for this investigative-services firm.

- Performed investigations, plus directed daily activities of up to 5 other investigators.
- Briefed clients on all investigations and information obtained.
- Provided diverse services, including surveillance, employee monitoring, activity checks, locates, backgrounds, and assets:

Surveillance. Accurately documented subject's activities, utilizing latest in high-tech video and photographic equipment.

Employee Monitoring. Observed and reported to client employee's activities and behavior.

Activity Checks. Performed discreet neighborhood interviews and analyzed subject's day-to-day capabilities, physical condition, surroundings, and lifestyle.

Locates. Determined location of subject, utilizing extensive network of local, state, and national sources.

Backgrounds. Conducted detailed investigation into subject's background and provided complete view of criminal, civil, and driving history.

Assets. Provided comprehensive review of financial sources and courthouse records to identify tangible assets, including information regarding both real and personal property.

The introductory section in the makeover presents Waterman's comprehensive background as a private investigator. Readers will be eager to learn more about her experience and will skim her retailing positions.

Harriet W. Waterman
2914 9th Street Court West
Bradenton, FL 34205

(941) 747-9128
Wwaterman@aol.com

PRIVATE INVESTIGATOR

Surveillance • Employee Monitoring • Activity Checks • Locates • Backgrounds • Assets

- Over 15 years' experience utilizing state-of-the-art techniques and equipment.
- Recognized for discretion, accuracy, and speed.
- Exceptional report preparation, including video and photo documentation.
- Hold A and C licenses.

EXPERIENCE

Payless ShoeSource, Tampa, FL. 2001 - Present
Area Training Supervisor for this nationwide retailer of footwear.

- Assist District Supervisor in hiring and training store management trainees and store associates for 23 locations.
- Implement skill-development programs for new hires, plus conduct management skill workshops for continuous training of Store Managers.
- Communicate merchandising needs of stores to District Supervisor, enhance displays and store layout, plus develop and conduct local promotions.

Etienne Aigner, Orlando, FL. 1999 - 2001
Assistant Manager at this upscale retailer of women's apparel.

- Hired, trained, scheduled, and supervised up to 10 sales associates.
- Managed all operations, including opening and closing store, sales, merchandising, displays, cash control, and inventory control.
- Trained associates individually as well as in group settings.
- Generated sales 10% above goal, plus set company record for achieving lowest personnel turnover.

Business Check, Inc., Tampa, FL. 1996 - 1998
Independent Contractor

- Contracted with marketing research firms across the country to evaluate operations of businesses, retail organizations, and apartment buildings.
- Assessed wide variety of factors, including appearance and attitude of employees, quality of services provided, prices offered, safety and cleanliness of facility, and decor.
- Prepared comprehensive reports on each assignment.

Tampa Surveillance, Tampa, FL. 1992 - 1995
Private Investigator for this investigative-services firm.

- Performed investigations, plus directed daily activities of up to 5 other investigators.
- Briefed clients on all investigations and information obtained.
- Provided diverse services, including surveillance, employee monitoring, activity checks, locates, backgrounds, and assets:

   Surveillance. Accurately documented subject's activities, utilizing latest in high-tech video and photographic equipment.

   Employee Monitoring. Observed and reported to client employee's activities and behavior.

   Activity Checks. Performed discreet neighborhood interviews and analyzed subject's day-to-day capabilities, physical condition, surroundings, and lifestyle.

   Locates. Determined location of subject, utilizing extensive network of local, state, and national sources.

   Backgrounds. Conducted detailed investigation into subject's background and provided complete view of criminal, civil, and driving history.

Problem 19: Recent Decreases in Responsibility

Lawrence shows promotions from servicing cars to selling them to becoming a Sales & Leasing Manager. Then he experiences decreases in responsibility, first taking a job as Service Manager, then as Finance & Insurance Manager, an even less responsible position. Lawrence appears to be burnt out, with a derailed background.

Floyd Lawrence

33 Ramblewood Place
Sarasota, FL 34237

Telephone: (941) 954-5244
E-mail: Flawrence111@aol.com

OBJECTIVE

Sales Management position with auto dealer seeking dramatic increase in sales and profits.

SUMMARY OF QUALIFICATIONS

A strong hands-on auto dealership sales manager with a record of success at increasing revenues and profits. Proven ability to hire and develop dedicated and motivated sales teams. Equally skilled at identifying problem areas and formulating effective solutions. An outstanding leader, communicator, and decision maker who ensures that all facets of the sales function are operating at optimum efficiency.

EXPERIENCE

TROPICAL CADILLAC AND OLDSMOBILE, Bradenton, FL.   Jan. '01 to Present
Finance & Insurance Manager
- Complete responsibility for preparing all documents required for financing, insurance, and title work, for both new and used vehicles.
- Established outstanding relationships with 5 lenders to ensure acceptance of maximum number of loan applications.
- Successfully elicited concessions from lenders to gain acceptance of marginal credit risks.
- Set company records for selling add-ons, including extended warranties, gap insurance, maintenance plans, and credit / life / disability insurance.

COAST CADILLAC, Sarasota, FL.   Mar. '97 to Dec. '00
Service Manager
- Managed 30+ employees generating up to $130,000 a month in labor sales. Responsibilities included hiring, training, managing, and motivating technicians, service advisors, the cashier, and warranty clerk.
- Consistently met profit goals while decreasing costs up to 10%.
- Maintained repair order fill rate of 98% and kept parts inventory at turn of 2X annually.
- Held obsolescence at less than $3000 over 12-month period.
- Operated department with minimum of personnel while providing outstanding service and customer satisfaction.
- Instituted numerous systems and procedures that improved efficiency of operations while decreasing time required to perform repair work up to 10%.
- Prepared all service operations, installing up to 400 operation codes in the computer.

POTAMKIN AUTO CENTER, New York, NY.   Oct. '91 to Jan. '97
Sales & Leasing Manager at flagship Manhattan location for this 50-unit chain.
- Increased revenues 100% from 1995 to 1997.
- Sold up to 1500 cars a year and wrote up to 2500 leases.
- Managed sales staff of 30, continuously training personnel in qualifying and closing techniques.
- Projected sales; ordered and paid for vehicles; established sales and leasing prices; negotiated credit lines and terms with lenders; billed and closed out all transactions; T.O.'d customers; instrumental in managing customer service and customer-relation problems.
- Initially joined company as Sales Associate in 1991; sold and leased over 400 vehicles in 1993, ranking #2 in 60-person sales force. Promoted to Leasing Manager in 1994. Promoted to Sales & Leasing Manager in 1995.

Earlier background includes 5 years' experience in auto sales after 5 years' experience servicing vehicles. High-school graduate.

In the introductory section in the revised resume, the reader immediately sees Lawrence as an extremely successful Sales & Leasing Manager with an outstanding record of accomplishments. When his decreases in responsibility become evident, readers will be more curious about the reasons for his job choices than they will be suspicious. Lawrence also de-emphasizes his time as Service Manager and Finance & Insurance Manager by deleting some of his activities in those positions.

Floyd Lawrence
33 Ramblewood Place
Sarasota, FL 34237

(941) 954-5244
Flawrence111@aol.com

SALES & LEASING MANAGER—AUTO DEALERSHIPS

- Managed sales and leasing at Potamkin's flagship Manhattan location.
- Doubled sales in 2-year period, managing sales staff of 30 selling 1500 cars and writing 2500 leases annually.
- Recognized for broad strengths in hiring, training, and developing topflight sales organizations that continuously meet or exceed sales goals.
- Background includes sales, leasing, and servicing new and used vehicles.

EXPERIENCE

TROPICAL CADILLAC AND OLDSMOBILE, Bradenton, FL. 2001 - Present
Finance & Insurance Manager

- Established outstanding relationships with 5 lenders, ensuring acceptance of maximum number of loan applications.
- Successfully elicited concessions from lenders to gain acceptance of marginal credit risks.
- Set company records for selling add-ons, including extended warranties, gap insurance, maintenance plans, and credit / life / disability insurance.

COAST CADILLAC, Sarasota, FL. 1997 - 2000
Service Manager

- Managed 30+ employees generating up to $130,000 a month in labor sales. Responsibilities included hiring, training, managing, and motivating technicians, service advisors, the cashier, and warranty clerk.
- Consistently met profit goals while decreasing costs up to 10%.
- Maintained repair order fill rate of 98% and kept parts inventory at turn of 2X annually.
- Held obsolescence at less than $3000 over 12-month period.

POTAMKIN AUTO CENTER, New York, NY. 1991 - 1997
Sales & Leasing Manager at flagship Park Avenue location for this 50-unit chain.

- Increased revenues 100% from 1995 to 1997.
- Sold up to 1500 cars in a year and wrote up to 2500 leases.
- Managed sales staff of 30, continuously training personnel in qualifying and closing techniques.
- Projected sales; ordered and paid for vehicles; established sales and leasing prices; negotiated credit lines and terms with lenders; billed and closed out all transactions; T.O.'d customers; instrumental in managing customer service and customer-relation problems.
- Initially joined company as Sales Associate in 1991; sold and leased over 400 vehicles in 1993, ranking #2 in 60-person sales force. Promoted to Leasing Manager in 1994. Promoted to Sales & Leasing Manager in 1995.

Earlier background includes 5 years' experience in auto sales after 5 years' experience servicing vehicles. High-school graduate.

Problem 20: The Resume Contains an Embarrassing Position

The problem with this resume is the two years Costello took off from the property appraisal business, 1992 to 1994, to own and operate a tavern. Many people will look unfavorably upon this experience and eliminate him from consideration.

FRANK D. COSTELLO
6504 Heron Lane
Sarasota, FL 34242
941-349-6620
fdcostello2@home.com

BACKGROUND

SUNSHINE BANK, Sarasota, FL. 1998 - 2002
Assistant Vice President
- Recruited by Senior Appraisal Officer to start up and manage Residential Appraisal Department for major residential lending institution.
- Staffed and trained most profitable appraisal team in the bank's system, managing up to 4 appraisers, with each one exceeding goal.
- Oversaw all internal and external work-flow processes.

FRANK D. COSTELLO APPRAISAL, INC., Sarasota, FL. 1994 - 1998
Founder / General Manager
- Started up this residential appraisal business, growing annual revenues to $215,000, with 5-month 1998 annual run rate of $250,000.
- Created business plan, staffed organization, and developed and implemented all policies and operating procedures, achieving 90% on-time performance, versus 80% industry average, and outstanding reputation for quality and accuracy.
- Developed and implemented segmented marketing plan, targeting banks, attorneys, mortgage brokers, and guardians.
- Networked through various business groups and organizations, including Power Network, Sarasota Chamber of Commerce, and United Cerebral Palsy, achieving 75% repeat business from referrals generated.
- Grew high-profit, niche, luxury-property market from 10% of business to 40%.
- Created and conducted cold-calling campaign to attorneys, generating 82% new business response rate.

SUNSET HOUSE, Sarasota, FL. 1992 - 1994
Co-owner
- Managed all bar operations, including hiring and overseeing 5 bartenders.
- Ensured outstanding service to guests and desired ambiance to generate repeat clientele.
- Established purveyors and performed extensive negotiating to secure lowest possible prices.
- Achieved all cost objectives and optimal inventory levels, keeping liquor costs below 20%, beer costs under 24%, and wine costs at less than 35%.
- Regularly attended wine tastings, purveyor promotions, and trade shows, developing and cultivating relationships with food and beverage personnel throughout Sarasota area.

KEY APPRAISAL SERVICES, Sarasota, FL. 1991 - 1992
Independent Fee Appraiser - Residential

SAVINGS OF AMERICA, Sarasota, FL. 1986 - 1991
Appraisal Supervisor, Chief Appraiser, Senior Staff Appraiser, Staff Appraiser
- Managed #1 producing appraisal team, overseeing staff of 4-6.

In the revised resume, Costello accounts for his work experience from 1992 to 1994 but provides no information as to what he was actually doing, giving readers no reason to reject him.

Frank D. Costello
6504 Heron Lane
Sarasota, FL 34242

941-349-6620
fdcostello2@home.com

RESIDENTIAL APPRAISAL

- Started up Sunshine Bank's Residential Appraisal Department and grew it into most profitable appraisal team throughout bank's system.
- Previously, operated appraisal company that generated $215,000 in annual revenues, with last year run rate at $250,000 level. Delivered 90% on-time performance versus 80% industry average.

EXPERIENCE

Sunshine Bank, Sarasota, FL. 1998 - 2003
Assistant Vice President

- Recruited by Senior Appraisal Officer to start up and manage Residential Appraisal Department for major residential lending institution.
- Staffed and trained most profitable appraisal team in the bank's system, managing up to 4 appraisers, with each one exceeding goal.
- Oversaw all internal and external work-flow processes.

Frank D. Costello Appraisal, Inc., Sarasota, FL. 1994 - 1998
Founder / General Manager

- Started up this residential appraisal business, growing annual revenues to $215,000, with 5-month 1998 annual run rate of $250,000.
- Created business plan, staffed organization, and developed and implemented all policies and operating procedures, achieving 90% on-time performance, versus 80% industry average, and outstanding reputation for quality and accuracy.
- Developed and implemented segmented marketing plan, targeting banks, attorneys, mortgage brokers, and guardians.
- Networked through various business groups and organizations, including Power Network, Sarasota Chamber of Commerce, and United Cerebral Palsy, achieving 75% repeat business from referrals generated.
- Grew high-profit, niche, luxury-property market from 10% of business to 40%.
- Created and conducted cold-calling campaign to attorneys, generating 82% new business response rate.

Sunset House, Sarasota, FL. 1992 - 1994
Co-owner

Sarasota Appraisal Services, Sarasota, FL. 1991 - 1992
Independent Fee Appraiser - Residential

Savings of America, Sarasota, FL. 1986 - 1991

- Held progressively responsible appraisal positions.
- Managed #1 producing appraisal team, overseeing staff of 4-6.

Previous experience includes: Independent Fee Appraiser, The Ratchford Group, Inc., 1985 - 1986; Staff Appraiser, The Robert W. Dunham Company, 1984 - 1985; Planner / Assistant Loan Officer, Community Development Block Grant Program, City of Sarasota, 1979 - 1984.

Problem 21: Dividing Key Accomplishments between Resume and Cover Letter

To avoid what Johnson considers to be repetition, he omits from his cover letter some of the most important accomplishments in his original resume (underlined), and he omits from this resume the two accomplishments that appear in his cover letter. By not providing this key information, he dilutes the impact of both documents.

Mathew B. Johnson, Jr.
4 Brookwood Drive
Downington, PA 19335
Tel: (610) 518-4591
E-mail: mbj1961@aol.com

March 22, 2003

Mr. George N. Simpson
Ward Howell International, Inc.
One Landmark Square, Suite 1810
Stamford, CT 06901

Dear Mr. Simpson:

I'm an accomplished senior executive with a record of success in general management, manufacturing, and sales management for companies with multi-plant operations. Key strengths include P&L, strategic planning, turnaround management, and organizational reengineering. At the present time I'm seeking a new opportunity and challenge and would like to apprise you of my background. My resume is enclosed for your review. Select highlights include:

- Turned around an industrial manufacturer with a 12% operating loss and delivered an operating income of 6% within 10 months, then achieved a 15% operating income 8 months later.
- Made sweeping changes at an industrial manufacturing company, improving on-time delivery from 79% to 96% while reducing direct labor 15%.
- Expert at leading-edge manufacturing techniques: Lean Manufacturing, JIT, Kaizen, Kanban, Flow Production.

Many of my accomplishments resulted from building dedicated and motivated teams to support me in my mission. I have the proven ability to recognize and attract top talent as well as create an environment where people work with commitment to achieve established goals.

In short, I combine outstanding human relations skills with the management knowledge, resourcefulness, and drive that are required to propel an organization to the next level of success and profitability.

My annual income is in the $175,000 area.

Please contact me at your convenience if you need any additional information. Otherwise, I look forward to hearing from you when my background is appropriate for a search.

Thank you in advance for reviewing my credentials.

Sincerely,

Mathew B. Johnson, Jr.

With Johnson's key accomplishments now appearing in both his revised resume and cover letter, the documents are as strong as they can be, which will translate into a maximum number of interviews.

Mathew B. Johnson, Jr.
4 Brookwood Drive
Downington, PA 19335
Tel: (610) 518-4591
E-mail: mbj1961@aol.com

March 22, 2003

Mr. George N. Simpson
Ward Howell International, Inc.
One Landmark Square, Suite 1810
Stamford, CT 06901

Dear Mr. Simpson:

I'm an accomplished senior executive with a record of success in general management, manufacturing, and sales management for companies with multi-plant operations. Key strengths include P&L, strategic planning, turnaround management, and organizational reengineering. At the present time I'm seeking a new opportunity and challenge and would like to apprise you of my background. My resume is enclosed for your review. Select highlights include:

- Turned around an industrial manufacturer with a 12% operating loss and delivered an operating income of 6% within 10 months, then achieved a 15% operating income 8 months later.
- Improved productivity for a multi-plant manufacturer 31% across all 3 plants, including increasing on-time delivery from 28% to greater than 90% in 7 months and improving the safety incident rate from 31.3 to 16.8 (less than the industry average).
- Turned around a stagnant sales force failing to meet goals—reorganized and restaffed the organization, generating revenues 18% ahead of plan.
- Made sweeping changes at several industrial manufacturing companies, reducing set-up times 45%, boosting machine utilization 40%, decreasing scrap 66%, and improving on-time delivery from 79% to 96% while decreasing direct labor 15%.
- Expert at leading-edge manufacturing techniques: Lean Manufacturing, JIT, Kaizen, Kanban, Flow Production.

Many of my accomplishments resulted from building dedicated and motivated teams to support me in my mission. I have the proven ability to recognize and attract top talent as well as create an environment where people work with commitment to achieve established goals.

In short, I combine outstanding human relations skills with the management knowledge, resourcefulness, and drive that are required to propel an organization to the next level of success and profitability.

My annual income is in the $175,000 area.

Please contact me at your convenience if you need any additional information. Otherwise, I look forward to hearing from you when my background is appropriate for a search.

Thank you in advance for reviewing my credentials.

Sincerely,

Mathew B. Johnson, Jr.

Mathew B. Johnson, Jr.
4 Brookwood Drive
Downington, PA 19335

Tel: (610) 518-4591
E-mail: mbj1961@aol.com

BACKGROUND PROFILE

Strong, well-rounded, performance-oriented general management / manufacturing / sales management executive with outstanding turnaround experience in rapid-growth environments. Successfully implemented ISO 9000 quality systems to become an approved supplier to automotive-based and other OEMs. Experienced in leading-edge techniques such as Lean Manufacturing, JIT, Kaizen, Kanban, and Flow Production. People-oriented motivator able to produce results in a fast-paced, turbulent environment with an emphasis on teamwork to achieve established goals.

EXPERIENCE

ALL-BODY INDUSTRIES, INC., Green Hills, PA.   2000-Present

VP - Operations at a $42 million, multi-plant operation manufacturing service bodies for the utility, wireless, telephone, and other service industries. Responsible for manufacturing, engineering, purchasing, logistics, environmental, safety, and human resources functions. Report to President.

- Improved productivity 31% across 3 plants, increased on-time delivery from 28% to greater than 90% in 7 months, plus improved safety incident rate from 31.3 to 16.8 (less than industry average).
- Introduced quality-measurement and root-cause, corrective-action system that improved quality from chronically poor levels to minor and infrequent complaints.
- Restructured, streamlined, and reduced headcount 50% while increasing production volume by changing plant layouts and improving management capabilities through both mentoring and replacing personnel as appropriate.
- Introduced Lean Manufacturing techniques and initiated major inventory reduction program after full implementation of new ERP system.

PAPEREX CORPORATION, Greenville, SC.   1999-2000

General Manager of a $45 million plant manufacturing paper machine components, recovering paper machine rolls, and servicing paper machines. P&L responsibility for manufacturing, engineering, accounting, purchasing, MIS, customer service, human resources, and sales organization covering Southeast U.S. Production processes included machining, assembly, welding, composites, rubber coating, polyurethane casting, and high-tech proprietary metal and ceramic flame-spray coating. Reported to Sr. VP-Operations.

- Turned around underperforming sales force failing to meet goal. Reorganized and restaffed organization, generating revenues 18% ahead of plan.
- Fostered facility-wide change in culture that emphasized teamwork, root-cause problem solving, greater levels of accountability, and commitment to the customer.
- Improved ISO 9000 audit results and increased annual inventory turns from 4 to 6 in 3 months, using Kanban, JIT, and inventory consignment.

ADVANCED BODY MANUFACTURING, INC., East St. Louis, MO.   1991-1999

VP - Manufacturing at a $70 million diversified Tier-1 supplier to heavy truck manufacturers and other OEM suppliers in North America. Processes included CNC metal fabrication, machining, complex assembly, welding, molded plastics, composites, and painting in manufacture of truck cabs, sleeper cabs, interior components, aircraft parts, jet-ski hulls, and other OEM components and assemblies. Member of Executive Committee setting company policy, strategy, goals, and business planning. Reported to President.

- Reduced CNC fabrication set-up time 45%, increased CNC machine utilization 40%, and decreased scrap 66%, using Kaizen events and techniques.
  - Facilitated implementation of 2 MRP II systems, achieving inventory accuracies greater than 98% and increasing turns from 4 to 12 per year.
  - Implemented SPC, achieving overall Cpk values in excess of 1.67.
  - Led creation of self-directed work teams in fabrication and assembly work cells. Introduced cross-functional teams in program management, new projects, and new product implementation.
- Improved workers' compensation industry rating to better than industry average, after having been placed in state's

Mathew B. Johnson, Jr.
4 Brookwood Drive
Downington, PA 19335

Tel: (610) 518-4591
E-mail: mbj1961@aol.com

SENIOR EXECUTIVE—GENERAL MANAGEMENT / MANUFACTURING / MULTI-PLANT EXPERIENCE

P&L • Strategic Planning • Turnaround Management • Organizational Reengineering • Sales Management

- Transformed auto parts manufacturer's 12% operating loss into 6% operating income after 10 months, then achieved 15% operating income 8 months later.
- Reengineered production operations for a multi-plant manufacturer, improving productivity 31% across all 3 plants, increasing on-time delivery from 28% to greater than 90% in 7 months, and reducing accident incident rate from 31.3 to 16.8 (less than the industry average).
- Revitalized stagnant sales force failing to meet goals—reorganized and restaffed the organization, delivering revenues 18% ahead of plan.
- Revamped operations at several industrial manufacturing companies, reducing set-up times 45%, boosting machine utilization 40%, decreasing scrap 66%, and improving on-time delivery from 79% to 96% while decreasing direct labor 15%.
- Accomplished at leading-edge manufacturing techniques: Lean Manufacturing, JIT, Kaizen, Kanban, Flow Production.

An innovative and energetic leader, skilled communicator / team builder, and adept negotiator. Accomplished at analyzing operations, then developing and implementing strategic and tactical solutions that improve competitive performance while increasing production, improving quality, and growing revenues and profits. Successful in fast paced, turbulent environments.

EXPERIENCE

ALL-BODY INDUSTRIES, INC., Green Hills, PA. 2000 - Present

VP - Operations at a $42 million, multi-plant operation manufacturing service bodies for the utility, wireless, telephone, and other service industries. Responsible for manufacturing, engineering, purchasing, logistics, environmental, safety, and human resources functions. Report to President.

- Improved productivity 31% across 3 plants, increased on-time delivery from 28% to greater than 90% in 7 months, plus improved safety incident rate from 31.3 to 16.8 (less than industry average).
- Introduced quality-measurement and root-cause, corrective-action system that improved quality from chronically poor levels to minor and infrequent complaints.
- Restructured, streamlined, and reduced headcount 50% while production volume increased by changing plant layouts and improving management capabilities through both mentoring and replacements as appropriate.

PAPEREX CORPORATION, Greenville, SC. 1999 - 2000

General Manager of a $45 million plant engaged in manufacture of paper machine components, recovery of paper machine rolls, and servicing of paper machines. P&L responsibility for manufacturing, engineering, accounting, purchasing, MIS, customer service, HR, as well as sales organization covering Southeast U.S. Production processes included machining, assembly, welding, composites, rubber coating, polyurethane casting, and high-tech proprietary metal and ceramic flame-spray coating. Reported to Sr. VP-Operations.

- Turned around underperforming sales force failing to meet goals. Reorganized and restaffed organization, generating revenues 18% ahead of plan.
- Fostered facility-wide change in culture that emphasized teamwork, root-cause problem solving, greater levels of accountability, and commitment to the customer.
- Improved ISO 9000 audit results and increased annual inventory turns from 4 months to 6 within 3 months, implementing Kanban, JIT, and inventory consignment.
- Improved on-time delivery from 79% to over 96% by reducing cycle times, using Lean Manufacturing, Flow Production, and cross training, also reducing direct labor 15%.

ADVANCED BODY MANUFACTURING, INC., East St. Louis, MO. 1991 - 1999

VP - Manufacturing at a $70 million diversified Tier-1 supplier to heavy truck manufacturers and other OEM suppliers in North America. Processes included CNC metal fabrication, machining, complex assembly, welding, molded plastics, composites, and painting in manufacture of truck cabs, sleeper cabs, interior components, aircraft parts, jet-ski hulls, and other OEM components and assemblies. Member of Executive Committee setting company policy, strategy, goals, and business planning. Reported to President.

- Turned around business with 12% operating loss and delivered 6% operating income after 10 months, achieving first positive month after 34 months of losses. Grew operating income to 15% just 8 months later.

Problems with Clarity and Word Choice
in Resumes

Problem 22: Failure to Discuss Accomplishments in Statements Beginning with Action Verbs

This resume looks as if Dunwoody wrote it as fast as he could, just jotting down his key successes. The lack of effort he put into preparing his resume suggests an individual who doesn't place much importance on his career, despite his impressive accomplishments.

Preston J. Dunwoody
2660 Hope Rd.
Cumming, GA 30041
Residence: (770) 889-0238
E-mail: pjdunwoody@aol.com

Work Experience:

Credex, Inc., August 1997 - Present
Regional Vice President, January 2000 - Present
Responsible for the hiring, management, and motivation of a sales force of up to 16 personnel covering the southeastern United States, selling small business owners an Internet-based, cash flow credit product via community banks. Oversight responsibility for some 200+ bank clients, with activities including development of relationships with senior management at key banks and with several key business accounts in providing quality service to those banks and business customers.

2002
- 2nd-ranked team overall (units & revenue), $7 million, 24% ahead of #3 team
- 1st in Q1 revenue; highest monthly units twice
- New customers equaled 30% of sales
- Hired three of seven reps; two qualified for President's Club
- Qualified for President's Club

2001
- Regional Manager of the Year
- Managed Regional Team of the Year
- Three of seven salespeople qualified for President's Club
- Qualified for President's Club

2000
- Highest per-rep revenue average, which exceeded $150,000 President's Club level
- Seven of eight salespeople qualified for President's Club
- Managed Co-Salesperson of the Year
- Managed a fifth-year, never-been-to-Club salesperson to Club
- Qualified for President's Club

Business Development Manager, May 1997 - December 1999
Responsible for the sale of an accounts-receivable financing program to small business owners via community banks. The sale required, first, the development of relationships with assigned banks; second, the implementation of an effective marketing strategy to target and meet with prospective candidates; third, the sale of the product to the prospect, including complex financial analysis; and, finally, the management of the approval and funding process.

1999
- Business Development Manager of the Year
- Qualified for Presidents Club ($14.2 million sales, #1)
- Diamond Club
- Grand Slam Award
- Promoted to Vice President

1998
- Qualified for President's Club ($8.6 million sales, #16)
- Diamond Club for selling $2 million in a month
- Triple Million Dollar Club for three months with sales in excess of $1 million

---

The rewritten resume now portrays a true business professional as well as an individual who carefully plans his work and takes pride in it, especially his successes. Dunwoody clearly has aspirations for career growth and increased responsibility.

Preston J. Dunwoody
2660 Hope Rd.
Cumming, GA 30041

Tel: (770) 889-0238
E-mail: pjdunwoody@aol.com

SENIOR SALES MANAGEMENT EXECUTIVE

- **Strategic Planning**
- **Training & Development**
- **Motivational Techniques**
- **Account Development & Management**

- Built and managed #2 sales team in nation, surpassing revenues of #3 team by 24%. Delivered highest monthly units twice, highest monthly revenue 3 times, and achieved #1 in nation for 2002 Q1 revenue.
- Earlier in career, won "Regional Manager of the Year," managed "Regional Team of the Year," and produced highest revenue per rep.

An accomplished sales manager, trainer, and motivator with the exceptional ability to hire and develop high-performance producers with outstanding product knowledge and skills in time management and opportunity management. Broad strengths in accessing key decision makers and closing business; adept at the consultative / solutions sales approach, selling in fast-paced, rapidly changing markets, plus developing long-term relationships with customers built on trust and exceptional service.

EXPERIENCE

Credex, Inc., 1997 - Present

Marketer of Internet-based cash flow credit product to small business owners via 200+ community banks.

Regional Vice President, 2000 - Present.

Complete responsibility for managing sales force of up to 16 covering southeastern United States.

2002

- Built and managed #2 ranking team in U.S., delivering over $7 million in revenues and eclipsing #3 team by 24%.
- Hired and developed 3 of the reps on the 7-person team; accompanied on sales calls as required, plus assisted in closing large sales.
- Generated new customers, accounting for 30% of total sales.
- Achieved highest monthly units twice, highest monthly revenue 3 times, and #1 in nation for Q1 revenue.
- Qualified for President's Club in addition to 2 sales reps qualifying for award.

2001

- Won "Regional Manager of the Year," plus managed "Regional Team of the Year."
- Qualified for President's Club along with 3 of 7 sales reps qualifying for Club.

2000

- Took over team of 8 and achieved highest per-rep revenue average, exceeding $150,000 President's Club level.
- Qualified for President's Club along with 7 of 8 sales reps qualifying.
- Managed "Co-Salesperson of the Year," plus developed sales rep who won President's Club for first time after 5 years with company.

Business Development Manager, 1997 - 1999

Responsible for the sale of accounts-receivable financing program to small business owners via community banks.

1999

- Won "Business Development Manager of the Year," achieving #1 ranking in nation and delivering sales of $14.2 million. Also achieved "Diamond Club," "Grand Slam Award," and promotion to Vice President.

1998

- Achieved President's Club with sales of $8.6 million, Diamond Club for selling $2 million in a month's time, and Triple Million Dollar Club for 3 months of sales in excess of $1 million.

Problem 23: Word Repetition, Especially in Beginning Statements

In this first resume, the continuous use of the same words (underlined) makes for boring reading. Moreover, it causes doubt about how creative a marketer Wilcox really is. (After all, he's trying to market himself with his resume!)

BENJAMIN J. WILCOX
146 Connecticut Street
San Francisco, CA 94107
415.552.3286
b_wilcox@earthlink.net

SUMMARY OF QUALIFICATIONS

- 8 years' experience working in sales and marketing, including 4 years in management positions.
- 6 years' experience developing promotions to increase sales and increase brand awareness.
- 2 years' experience developing ad campaigns, using print, radio, television, and web sites.

PROFESSIONAL EXPERIENCE

Telcom Services of California, San Francisco, CA.   2001 to 2002

Marketing Manager for this start-up provider of long-distance telecommunication services.
- Developed marketing campaigns to attract new customers.
- Developed campaigns to increase sales through channel partners.
- Wrote case studies and press releases, plus designed marketing collateral materials.

Alltel, Inc., Little Rock, AR.   1994 to 2001

$6+ billion, NYSE-listed provider of telecommunication and information services.

Regional Marketing Manager - West Coast, 1999 to 2001
- Developed marketing campaigns to gain new customers, retain existing customers, plus position company as a market leader—exceeded goal each year from 10-20%.
- Managed $15 million advertising budget covering 3-state region.
- Developed marketing campaigns to introduce new products and services.
- Developed and managed direct marketing campaigns and web-advertising initiatives, exceeding plan by 4-10%.
- Negotiated and managed advertising sponsorships with $500,000 annual value.
- Developed and managed customer events.
- Developed collateral and sales materials for retail stores.

Regional Pricing Manager - West Coast, 1998 to 1999
- Developed plan for identifying customer needs, then developed pricing structure that was competitive yet increased profits 5%.
- Managed launch of new products and services.
- Analyzed competitors and monitored changes in wireless industry.
- Developed and managed customer retention programs, resulting in 15% decrease in customer disconnects.

Sales Manager - West Coast, 1997 to 1998
- Managed 18-person team of sales representatives, with each rep responsible for generating annual sales of $1.4 million from new customers—achieved 104% of goal.
- Hired, trained, motivated, and monitored sales organization.

Regional Marketing Associate - West Coast, 1994 to 1997
- Developed retail promotions to acquire new customers.
- Managed internal audits to ensure compliance with company policies.

The rewritten resume continuously uses different words, resulting in a fresh and exciting presentation of Wilcox's background and successes.

Benjamin J. Wilcox
146 Connecticut Street
San Francisco, CA 94107

Tel: (415) 552-3286
E-mail: b_wilcox@earthlink.net

SALES & MARKETING MANAGEMENT—Telecommunications

Account Development / Management • New Product & Service Launch • Internet Marketing • Start-ups

- Built and led 18-person sales organization that consistently exceeded goals, achieving as high as 120% of plan.
- Managed $15 million advertising budget, plus developed and conducted marketing programs that exceeded goal by as much as 10%.
- Performed competitive intelligence, then implemented new pricing strategy that increased profits 5%.

An innovative and energetic leader, skilled communicator / team builder, and adept negotiator. Proven ability to analyze products, services, markets, and growth opportunities, then introduce initiatives that increase sales and profits.

EXPERIENCE

Telcom Services of California, San Francisco, CA. 2001 - 2002

Marketing Manager for this start-up provider of long-distance telecommunication services.

- Originated marketing campaigns to attract new customers.
- Created programs to increase sales through channel partners.
- Wrote case studies and press releases, plus developed innovative marketing collateral materials.

Alltel, Inc., Little Rock, AR. 1994 - 2001

$6+ billion, NYSE-listed provider of telecommunication and information services.

Regional Marketing Manager - West Coast, 1999 - 2001

- Designed marketing initiatives to gain new customers, retain existing accounts, plus position company as a market leader—exceeded goal each year from 10-20%.
- Planned and administered $15 million advertising budget covering 3-state region.
- Developed marketing programs to introduce new products and services.
- Created and implemented direct marketing campaigns and web-advertising initiatives, exceeding plan by 4-10%.
- Negotiated and managed advertising sponsorships with $500,000 annual value.
- Originated and conducted customer events.
- Created and produced collateral and sales materials for retail stores.

Regional Pricing Manager - West Coast, 1998 - 1999

- Initiated plan for identifying customer needs, then formulated pricing structure that was competitive yet increased profits 5%.
- Planned and conducted launch of new products and services.
- Analyzed competitors and monitored changes in wireless industry.
- Developed and managed customer retention programs, resulting in 15% decrease in customer disconnects.

Sales Manager - West Coast, 1997 - 1998

- Led 18-person team of sales representatives, with each representative responsible for generating annual sales of $1.4 million from new customers—achieved 104% of goal.
- Hired, trained, motivated, and monitored sales organization.

Regional Marketing Associate - West Coast, 1994 - 1997

- Conceived of, designed, and conducted retail promotions to acquire new customers.
- Managed internal audits to ensure compliance with company policies.

Problems with Clarity and Word Choice in Resumes

Problem 24: Using "I" and "My," Especially to Begin Statements

Beginning statements with "I" and "My," as Daniels did in this resume, automatically dilutes the power of those statements. Additionally, what's being said takes on a juvenile and unprofessional tone that turns off many readers.

HAROLD W. DANIELS
5624 Bridle Bend Trail • Plano, TX 75093 • 214-616-7689 • hwdaniels@aol.com

CAREER PROFILE

I have a long history of growing responsibility and strong commitment towards achieving business results. For business and technical professionals, focusing on improving business measures is a challenging effort, usually due to different views on priorities. My balancing technical utilization with costs to achieve business value will continue to be a focus for me in the current business climate and is one of my key strengths. My last two years have been spent transforming an international start-up into an operationally stable business. Managing this business through the last two turbulent years has been challenging and rewarding for me. This recent international experience provided me with new executive leadership and management skills, additional personnel sensitivity and management skills, and continued technical and business delivery of major OSS application components.

EXPERIENCE

TELECOMMUNICATIONS INTERNATIONAL, Dallas, TX. Jan. 2000 - Mar. 2003

Chief Information Officer - CLEC Broadband Services Provider

As CIO and part of a six-person Executive Management team, I oversaw the closing of nonprofitable business ventures, consolidation of business units to gain synergies, and alignment of resources to increase sales and operational efficiency in order to make the business more profitable. During this time I also led the relaunch of our complete OSS, automating primary business processes that allowed us to align our cost structure and launch new xDSL services. Highlights include:

- I maintained IT budget control even while the business and network services were inappropriately growing between 20-30%. Total IT investments as a percentage of revenue for 2000 to 2001 were reduced from 14.9% to 6.7%. Ultimate downsizing of company had little impact on IT.
- I decreased voice provisioning timeframe from several minutes to real-time, allowing new wholesaler marketing plans that supported as many as 20,000 activations and deactivations per day.
- I improved E2E order entry for basic voice services from forty-five minutes to less than seven minutes for internally entered orders and zero minutes for externally entered orders through process simplification and EAI integration between Web, CRM, billing, and switch activation applications. This improvement supported a rationalization of our back-office departments by between 20-30%.
- I extended new architected OSS to support semi-automated order to activation of xDSL services in three to four months.
- I reduced company SG&A from 117% of sales to 60% while growing sales by over 52%.

ACCENTURE / ANDERSEN CONSULTING, Chicago, IL. Apr. 1985 - Dec. 1999

Business and Systems Integrator and **Associate Partner**

My fifteen-year career with this firm has enabled me to work on over 30 projects in a variety of industries, including retail, manufacturing, advertising, banking, and telecommunications. The skills that I developed were comprehensive in both depth and breadth, and they included programming, business analysis, technical design, project management, sales, business results delivery, customer relationship development, financial / budget management, recruiting and many others. My scope of responsibility also increased as I was promoted from my initial position of Analyst. My promotion timeframe is as follows: Supervisor 1988, Manager 1990, Associate Partner 1996. Two selected client engagements are described below as a representative example of the skills I developed over my fifteen-year career. These two engagements are projects for which I was responsible for selling and delivering the business results promised to the client.

National Long Distance Middle Market Service Provider, Oct.1997 - Dec. 1999

Over a year-and-a-half period I served three roles, two as a client executive and one as a traditional consultant: Interim CIO, Interim VP IT, and Billing Center Operations Support Manager, respectively. In the Interim CIO position, I worked with a twelve-member Executive Management team and seven IT Directors to organize and manage the 500+ person IT department. The focus was on developing better accountability for business solution delivery and meeting budget goals. A primary goal was to set the stage for the new CIO to come on board and provide a healthier environment with which to begin. After a brief transition with the new CIO, I was asked to manage a small newly acquired facilities-based casual calling long distance company and facilitate the smooth transition of the two IT organizations. Finally, as the Billing Center Operations Support Manager, I quickly developed a team of thirty to ensure $50 million in revenue would not be placed at risk due to the large number of employees leaving. Highlights include:

- Within two months I reduced the overall project list by over 30% and reduced the associated monthly consultant burn rate by over $1.5 million per month.

By rewriting the resume so that "My" and "I" don't appear and accomplishments begin with action verbs, the resume has impact and is a convincing document.

Harold W. Daniels
5624 Bridle Bend Trail
Plano, TX 75093

214-616-7689
hwdaniels@aol.com

CHIEF INFORMATION OFFICER

- **Strategic Planning**
- **Organizational Restructuring**
- **Efficiency Enhancement**
- **Cost Reduction**
- **New Service Launch**
- **Information Technology**

- Maintained IT budget control despite business and network services growing at 20-30% rate; concurrently, reduced IT investments as percentage of revenue from 14.9% to 6.7% within 1 year.
- Decreased order entry from 45 minutes to less than 7 while cutting SG&A from 117% of sales to 60% despite sales growing by over 52%.
- Delivered billing revenue of over $50 million per month within 45 days, overseeing approximately 30 consultants.

A multifunctional executive with broad strengths in IT, business analysis, technical design, project management, business development, customer relationship development, and financial / budget management.

EXPERIENCE

Telecommunications International, Dallas, TX. 2000 - 2003

CLEC broadband services provider.

Chief Information Officer

Member of 6-person Executive Management team, led closing of nonprofitable business ventures, consolidation of business units to gain synergies, and alignment of resources to increase sales and operational efficiency. Concurrently, led relaunch of complete OSS, automating primary business processes that allowed alignment of cost structure and launch new xDSL services.

- Maintained IT budget control despite business and network services growing at rapid rate of 20-30%.
- Reduced IT investments as percentage of revenue from 14.9% in 2000 to 6.7% in 2001. Ultimate downsizing of company had little impact on IT.
- Decreased voice provisioning timeframe from several minutes to real-time, enabling new wholesaler marketing plans supporting as many as 20k activations and deactivations per day.
- Improved E2E order entry for basic voice services from 45 minutes to less than 7 for internally entered orders and zero minutes for externally entered orders through process simplification and EAI integration between Web, CRM, billing, and switch activation applications. Improvement supported rationalization of back-office departments by 20-30%.
- Extended new architected OSS to support semi-automated order to activation of xDSL services in 3-4 months.
- Reduced SG&A from 117% of sales to 60% while growing sales by over 52%.

Accenture / Andersen Consulting, Chicago, IL. 1985 - 1999

Business and Systems Integrator and **Associate Partner**

Responsible for over 30 projects in diverse industries, including retail, manufacturing, advertising, banking, and telecommunications. Utilized broad skills in programming, business analysis, technical design, project management, sales, business results delivery, customer relationship development, financial / budget management, and recruiting. Representative engagements include:

National Long Distance Middle Market Service Provider, 1997 - 1999

Served in 3 separate roles: Interim CIO, Interim VP of IT, and Billing Center Operations Support Manager. In Interim CIO position, worked with 12-member Executive Management team and 7 IT Directors to organize and manage the 500+ person IT Department, with focus on developing better accountability for business solution delivery and meeting budget goals. As Interim VP of IT, managed small newly acquired facilities-based casual calling long distance company, plus facilitated smooth transition of the 2 IT organizations. As Billing Center Operations Support Manager, quickly developed team of 30 to ensure $50 million in revenue would not be placed at risk due to large number of employees leaving company.

- Reduced overall project list by over 30%, plus reduced associated monthly consultant burn rate by over $1.5 million per month, both accomplished within 2 months.
- Secured monthly billing revenue of over $50 million within 45 days, working with approximately 30 consultants.

Problems with Clarity and Word Choice in Resumes

Problem 25: Beginning Statements in an Inconsistent Way

In this resume, statements begin with nouns, verbs, adjectives, and prepositions, making for a disjointed, uneven read that has no impact.

CONNIE E. DAVIS
1231 Circle Wood Drive
Sarasota, FL 34231
Home Phone: (941) 924-1403

EXPERIENCE:

SUNTRUST, Venice, FL. 2000 - Present
<u>**Assistant Manager**</u>
Responsible for New Account Development, Teller Operations, Loan Applications, and Loan Processing.

- Responsible for performing cold-calling throughout local community to develop new business.
- Within 12 months, new checking accounts increased 232% and short- and long-term certificates of deposit grew by 46%.
- Designed and implemented promotional programs that contributed to 32% increase in deposits.
- Supervisory responsibility for small group in areas of Operations, Security, and Customer Service.
- Training of staff in new and existing products and services as well as in cross-selling techniques.
- Interview and hire new personnel.

HUNTINGTON BANK, Sarasota, FL. 1995 - 2000
<u>**Sales & Service Associate / Financial Representative**</u>

- Sold life insurance, fixed and variable annuities, and mutual funds to new and existing customers. Also opened up new accounts, including checking, savings, CDs, and IRAs.
- Brought in over $8 million during 2000, exceeding all monthly and annual goals.
- Responsible for processing consumer loans, from initial application to close, handling all details and required information.
- Maintenance of customers' accounts and resolution of problems that arose.
- Due to previous experience with computer and word-processing systems, was chosen to learn new systems.

SOUTHEAST BANK, Sarasota, FL. 1988 - 1995
<u>**Trust Associate / Assistant,**</u> Personal Trust Division

- Responsible for supporting Trust Officer in daily operation and maintenance of trust accounts as well as ensuring that department complied with all provisions of federal and state laws.
- Extensive client contact maintenance, with activities including opening new accounts, collecting assets, paying monthly bills, answering questions, and researching documents.
- Coordinating activities with attorneys, CPAs, insurance companies, banks, stockbrokers, and personnel at nursing / retirement homes.
- Worked closely with Investment Department in execution of stock / bond purchase and sell orders.
- Management of estate procedures, including inventorying assets, contacting beneficiaries, and preparing miscellaneous documents.
- Was selected to learn new computer and word-processing systems, plus train other Trust Associates.

EDUCATION / LICENSURE:

Bachelor of Business Administration, City College of New York. 1988
Series 6 - Variable Annuities, Mutual Funds.
State of Florida Insurance License - Life Insurance, Fixed Annuities.

In her revised resume, all statements begin with verbs. The accomplishments and descriptions of job duties now flow and have power.

Connie E. Davis
1231 Circle Wood Drive
Sarasota, FL 34231

(941) 924-1403

NEW ACCOUNT DEVELOPMENT & MANAGEMENT—CONSUMER & COMMERCIAL BANKING

- Grew Suntrust's number of checking accounts 232% and number of CDs 46%, both within 12 months; concurrently, developed promotional programs that led to 32% increase in commercial and consumer deposits.
- Delivered over $8 million in new consumer business for Huntington Bank during 2000, exceeding all monthly and annual goals.

An accomplished business developer with outstanding communication and interpersonal skills.
Recognized for high energy level as well as strengths in prospecting and building effective referral networks.

EXPERIENCE

SUNTRUST, Venice, FL. 2000 - Present

Assistant Manager

Responsible for New Account Development, Teller Operations, Loan Applications, and Loan Processing.

- Perform cold-calling throughout local community to develop new business.
- Increased number of new checking accounts 232% within 12 months while growing number of short- and long-term certificates of deposit 46%.
- Designed and implemented promotional programs that contributed to 32% increase in deposits.
- Supervise small group in areas of Operations, Security, and Customer Service.
- Train staff in new and existing products and services as well as in cross-selling techniques.
- Interview and hire new personnel.

HUNTINGTON BANK, Sarasota, FL. 1995 - 2000

Sales & Service Associate / Financial Representative

- Sold life insurance, fixed and variable annuities, and mutual funds to new and existing customers. Also opened up new accounts, including checking, savings, CDs, and IRAs.
- Generated over $8 million in new business during 2000, exceeding all monthly and annual goals.
- Processed consumer loans, from initial application to close, handling all details and required information.
- Maintained customers' accounts and resolved problems that arose.
- Selected to learn new computer and word-processing systems due to previous systems experience.

SOUTHEAST BANK, Sarasota, FL. 1988 - 1995

Trust Associate / Assistant, Personal Trust Division

- Supported Trust Officer in daily operation and maintenance of trust accounts as well as in ensuring that department complied with all provisions of federal and state laws.
- Maintained extensive contact with clients, with activities including opening new accounts, collecting assets, paying monthly bills, answering questions, and researching documents.
- Coordinated activities with attorneys, CPAs, insurance companies, banks, stockbrokers, and personnel at nursing / retirement homes.
- Worked closely with Investment Department in execution of stock / bond purchase and sell orders.
- Managed estate procedures, including inventorying assets, contacting beneficiaries, and preparing miscellaneous documents.
- Chosen to learn new computer and word-processing systems, plus train other Trust Associates.

EDUCATION / LICENSURE:

Bachelor of Business Administration, City College of New York. 1988
Series 6 - Variable Annuities, Mutual Funds.
State of Florida Insurance License - Life Insurance, Fixed Annuities.

Problems with Clarity and Word Choice in Resumes

Problem 26: Continuous Use of Clichés and Buzz Words in the Introductory Section

Nothing turns off employers and recruiters more than the excessive use of clichés and buzz words in the introductory section. Costello's use of such verbiage (underlined) in his first resume leads readers to believe that he has no originality or creativity and is more of a follower than a leader, despite the glowing claims he makes about his outstanding leadership strengths.

STEVEN D. COSTELLO
8701 Shore Road
Brooklyn, NY 11209
Telephone: 718.745.7612
E-mail: Scostello@nyc.rr.com

PROFILE:

A visionary, self-motivated, results-oriented restaurateur with a record of success at meeting or exceeding growth goals through developing and implementing cutting-edge business processes. Recognized as a driven change agent, mentor, and coach with outstanding interpersonal, communication, and cross-functional team-building skills who thrives on challenge and problem solving. An out-of-the-box thinker and shirt-sleeves leader who empowers employees through fostering a nurturing management style and open-door policy.

EXPERIENCE DETAILS:

JACK'S CHOPHOUSE, Brooklyn, New York.   1999 - 2003
General Manager of this facility seating 270 guests in the restaurant and 175 in the nightclub. P&L responsibility for all operations, overseeing 95 employees, including 5 Managers and a Dining Room Supervisor.
- Rigorously analyzed all operations, then developed and implemented strategic turnaround plan that transformed a neglected, unprofitable restaurant / nightclub into a topflight, profitable business.
- Upgraded facility to dramatically improve its appearance.
- Reduced breakeven point from $237,000 in monthly revenues to $192,000.
- Decreased food costs from 42% to 32%, liquor expenses from 32% to 20%, beer costs from 30% to 24%, wine expenses from 49% to 35%, and labor costs from 39% to 25%.
- Instituted new systems, procedures, and controls to significantly improve efficiency of operations and quality of guest service, including developing and introducing facility's first formal staff training program in over 2 years.
- Performed extensive hiring of new personnel and developed professional and motivated staff, resulting in reducing annual turnover from 75% to 20%, a record for the establishment.
- Closely monitored all operations to ensure that staff provided personal attention to guests and continuously met their needs.
- Planned and set up banquets for up to 140 patrons.

DURANGO'S RESTAURANT, New York, New York.   1996 - 1999
General Manager of this restaurant that seated 330 patrons and served Southwestern cuisine.
- Directed 60 employees, including 3 Managers.
- Aggressively marketed restaurant throughout Manhattan, increasing revenues 20% over 3-year period.
- Improved quality of service and professionalism of staff, ensuring personal attention to guests.
- Decreased food costs from 32% to 29%, liquor expenses from 25% to 20%, labor costs from 25% to 21%, and turnover from 50% to 23%, a record for the restaurant.

CASA LUPITA, New York, New York.   1993 - 1996
Associate General Manager of this restaurant serving Mexican cuisine.
Responsible for both front-of-the-house and kitchen operations, with activities including hiring and training staff, marketing, plus overseeing purchasing and bookkeeping.

The rewritten introductory section omits all clichés and buzz words and focuses on accomplishments and documentable strengths. Costello is seen as a driven, top-producing restaurateur with outstanding skills in developing and managing staff members.

Steven D. Costello
8701 Shore Road
Brooklyn, NY 11209

(718) 745-7612
Scostello@nyc.rr.com

RESTAURANT & NIGHTCLUB MANAGEMENT

P&L • Strategic Planning • Turnaround Management • Employee Motivation & Enhancement

- Turned around unprofitable restaurant / nightclub, reducing breakeven level 19%, slashing operating costs 29%, and decreasing turnover 73% to record level.
- Grew revenues 20% at Southwestern-cuisine restaurant while reducing operating costs 29% and turnover 54%, the latter to an all-time low.

An accomplished restaurateur with a record of success at increasing operating efficiencies, revenues, and profits. Recognized for broad strengths in cost reduction and employee training / motivation, the latter resulting in outstanding guest service and record low turnover at all employers.

EXPERIENCE

JACK'S CHOPHOUSE, Brooklyn, NY. 1999 - 2003

General Manager of this facility seating 270 guests in the restaurant and 175 in the nightclub. P&L responsibility for all operations, overseeing 95 employees, including 5 Managers and a Dining Room Supervisor.

- Rigorously analyzed all operations, then developed and implemented strategic turnaround plan that transformed a neglected, unprofitable restaurant / nightclub into a topflight, profitable business.
- Upgraded facility to dramatically improve its appearance.
- Reduced breakeven point from $237,000 in monthly revenues to $192,000.
- Decreased food costs from 42% to 32%, liquor costs from 32% to 20%, beer costs from 30% to 24%, wine costs from 49% to 35%, and labor costs from 39% to 25%.
- Instituted new systems, procedures, and controls to significantly improve efficiency of operations and quality of guest service, including developing and introducing facility's first formal staff training programs in over 2 years.
- Performed extensive hiring of new personnel and developed professional and motivated staff, resulting in reducing annual turnover from 75% to 20%, a record for the establishment.
- Closely monitored all operations to ensure that staff provided personal attention to guests and continuously met their needs.
- Planned and set up banquets for up to 140 patrons.

DURANGO'S RESTAURANT, New York, NY. 1996 - 1999

General Manager of this restaurant that seated 330 patrons and served Southwestern cuisine.

- Directed 60 employees, including 3 Managers.
- Aggressively marketed restaurant throughout Manhattan, increasing revenues 20% over 3-year period.
- Improved quality of service and professionalism of staff, ensuring personal attention to guests.
- Decreased food costs from 32% to 29%, liquor expenses from 25% to 20%, labor costs from 25% to 21%, and turnover from 50% to 23%, a record for the restaurant.

CASA LUPITA, New York, NY. 1993 - 1996

Associate General Manager of this restaurant serving Mexican cuisine.

Responsible for both front-of-the-house and kitchen operations, with activities including hiring and training staff, marketing, plus overseeing purchasing and bookkeeping.

Problems with Clarity and Word Choice in Resumes

Problem 27: Using Unclear, Confusing, or Generally Poor Language

The poor wording in Merriman's resume (underlined) shows him to be an ineffective communicator, which makes his glowing accomplishments in human resources and sales management suspect. Hence, his poor communication skills will cause people to reject him for interviews.

BRUCE A. MERRIMAN

12 Marquette Avenue
Naperville, IL 60565
e-mail: bamerriman@aol.com
Tel: (630) 527-3498
Cell: (630) 531-4392

Career Objective

Obtain a senior management position in human resources or operations within a growth industry, contributing significantly to the success of the line organizations by maximizing my management skills and HR leadership experience.

Employment Experience

Allied Industries International, Chicago, IL. January 1973 to December 2002
$1 billion conglomerate with subsidiaries in diversified industries.

Manager - Human Resources, Western Area, April 1996 to December 2002

Ranked as best in class in resource planning, sourcing, staffing, and retention of management and sales personnel. Senior HR leader for Sr. VP - GM and 14 Sales VPs in all operations management issues in western United States territory with 1000 employees.

- Clean sheet design, development, and implementation of organizational human resources policies.
- Developed and implemented first web-based training for field sales force. Results measurements showed 23% increased sales in targeted skills area.
- Filled 70 sales assignments in 5 months, supporting $77 million in planned revenues.
- Achieved 90% people retention by implementing targeted retention strategies for key populations.
- Top-rated manager - directed management responsibilities for 6 human resources professionals in 5 field and headquarters locations.

Manager - Employee Development, Illinois Operations, September 1995 to April 1996

Major responsibilities included direct responsibility for quality programs, employee training programs, customer loyalty program management, and internal communications.

- Designed and implemented field-empowerment process enabling decision making at the first-line employee level. Increased sales force satisfaction 25% with workflow and paperwork reductions.
- Launched high-performance work systems from concept development to implementation and measurement. Saved $1 million dollars in first-year savings.
- Launched first employee training programs team-based high-performance employee workgroups.
- Managed internal communications programs and staff management processes for $100 million, 250-employee operation.

District Manager, Customer Service - Illinois Operations, October 1992 to September 1995

Key areas of responsibility included direct responsibility for top-tier account customer relationships and general management for Illinois operations field customer service / technical teams.

- Delivered highest profit +22% and revenue +18% growth in midwest operations group through intense focus on growing and retaining the business and managing costs.
- Provided leadership and management for 50-person technical support, software, and hardware field-service force. Repeatedly recognized by corporate management as role model leader.
- Effective management processes directing the outcomes of 4 line managers.
- Improved customer satisfaction 15 points to 99% satisfied in 6 months.

After improving the language, Merriman's accomplishments have complete credibility, and readers have every reason to want to interview him.

Bruce A. Merriman
12 Marquette Avenue
Naperville, IL 60565
Tel: (630) 527-3498

e-mail: bamerriman@aol.com
Cell: (630) 531-4392

HUMAN RESOURCES & OPERATIONS MANAGEMENT

- **Staffing**
- **Compensation**
- **Benefits**
- **Training**
- **Organizational Development**

- **Internal Communications**
- **Quality Management**
- **Call Center Operations**
- **Customer Service**
- **Employee Relations**

A record of progressively responsible positions in both Human Resources and Operations, supporting up to 7100 employees:

- Ranked as best in class in resource planning, sourcing, staffing, and personnel retention.
- Created and introduced first web-based training initiative for field sales force, resulting in 23% increase in sales; concurrently, introduced strategies that achieved 90% retention rate.
- Achieved highest profit increase—22%—and revenue growth—18%—at midwest operations group.
- Led internal communications programs and staff management processes for $100 million, 250-employee operation.
- Turned around call center and achieved 99% customer satisfaction level, winning Malcolm Baldridge National Quality Award.

EXPERIENCE

Allied Industries International, Chicago, IL. 1973 - 2002

$1 billion conglomerate with subsidiaries in diversified industries.

Manager - Human Resources, Western Area, 1996 - 2002
Senior HR leader supporting Sr. VP - GM and 14 Sales VPs in all operations management issues in 7100-employee western United States territory.

- Achieved best-in-class ranking for resource planning, sourcing, staffing, and retention of personnel.
- Conceived of, designed, and implemented human resources policies.
- Developed and implemented first web-based training initiative for sales force, achieving 23% increase in sales.
- Hired 70 sales personnel in 5 months, enabling achievement of $77 million revenue goal.
- Delivered 90% retention rate through implementing targeted retention strategies for key populations.
- Won recognition as top-rated manager, directing 24 human resources professionals in 22 field and headquarters locations.

Manager - Employee Development, Illinois Operations, 1995 - 1996

Complete responsibility for quality, employee training, customer-loyalty program management, and internal communications.

- Designed and implemented process that empowered sales force to make key decisions in the field, increasing job satisfaction 25%; concurrently, reduced administrative paperwork.
- Developed and instituted high-performance work systems that achieved $1 million in first-year savings.
- Launched first team-based training programs for high-performance personnel.
- Managed internal communications programs and staff management processes for $100 million, 250-employee operation.

District Manager, Customer Service - Illinois Operations, 1992 - 1995

Responsible for strengthening relationships with top-tier accounts as well as for general management of Illinois operations field customer service / technical teams.

- Delivered highest profit growth rate—22%—and revenue growth rate—18%—in midwestern operations group through strictly adhering to business plan, including rigorous management of costs.
- Achieved repeated recognition from corporate management as model leader for management of 225-person technical support, software, and hardware field-service force.
- Led management processes designed to ensure attainment of goals set for 14 line managers.
- Improved customer satisfaction 15 points within 6 months, achieving 99% level.

Problem 28: Making Rambling Statements versus Crisp, Concise Ones

In this resume, many of Edwards's statements are long-winded, and they lose power as a result. He doesn't appear to be the "take-charge leader" that he represents himself to be in the introductory section.

Torrey S. Edwards
71 Seasons Drive
Wexford, PA 15090
724-934-1187
TSEdwards@attbi.com

Profile:

A take-charge leader who leads by example, with broad-based business knowledge to support hands-on management style. Able to motivate subordinates, with proven operations and manufacturing management background. Capable financial and cost manger. Experienced at managing R&D operations. A reliable and cooperative team player with strong teaching and training skills. Hard working with a great capacity to learn new things. Good working knowledge of mainframe and PC operations. Proficient with most business-related PC applications.

Work History:

H.J. HEINZ COMPANY, Pittsburgh, PA. 1980 - Present

Corporate Program Manager - Bakery Products, 1998 - Present

Responsible for the strategic planning, leadership, management, and direction of capital projects requiring the application of both engineering and technology to improve manufacturing facilities, with the goal of achieving productivity gains, cost reduction, and improved quality. Projects have ranged in value to date from $2 million to $6 million.

- Acquired bakery skills and knowledge (a new field for me) in a relatively short time, then successfully managed the consolidation and technological changes from 5 small family-run bakery businesses into a bigger corporate structure, achieving all objectives on schedule.

- Completed the consolidation of 2 plants into 1 major operation (a $5 million project) in 6 months by expanding 1 plant to absorb another plant in the same city, resulting in cost savings of 25% and improved efficiency.

- Identified, negotiated with, and selected vendors from the UK, Germany, France, and Italy for timely delivery of various pieces of equipment that provided best performance for dollars invested in major capital projects, increasing productivity 10% at 5% lower cost. Successfully completed all projects on time and on budget (projects ranged from $2 million to $6 million), meeting corporate goals and objectives.

- Upgraded an old, inefficient plant on the East Coast (a $2 million project); project was completed with minimal disruption to the operation and started to generate significant benefits as planned.

- Set up policy, procedures, and controls for the $23 million capital expenditure of a newly formed bakery affiliate; personally controlled and monitored the process at the corporate level to ensure that all timetables and milestones would be met so that production would begin on schedule and achieve all revenue and profit goals.

General Manager, 1993 - 1997

Promoted to position with P&L responsibility for the performance of an unprofitable joint venture producing and marketing a wide variety of infant / children foods, with annual sales of over $20 million and employing 250 people.

- Increased market growth from 5 major cities to 23 major cities through developing and implementing highly effective sales and marketing strategies and programs, resulting in total sales increasing from $7 million to over $20 million in 3 years and producing a significant profit.

- Achieved a 60% market penetration in one geographic territory alone.

- Managed the company from an unprofitable operation (10% loss on sales) to an operating profit in excess of 20% of sales through developing and implementing operations controls and cost-reduction initiatives, the latter including reducing headcount of both management and hourly workers, personally renegotiating contracts with suppliers, instituting new purchasing procedures, and finding more cost-effective suppliers.

- Installed sound financial controls and systems to monitor the company's pricing, cost controls, and financial resource utilization to reach corporate objectives and goals.

- Achieved significant product and company awareness through careful development of marketing and advertising strategies that attained unaided brand awareness of over 70% in 3 major markets surveyed.

By stating accomplishments concisely and deleting extraneous information, Edwards's statements portray him as a proactive executive who can lead companies to the next level of success. Whereas his original resume contained 462 words in the discussion on responsibilities and accomplishments, the makeover uses only 256, a 45 percent decrease.

Torrey S. Edwards
71 Seasons Drive
Wexford, PA 15090

724-934-1187
TSEdwards@attbi.com

GENERAL MANAGEMENT & MANUFACTURING EXECUTIVE

- **P&L**
- **Strategic Planning**
- **Turnaround Management**
- **Productivity Improvement**
- **Cost Reduction**
- **Quality Enhancement**

- Increased productivity 10% while reducing operating costs 5% through installing new manufacturing equipment sourced internationally. Personally located all vendors and negotiated contracts.
- Integrated 5 bakery plants into single Heinz facility, completing project ahead of schedule despite no previous experience in baking industry. Earlier during tenure, reduced manufacturing costs 25% through consolidating 2 plants into single location.
- Turned around Heinz food manufacturing operation, reversing 10% loss on sales and delivering 20% operating profit. Grew sales almost 200% in 4 years while achieving penetration as high as 60% in key markets.

An accomplished executive with broad strengths in general management and manufacturing. Proven ability to analyze operations, products, markets, and growth opportunities, then introduce strategic and tactical solutions that increase sales, reduce costs, improve efficiency of operations, and grow profits.

EXPERIENCE

H.J. HEINZ COMPANY, Pittsburgh, PA. 1980 - Present
Corporate Program Manager - Bakery Products, 1998 - Present
Responsible for planning and implementing capital projects to improve manufacturing productivity, reduce costs, and improve quality, with projects ranging in value from $2 million to $6 million.

- Planned and implemented consolidation of 5 bakery plants into single Heinz location, achieving all goals ahead of schedule despite no previous experience in baking industry.
- Consolidated 2 plants into 1 operation in 6 months, decreasing costs 25% while improving operating efficiency.
- Installed production equipment from Europe, increasing productivity 10% while decreasing costs 5%. Personally performed all sourcing and contract negotiations.
- Upgraded underperforming plant on East Coast, completing project with minimal disruption to business and delivering immediate targeted results.
- Planned and led $23 million capital expenditure for newly formed bakery affiliate; set up process to ensure that all timetables and milestones would be successfully met.

General Manager, 1993 - 1997
Promoted to position with P&L responsibility for unprofitable infant / children foods joint venture, with annual sales of over $20 million and employing 250 personnel.

- Developed and implemented strategic turnaround plan that transformed 10% loss on sales into 20+% operating profit.
- Expanded customer base from 5 major markets to 23, driving annual sales from $7 million to over $20 million and achieving market shares as high as 60%.
- Introduced successful programs to reduce and control costs, personally renegotiated contracts with existing suppliers, secured new, cost-effective suppliers, and instituted new purchasing procedures.
- Installed sound financial controls and systems to monitor pricing, cost controls, and financial resource utilization.
- Achieved widespread company and product recognition through implementing marketing programs that attained unaided brand awareness of over 70% in select markets.

Problems with Clarity and Word Choice in Resumes

Problems with Composition/Appearance/
Formatting in Resumes

Problem 29: Four or More Pages in Length

Due to the resume's four-page length, many recruiters and prospective employers won't even read the document.

LAWRENCE N. RABINOWITZ
8000 S.W. 72nd Avenue, #320-E
Miami, FL 33143
Cell: 305.495.8733
Tel: 305.666.4912
LNR@ix.netcom.com

EXPERIENCE:

Encore Digital Communications, Inc., Miami, Florida.   2000 - Present
Provider of long-distance and local telephone services.

Chief Information Officer and **Vice President**

Responsible for the technology vision and leadership by developing and implementing IT initiatives that create and maintain leadership for the enterprise. Report to CEO with functional responsibility for 332 personnel nationwide. Work in close cooperation with leaders of 2 subsidiaries to lead regional IT teams. Developed strategic information systems plan for systems alignment synchronizing information systems plans with business plan. Responsible for creating and managing call centers and technology supporting fulfillment, field operations support, and 4 multiple network operations centers. Provided the leadership and development of an integrated Operating Support System (OSS) plan supporting flow-through provisioning for eBusiness applications. The OSS must support the convergence of technology on an integrated communications provider environment. The strategies include a global access to the customer, creating an environment where the cost to sell will be lowered to increase market share and products' margins. Responsible for the design and development of an IT organizational structure that is responsive to corporate needs. Serve as a strategic leader capable of identifying and evaluating new technology developments and gauge their appropriateness for the organization. Also guide the next level of products, services, and technology development. Oversee $100 million budget. Member of Due Diligence Team responsible for acquisition identification and negotiation.

- Implemented processes to support Systems Development Life Cycle (SDLC).
- Reorganized IT Department to support Internet style infrastructure buffering the users from major changes in the back-office applications.
- Developed and implemented enterprise policies and procedures by which users could request support on new projects from IT organization.
- Outsourced desktop side support to Compaq, improving service level agreement nationwide and saving $3.4 million in maintenance capital budget.
- Delivered 24 IT initiative projects on time and under budget, reducing capital outlay by $5 million.
- Formulated security strategy and policies to support Web-enabled applications.
- Implemented computer telephony interfaces in order to integrate 2 call centers.
- Provided leadership and direction on development off new technology architecture supporting back-office and front- office systems.
- Provided leadership on e-commerce strategies, including customer relationship management.
- Closed year under budget by $43,000.

ReadySportsLine, Tampa, Florida.   1999 - 2000
On-line sports service.

Director of Information Technology

Responsible for all aspects of the enterprise's IT and systems development. Oversaw over 25 developers with 3 direct reports. Accountable for on-time delivery of major applications, including continuous support availability of production systems and databases in 24 / 7 environment. Responsible for strategic planning, fault tolerance, disaster recovery, stress testing, and capacity planning, Also responsible for customer relation database development, including the e-commerce, image content, personalization / targeting, customer relation management (call center), and data warehousing / data mining project for customer information initiative. Accountable for traditional MIS Department, including networks, telecommunications, technical support, and production control.

- Developed company's strategy technology vision and provided leadership during implementation.
- Implemented Lawson Enterprise Resource Planning modules for finance and human resources.
- Developed and implemented with the business users the eCommerce data warehouse, including the installation of the infrastructure.

- Evaluated the Customer Relation Management software and the inbound e-mail software vendors in support of the Customer Care Call Center. These products were intrinsically integrated to support back-office functions, with back office architecture integrating the disparate data sources.
- Installed and implemented personalization and targeting software packages.
- Reorganized MIS Department to support growth of the enterprise.

University of Miami, Coral Gables, Florida.   1983 - 1999

Assistant Vice President - Information Technology

Responsible for all aspects of the institution's information technology as well as directing the information and data integrity policies of the institution and its groups and for all IT functions. Activities included all data centers, administrative centers, academic and research centers, technical service centers, production scheduling functions, call centers, communication networks, the network operations center, computer program development, medical network services, and telecommunications, including customer service delivery and computer systems operations. Possess in-depth knowledge of both technology and business processes with cross-functional perspective. Demonstrated ability to bring the benefits of IT to solve business issues while also managing costs and risks. Skilled at identifying and evaluating new technological developments and gauging their appropriateness. Adept at communicating with and understanding the needs of non-technical internal clients. Proven ability to conceptualize, launch, and deliver multiple IT projects on time and within budget. An excellent listener who is able to mesh well with the existing management teams as well as a team builder who can articulate the IT vision.

- Provided leadership on implementation of Academic / Business On-Line Applications development systems. The Long-Range Information Systems Pan was successfully completed in 4 years, on time and under budget, including a Business Reengineering Plan for all administrative units. During the development cycle of the on-line systems, the hardware platform supporting the legacy systems was converted without interruption from the Sperry Univac hardware platform to an IBM platform.
- Led the development and implementation of the telecommunications strategic plan under budget and on time.
- Developed and directed the Business Process Reengineering Plan (BPR) that supported the Long-Range Information Systems Plan. Due to the rapid change in technology the BPR had been converted into an ongoing continuous improvement plan centered on obtaining high users' satisfaction.
- Formulated and implemented Y2K audits, assessments, and inventory plan.
- Led the development and implementation of the 5-year Hardware Strategic Plan supporting the academic and administrative functions.
- Directed the development of an integrated wide area network (WAN) and campus area network (CAN), including local area network standards.
- Merged the Information Systems Computer Operations with the Telecommunications Department, balancing the technology needs of the university's users.
- Developed and implemented the Business Continuity / Disaster Recovery Plan (DRP) for the entire enterprise as well as the IT organization. DRP was rigorously tested during and after the onslaught of Hurricane Andrew in August 1992.
- Directed the design and implementation of the 900 MHZ emergency radio system.
- Designed and implemented a Jump Level Management process for the staff to communicate and understand the university's strategic directions, including total quality management.
- Member of team that developed the Internet and Intranet policies and procedures.
- Participated as active member of the telecommunications committee supporting the Summit of the Americas in Miami, Florida.
- Former adjunct professor / lecturer in the School of Business Administration, Computer Information Systems Department. Established, negotiated, and implemented partnerships with IBM, BellSouth, Lucent Technologies, and Cabletron.
- Former member of the Hemisphere Summit's of the Americas Informatic / Telecommunications Subcommittee held in Miami in December 1994.
- Member, Board of Directors, University Credit Union; member, Greater Miami Chamber of Commerce, Information Technology Subcommittee.
- Participated as member of the Technology Expert Panel of the Blue Ribbon Task Force overseeing City of Miami financial recovery.
- Directed and completed a $7 million residential colleges network.
- Directed the implementation of 6 new voice switches costing $9 million.

Sperry Univac, Miami, Florida.   1972 - 1983

Systems Analysts Manager / Project Manager / Senior Systems Analyst / Consultant

Responsible for all Sperry Univac 1100 series in South Florida. Supported the Marketing Department on the pre-sale analysis, design, and implementation of large-application systems. Supported the branch consulting efforts by providing the assistance on the management of technology engagements. Developed on-line application packages for several industries. Managed 27 systems engineers and analysts. Managed multiple IT projects on time and within budget.

- Exceeded branch's assigned revenue quota 4 consecutive years and managed 6 concurrent projects successfully.
- Led and developed relocation plans to move Walt Disney Productions' MIS operations from Anaheim, California, to Lake Buena Vista, Florida.
- Led development requirements for Carnival Cruise Lines' reservation, financial, and operations systems.
- Managed Sperry Univac's project team responsible for developing and implementing $27 million State of Florida contract. Project developed the State Capitol Systems, Department of Revenue, and Department of Business and Professional Regulation (liquor licenses, tobacco and fire arms, and restaurant and elevator inspections).
- Managed City of Tampa technical support team.
- Project Manager responsible for development and implementation of Southeast Toyota Distributors systems.
- Manager responsible for assisting Coral Gables Federal Bank in implementing their new hardware / software systems. Assisted MIS executives in formulation and presentation of business plans, strategic planning, and IT policies and procedures.
- Designed and implemented the conversion of the total-market-coverage circulation package for Cox Publishing Company at "Des Moines Register and Tribune" and "Palm Beach Post" newspapers.
- Designed and implemented communications network for the nationwide operations of Alterman Transport, Mercury Motors, and Southeast Toyota Distributors.
- Led implementation of the U.S. Navy engineering packages supporting the naval air station stock points nationwide.
- Managed relocation of the Department of Health and Welfare to Tallahassee.

Control Data Corporation, Minneapolis, Minnesota.   1967 - 1972

Systems Engineer assigned to U.S. Naval Research and Development Center.

- Designed and developed scientific programming for the U.S. Navy as well ass instructing systems installation techniques.
- Assigned to engineering team that designed the speed-up feature for the CDC 6600 processor series with Seymour Cray.
- Developed a model to simulate anti-submarine warfare rotorcraft landing on ships. Wrote the analog / digital conversion programs to interpret structure measurements.
- Identified and engineered the changes to correct a hardware deficiency affecting the disk access storage unit, resulting in an assignment to work with Mr. Cray at CDC Research and Development Laboratory.
- Developed a field customer service organization to support the federal government with 24x365 technical customer support in the Naval and Research Laboratories.
- Led selection of systems integration project for large federal agency. The integration product eliminated need for point-to-point interfaces between heterogeneous application platforms.

Radio Corporation of America, Burlington, Massachusetts.   1963 - 1966

Engineer

Member of team supporting systems test group responsible for developing and supervising the troubleshooting procedures for the SPECTRA 70 processor series. Assisted design engineers in R&D Laboratory by testing the logic circuitry prototypes, troubleshooting, and designing the engineering field changes.

- Developed test programming and diagnostic software for new logic circuitry designs in R&D Laboratory in order to properly test performance in accordance with design guide and its specifications.
- Designed and developed testing software for off-line and on-line troubleshooting hardware malfunctions.
- Coordinated NASA's scientists, vendors, and technical teams assigned to Gemini and Apollo programs.
- Maintained synergy on transition from Gemini to Apollo programs while working for RCA Global Communications.

EDUCATION:

M.B.A., University of Miami.
B.A., Mathematics, University of Miami.

CERTIFICATES:

RETS
Electronic Engineering Technology
RCA Data Processing Institute
Control Data Corporation
Sperry Univac Education Center

PROFESSIONAL AFFILIATIONS:

University Credit Union - Member, Board of Directors
IT Committee - Greater Miami Chamber of Commerce
Miami-Dade Beacon Council
Data Processing Management Association
Association for IT Professionals in Higher Education
Colleges and Universities Association of Computer Machines
Florida Telecommunications Association
Southeast Telecommunications Association
Society of Information Management
Miami CIO Council

SECURITY:

U.S. Secret Industrial (DISCO)

LICENSES:

Federal Communications Commission: Commercial General Class Radio Telephone and Advanced Class Amateur Radio
Operation
Federal Aviation Administration – Pilot
Florida Real Estate Board – Salesman

PUBLICATIONS:

Authored dozens of articles appearing in industry publications.

The resume has been streamlined to two pages by (1) eliminating the less important information, especially with Control Data Corporation and Radio Corporation of America, and (2) deleting the Certificates, Professional Affiliations, Security, Licenses, and Publications sections.

Lawrence N. Rabinowitz
8000 S.W. 72nd Avenue, #320-E
Miami, FL 33143
Tel: 305-666-4912

Cell: 305-495-8733
LNR@ix.netcom.com

CHIEF INFORMATION OFFICER

- **Strategic Planning**
- **System Development**
- **Product Development**
- **Business Process Reengineering**
- **Productivity Improvement**
- **Organizational Development**

- Progressively responsible IT experience leading companies' technology growth.
- Accomplished at partnering with executives organization-wide to balance strategic plans and technology innovation with tactical business goals, continuously delivering cost-effective, value-adding IT solutions.
- Nominated for "CIO of the Year," Miami CIO Council—won "Runner-up."
- Received "2001, CIO IT Staff Of the Year Award" from Miami CIO Council.

A driven corporate strategist tireless in the pursuit of quality business processes and organizational growth. Proven ability to develop and direct high-performance teams that consistently complete projects on time and under budget. Extensively published on IT issues and solutions. MBA.

EXPERIENCE

Encore Digital Communications, Inc., Miami, Florida. 2000 - Present

Provider of long-distance and local telephone services.

Chief Information Officer and **Vice President**

Complete responsibility for technology vision and leadership of all IT initiatives, overseeing $100 million budget and 330+ IT personnel nationwide. Report to CEO.

- Developed strategic information systems plan for systems alignment synchronizing information systems plans with business plan. Also designed and developed IT organizational structure to support corporate growth goals.
- Created and managed call centers and technology supporting fulfillment, field operations support, and 4 multiple network operations centers.
- Led development of integrated Operating Support System (OSS) plan supporting flow through provisioning for e-Business applications. OSS must support convergence of technology in integrated communications provider (ICP) environment. Strategies include global access to customer and creating environment with lower sales costs, enabling increase in market share and profit margin.
- Serve as strategic leader on executive team, guiding development of next level of products, services, and technology development.
- Member of due diligence team responsible for acquisition identification and negotiation.
- Technical accomplishments include:
  - Implemented processes to support Systems Development Life Cycle (SDLC).
  - Reorganized IT department to support Internet style infrastructure, buffering users from major changes in back-office applications by hiring, retaining, and retooling current staff.
  - Developed and implemented enterprise policies and procedures where users can request support on new projects from IT organization.
  - Outsourced desktop side support to Compaq, improving service level agreement nationwide and saving $3.4 million in maintenance capital budget.
  - Delivered 24 IS projects on time and under budget, reducing capital outlay by $5 million.
  - Formulated security strategy and policies to support Web-enabled applications.
  - Implemented computer telephony interfaces features to integrate 2 call centers.
  - Provided leadership on e-commerce strategies, including CRM.

ReadySportsLine, Tampa, Florida. 1999 - 2000

On-line sports service.

Director of Information Technology

Responsible for all aspects of IT and systems development in 24 / 7 environment, overseeing over 25 developers with 3 direct reports. Activities consisted of strategic planning; fault tolerance; disaster recovery; stress testing; capacity planning; customer relation database development, including e-commerce, image content, personalization / targeting, and customer relation management (call center); data warehousing / data mining project for customer information initiative; and traditional MIS functions, including networks, telecommunications, technical support, and production control.

- Developed company's IT strategy and technology vision, providing leadership during implementation phase.
  - Implemented Lawson Enterprise Resource Planning modules for finance and human resources.
  - Developed and implemented with business users the eCommerce data warehouse, including installation of infrastructure.
  - Evaluated CRM software and in-bound e-mail software vendors to support Customer Care Call Center. Products were intrinsically integrated to support back-office functions, with back-office architecture designed to integrate disparate data sources.
  - Installed and implemented personalization and targeting software packages.
  - Reorganized MIS Department to support growth of enterprise.

University of Miami, Coral Gables, FL. 1983 - 1999

Assistant Vice President - Information Technology

Responsible for all aspects of institution's information technology, including data centers, technical service centers, production scheduling functions, call centers, communication networks, the network operations center, computer program development, medical network services, telecommunications, including customer service delivery and operations, and computer systems operations.

- Led implementation of Academic / Business On-line Applications development systems, with hardware platform supporting legacy systems converted from the Sperry Univac hardware platform without interruptions to IBM platform.
- Directed development and implementation of telecommunications strategic plan, plus developed and directed Business Process Reengineering (BPR) Plan that supported Long-Range Information Systems Plan. Due to rapid change in technology, BPR Plan was converted into ongoing continuous improvement plan focused on obtaining high users' satisfaction.
- Managed development and implementation of 5-year Hardware Strategic Plan supporting academic and administrative functions.
- Directed development of an integrated WAN and campus area network (CAN), including local area network standards.
- Merged Information Systems Computer Operations with Telecommunications Department.
- Developed and implemented Business Continuity / Disaster Recovery Plan (DRP) for entire enterprise as well as the IT organization.
- Designed and implemented Jump Level Management process for the staff to communicate and understand the university's strategic directions, including total quality management.

Sperry Univac, Miami, FL. 1972 - 1983

Systems Analysts Manager / Project Manager / Senior Systems Analyst / Consultant

Responsible for all Sperry Univac 1100 series in South Florida. Activities included supporting Marketing Department on pre-sale analysis, design, and implementation of large application systems; supporting branch consulting efforts by providing assistance on management of technology engagements; developing on-line application packages for several industries. Managed 27 systems engineers and analysts.

Previous employers included Control Data Corporation and Radio Corporation of America, holding positions of Systems Engineer and Test Engineer.

EDUCATION

M.B.A., University of Miami.
B.A., Mathematics, University of Miami.

Problem 30: Insufficient White Space

This resume looks like a "wall of words" and is cumbersome to read, with no white space between the various elements. Many resume reviewers will move to the next submission, especially if they have a large number of resumes to read.

WENDY A. ALPER   1340 Bradenton Road • Sarasota, FL 34234 • (941) 951-9812 • Waalper@gte.net

Objective:
Speech-Language Pathologist at preschool level.

Education:
MS, Speech-Language Pathology, University of South Florida, 1994
BA, Elementary Education, University of South Florida, 1985
Kappa Delta Pi, National Honor Society Member
Suncoast Area Teacher Training Honors Program (SCATT) graduate

Work Experience:
Sarasota County School Board, Sarasota, FL. 1994 - Present
Gulf Gate Elementary School
Speech-Language Pathologist
- Work in both preschool and elementary school settings serving pre-kindergarten through grade 5 population with cerebral palsy, autism, developmental delays, emotional handicaps, learning disabilities, fluency, language, and articulation disorders.
- Administer diagnostic evaluations, fulfill duties as Local Education Agent, and complete Individual Education Plans, including therapeutic interventions for students in varying exceptionalities and regular education classes.
- Provide training to new teachers, other therapists, and parents.
- Utilize AC devices and picture symbols for children with autism / developmental delay.

Asolo Theatre Company, Sarasota, FL. Summers 1996, 1997
Summer Program with Asolo Theatre Company and Children's Haven and Adult Community Services, Inc.
Speech-Language Pathologist
- Worked with teens and adults with physical, mental, and developmental disabilities.
- Assessed and developed ongoing oral-motor, voice, language, and pragmatic interventions to enhance and improve performance abilities for theatrical productions.
- Trained staff on individual strengths and weaknesses related to specific disabilities and impact on communication.

Hospital Homebound Program, Charter Hospital, Bradenton, FL. 1998, 1999
Speech-Language Pathologist
Sarasota County School Board, Sarasota, FL. 1994
Head Start Program
Speech-Language Pathologist
- Worked with preschool children with phonological processing disorders and language delays.

Professional Memberships:
- American Speech / Language and Hearing Association (ASHA), 1994 - present.
- Florida Association of Speech-Language Pathologists and Audiologists (FLASHA), 2000 - present.
- Suncoast Speech and Hearing Association, Sarasota, FL, 1995 - 1999; Secretary 1996 - 1997.

Recent Supplemental Education
- Attended 4 Van Wezel / Kennedy Center for the Performing Arts-sponsored workshops instructing teachers in use of performing arts to teach Sunshine State Standards, 1998 - Present.
- 1988 - Present: Addressing the Needs of Culturally and Linguistically Diverse Populations; Jose Lozano, M.S., CCC-SLP, Sarasota, FL, 2002.
- Arts Odyssey Workshop, Sarasota, FL, 2002.
- Unlocking a Child's Potential, Dr. Jeffrey Bradstreet, Sarasota, FL, 2002.
- Literacy-based Language Strategies for SLP's, Carolyn Ford, Ph.D., CCC-SLP, 2001.
- ASHA Conference, New Orleans, LA, 2001.
- Arts Odyssey Workshops, "There's More to the Story," Sarasota, FL, 2001.
- Arts Odyssey Workshop, "Order for the Day: Classroom Management Through Drama," 2000.
- Asha Conference, San Antonio, TX, 1998.
- Arts Odyssey Workshop, "Bringing Literature to Life II," Sarasota, FL, 1998.
- Asha Conference, Boston, MA, 1997.

Grants Received
- $1000, Manatee County School Board - involved students, parents, and teachers in the creation of a xeriscape garden and use of science equipment to study plant and animal life, 1998-1999.

With the appropriate amount of white space, the reworked resume has an excellent appearance and is inviting to read.

Wendy A. Alper
1340 Bradenton Road
Sarasota, FL 34234

(941) 951-9812
Waalper@gte.net

SPEECH-LANGUAGE PATHOLOGIST
Elementary Schools • Community Service Programs

- 10 years' experience working with preschool speech-language-impaired children.
- Utilize augmentative-communication (AC) devices and picture symbols for children with autism / developmental delay.
- Attended 5 national speech-language pathology conferences.
- Awarded 2 grants for hands-on environmental / science studies.
- Attended 4 Van Wezel / Kennedy Center for the Performing Arts-sponsored workshops instructing teachers in use of performing arts to teach Sunshine State Standards.
- MS, Speech-Language Pathology.

EXPERIENCE

Sarasota County School Board, Sarasota, FL. 1994 - Present
Gulf Gate Elementary School
Speech-Language Pathologist

- Work in both preschool and elementary school settings, serving pre-kindergarten through grade 5 population with cerebral palsy, autism, developmental delays, emotional handicaps, learning disabilities, fluency, language, and articulation disorders.
- Administer diagnostic evaluations, fulfill duties as Local Education Agent, and complete Individual Education Plans, including therapeutic interventions for students in varying exceptionalities and regular education classes.
- Provide training to new teachers, other therapists, and parents.
- Utilize AC devices and picture symbols for children with autism / developmental delay.

Hospital Homebound Program, Charter Hospital, Bradenton, FL. 1998, 1999
Speech-Language Pathologist

Asolo Theatre Company, Sarasota, FL. Summers 1996, 1997
Summer Program with Asolo Theatre Company and Children's Haven and Adult Community Services, Inc.
Speech-Language Pathologist

- Worked with teens and adults with physical, mental, and developmental disabilities.
- Assessed and developed ongoing oral-motor, voice, language, and pragmatic interventions to enhance and improve performance abilities for theatrical productions.
- Trained staff on individual strengths and weaknesses related to specific disabilities and impact on communication.

Hospital Homebound Program, Charter Hospital, Bradenton, FL. 1998, 1999
Speech-Language Pathologist

Sarasota County School Board, Sarasota, FL. 1994
Head Start Program
Speech-Language Pathologist

- Worked with preschool children with phonological processing disorders and language delays.

Problem 31: Lacking Bold Type to Highlight Key Parts of the Resume

Because there's no bold type to separate its different elements, this resume lacks eye appeal and isn't inviting to read.

Alberto Gabelli
4701 Shore Road
Brooklyn, N.Y. 11209
Telephone: 718.745.8346
E-mail: agabelli@nyc.rr.com

EXPERIENCE SUMMARY

18 years of progressively responsible accounting and financial management experience, with concentration in technology and service industries. Heavy information technology experience, including implementation and supervision of financial systems. Skilled at creating and enhancing processes to meet changing business requirements.

EMPLOYMENT BACKGROUND

Internet Consulting Solutions, Inc., New York, NY.   08/'00 to Present

Privately held $10 million web design / internet consulting firm.

Director of Finance

Complete responsibility for all financial functions, reporting to COO.

- Revamped all financial and accounting policies, procedures, and processes to ensure more efficient operation while playing key role in driving net income from $46,000 in 2000 to $400,000 in 2001.
  - Streamlined accounting staff, saving $124,000 a year, plus reduced audit and accounting fees $44,000 annually.
  - Developed accurate picture of cash position through posting receipts on daily basis, writing computerized checks versus manual, performing bank reconciliations within 2 weeks of month-end, plus instituting monthly cash flow projections and weekly scheduling of expected receipts and disbursements.
  - Brought accounts receivable from 51% current to 85% level.
  - Achieved zero bad debt over 21-month period.
  - Instituted process to accelerate billing cycle.
- Resolved problems with 43 vendors threatening lawsuits during Q4 2000, negotiating extended payment terms with 37 and long-term payouts with the 6 that had been sent to collection.
- Established procedure for tracking work in process and projects to be initiated.
- Created company's first revenue-projection system.
- Developed first Billing Rates / Cost Rates System, enabling accurate understanding of project profitability, plus increased revenues through creating Standard Pricing Worksheet.
- Instituted first Project Status Reports and Utilization Reports systems.

New York Web Design / Internet Consultants, New York, NY.   11/'98 - 06/'00

Global web design / internet consulting firm with over 500 employees in 10 offices worldwide.

Controller / Director of Accounting

- Expanded department from 5 to 20 to support revenue growth goals.
- Performed financial integration of 9 merged companies.
- Successfully implemented and oversaw support function of integrated time / billing / financial system with over 800 worldwide users.
- Coordinated monthly closings, quarterly reviews, and certified audits.

Computer-Aided Solutions, Inc., New York, NY.   03/'97 - 10/'98

National diversified computer sales, services, and integration company.

Manager of Financial Reporting

By highlighting "Experience" as well as names of employers and job titles, the new resume's appearance is improved and will attract readers.

Alberto Gabelli
4701 Shore Road
Brooklyn, N.Y. 11209

(718) 745-8346
agabelli@nyc.rr.com

ACCOUNTING & FINANCE EXECUTIVE— Technology & Service Industries

Cost Reduction • Efficiency Enhancement • Productivity Improvement • Information Technology • CPA

- Revamped Internet company's financial and accounting processes, playing lead role in driving net income from $46,000 to $400,000 level within 1 year.
- Performed financial integration of 9 merged companies into parent organization.

An accomplished financial planner and strategist recognized for broad strengths in evaluating financial and accounting systems and processes, then instituting initiatives that dramatically improve efficiencies and productivity while reducing costs.

EXPERIENCE

Internet Consulting Solutions, Inc., New York, NY. 2000 - Present

Privately held $10 million web design / internet consulting firm.

Director of Finance

Complete responsibility for all financial functions, reporting to COO.

- Revamped all financial and accounting policies, procedures, and processes to ensure more efficient operation while playing key role in driving net income from $46,000 in 2000 to $400,000 in 2001.
  - Streamlined accounting staff, saving $124,000 a year, plus reduced audit and accounting fees $44,000 annually.
  - Developed accurate picture of cash position through posting receipts on daily basis, writing computerized checks versus manual, performing bank reconciliations within 2 weeks of month-end, plus instituting monthly cash flow projections and weekly scheduling of expected receipts and disbursements.
  - Brought accounts receivable from 51% current to 85% level.
  - Achieved zero bad debt over 21-month period.
  - Instituted process to accelerate billing cycle.
- Resolved problems with 43 vendors threatening lawsuits during Q4 2000, negotiating extended payment terms with 37 and long-term payouts with the 6 that had been sent to collection.
- Established procedure for tracking work in process and projects to be initiated.
- Created company's first revenue-projection system.
- Developed first Billing Rates / Cost Rates System, enabling accurate understanding of project profitability, plus increased revenues through creating Standard Pricing Worksheet.
- Instituted first Project Status Reports and Utilization Reports systems.

New York Web Design / Internet Consultants, New York, NY. 1998 - 2000

Global web design / internet consulting firm with over 500 employees in 10 offices worldwide.

Controller / Director of Accounting

- Expanded department from 5 to 20 to support revenue growth goals.
- Performed financial integration of 9 merged companies.
- Successfully implemented and oversaw support function of integrated time / billing / financial system with over 800 worldwide users.
- Coordinated monthly closings, quarterly reviews, and certified audits.

Computer-Aided Solutions, Inc., New York, NY. 1997 - 1998

National diversified computer sales, services, and integration company.

Manager of Financial Reporting

Problem 32: Excessive Use of Bold Type

In this resume, Brinkley is trying to get readers' attention by using bold type to highlight the action verbs that begin his statements. By using so much bold type, nothing stands out. Worse, the excessive use of this type makes the resume look cluttered, deterring people from reading it.

David W. Brinkley
7329 NW Hawkins Blvd.
Portland, OR 97229
(503) 297-2014
Dbrinkley@hotmail.com

WORK HISTORY

PORTLAND CLOSURES, Portland, Oregon. 1997 - Present
Manufacturer and distributor of bottle caps.
<u>Production Scheduler</u>

- **Coordinated production** for 31 injection molding machines, 15 lining machines, and 3 printers producing 2500 units per day.
- **Increased throughput as much as 10%** through developing and implementing more efficient scheduling system.
- **Assisted in software conversion** from Providex / Windex to J.D. Edwards.
- **Expedited orders** from inception to shipment.
- **Created multilevel bill of materials** in both Providex and J.D. Edwards/MRP system.
- **Developed and implemented** product code numbers.

QUALITY WALL SYSTEMS, Seattle, Washington. 1995 - 1997
Developer and manufacturer of removable wall systems and room dividers.
<u>Production Foreman</u>

- **Hired, trained, and supervised** crew of up to 17 personnel at this start-up company producing concrete walls for manufactured homes.
- **Developed and implemented effective production processes** as well as quality assurance program.
- **Continuously analyzed and improved processes,** resulting in increasing productivity as much as 12% and reducing costs to 15%.
- **Produced products ahead of schedule** while maintaining quality standards.
- **Reviewed, revised, and translated** blueprints.

PACIFIC NORTHWEST LUMBER, Corvallis, Oregon. 1993 - 1995
Wholesale and retail lumber dealer and home improvement center.
<u>Assistant Foreman</u>

- **Trained and supervised** 8-person crew to assemble and ship pre-hung door systems.
- **Reduced inventories up to 20%** through instituting new inventory management system.

EDUCATION

A.S., Computer Network Administration, Keiser College, Sarasota, FL. 1998
Honor Roll Graduate.
Key courses included Novell 4.1, Windows NT 4.0, Microsoft Office, Unix, J.D. Edwards, Access, WordPerfect.

In his revised resume, Brinkley uses the introductory section to highlight the key parts of his background and now achieves the impact he was striving for in his original resume.

David W. Brinkley
7329 NW Hawkins Blvd.
Portland, OR 97229

Tel: (503) 297-2014
E-mail: Dbrinkley@hotmail.com

PRODUCTION SCHEDULING / PRODUCTION MANAGEMENT

- Introduced new production scheduling system that increased output up to 10%.
- Developed and implemented new production processes that boosted throughput 12% while reducing costs 15%.
- Decreased inventories 20% through creating state-of-the-art inventory management system.
- Hired, trained, and led teams of up to 17 personnel.

EXPERIENCE

Portland Closures, Portland, OR. 1997 - Present
Manufacturer and distributor of enclosures for bottles.

Production Scheduler

- Coordinated production for 31 injection molding machines, 15 lining machines, and 3 printers producing 2500 units per day.
- Increased throughput as much as 10% through developing and implementing more efficient scheduling system.
- Assisted in software conversion from Providex / Windex to J.D. Edwards.
- Expedited orders from inception to shipment.
- Created multilevel bill of materials in both Providex and J.D. Edwards / MRP system.
- Developed and implemented product code numbers.

Quality Wall Systems, Seattle, WA. 1995 - 1997
Developer and manufacturer of removable wall systems and room dividers.

Production Foreman

- Hired, trained, and supervised crew of up to 17 personnel at this start-up company producing concrete walls for manufactured homes.
- Developed and implemented effective production processes as well as quality assurance program.
- Continuously analyzed and improved processes, resulting in increasing productivity as much as 12% and reducing costs to 15%.
- Produced products ahead of schedule while maintaining quality standards.
- Reviewed, revised, and translated blueprints.

Pacific Northwest Lumber, Corvallis, OR. 1993 - 1995
Wholesale and retail lumber dealer and home improvement center.

Assistant Foreman

- Trained and supervised 8-person crew to assemble and ship pre-hung door systems.
- Reduced inventories up to 20% through instituting new inventory management system.

EDUCATION

A.S., Computer Network Administration, Keiser College, Sarasota, FL. 1998. Honor Roll Graduate.
Key courses included Novell 4.1, Windows NT 4.0, Microsoft Office, Unix, J.D. Edwards, Access, WordPerfect.

Problem 33: Using a Fancy Font

Some job hunters try to gain readers' attention by using a fancy font, as does Atkins in this resume. This doesn't work because it makes the document extremely difficult to read. Many people will set the resume aside.

Christopher R. Atkins

1047 Olentary St.
Sarasota, FL 34231
941.926.2978

Experience

Poseidon Restaurant, Longboat Key, FL. July 1998-2002
Chef at this fine-dining restaurant seating 160 guests.
- Responsible for prep, setting line, working sauté, plus ensuring that all 5 kitchen personnel were properly set up.
- Developed menu with executive chef, including creating daily specials.
- Performed closing duties.

Michael's Seafood Grille, Sarasota, FL. May 1996-July 1998
Sous chef at this fine-dining establishment seating 300 patrons upstairs and 170 downstairs. Responsible for 2 kitchens accommodating 500-600 diners Friday and Saturday nights.
- Recruited by leading local restaurateur to play key role in turning around poorly performing kitchen, especially in areas of food cost, quality, consistency, line operations, and cleanliness.
- Turned around poorly performing kitchen, plus hired, trained, and developed 25-30 personnel.
- Created and implemented new kitchen systems, procedures, and controls.
- Redesigned menus and ordered all food and supplies.
- Reduced food cost 25 points, while improving quality, plus decreased labor cost 15 points.
- Prepared food for 25-30 banquet parties a month as well as for buffets and sit-down dinners for 20-200 people.
- Planned and built new kitchen for downstairs facility. Created menu, hired and trained staff, and instituted efficient and effective operating procedures and controls.

Michael's on East, Sarasota, FL. October 1993-May 1996
Catering chef at this fine-dining restaurant.
- Prepared breakfasts, lunches, and dinners for ballroom parties of from 10-1500 people.
- Specialized in private house parties with wine dinners, fine dining, and 5-course meals. Supervised staffs of up to 12.

Sarasota Brewing Company, Sarasota, FL. August 1992-March 1993
Assistant kitchen manager at this full-service, casual dining establishment seating 100 guests.

By using a traditional font such as Times Roman, the revised resume is now a pleasure to read.

Christopher R. Atkins
1047 Olentary St.
Sarasota, FL 34231

(941) 926-2978

SOUS CHEF—FINE DINING & CATERING

- Recognized for broad strengths in creative menu design, food preparation, cost reduction, and management of kitchen personnel.
- Rectified kitchen and turned around underperforming operation, improving food quality while reducing food costs 25 points and labor costs 15 points.
- Managed kitchens serving up to 600 diners on weekend nights; catered sit-down parties for up to 200 guests.
- A.O.S., Culinary Institute of America, Hyde Park, NY.

EXPERIENCE

POSEIDON RESTAURANT, Longboat Key, FL. 1998 - 2002
Sous Chef at this fine-dining restaurant seating 160 guests.

- Responsible for prep, setting line, working sauté, plus ensuring that all 5 kitchen personnel were properly set up.
- Developed menu with Executive Chef, including daily specials.
- Performed closing duties.

MICHAEL'S SEAFOOD GRILLE, Sarasota, FL. 1996 - 1998
Sous Chef at this fine-dining establishment seating 300 patrons upstairs and 170 downstairs. Responsible for 2 kitchens accommodating 500-600 diners Friday and Saturday nights.

- Recruited by leading local restaurateur to play key role in turning around poorly performing kitchen, especially in areas of food cost, quality, consistency, line operations, and cleanliness.
- Turned around poorly performing kitchen, plus hired, trained, and developed 25-30 personnel.
- Created and implemented new kitchen systems, procedures, and controls.
- Redesigned menus and ordered all food and supplies.
- Reduced food cost 25 points, while improving quality, plus decreased labor cost 15 points.
- Prepared food for 25-30 banquet parties a month as well as for buffets and sit-down dinners for 20-200 people.
- Planned and built new kitchen for downstairs facility. Created menu, hired and trained staff, and instituted efficient and effective operating procedures and controls.

MICHAEL'S ON EAST, Sarasota, FL. 1993 - 1996
Catering Chef at this fine-dining restaurant.

- Prepared breakfasts, lunches, and dinners for ballroom parties of from 10-1500 people.
- Specialized in private house parties with wine dinners and fine-dining, 5-course meals. Supervised staffs of up to 12.

SARASOTA BREWING COMPANY, Sarasota, FL. 1992 - 1993
Assistant Kitchen Manager at this full-service, casual dining establishment seating 100 guests.

- Supervised staff of 4; assisted Kitchen Manager with lunch, dinner, inventories, and labor costs; helped with prep.

EDUCATION

A.O.S., Culinary Institute of America, Hyde Park, NY. 1990
Certified Food Manager, Florida Department of Business & Professional Regulation, 1993.

Problems with Composition/Appearance/Formatting in Resumes

Problem 34: Using Multiple Fonts

In this resume, Tomlinson uses multiple fonts to attract readers' attention. This approach is ineffective because it makes the resume extremely busy. The way to dazzle readers is with accomplishments, not with varied fonts.

HARDING R. TOMLINSON

35 MORTON STREET
NEW YORK, NY 10012

212-677-6443
HRTOM@AOL.COM

_____SUMMARY_____

Communications professional with 15 years' marketing, public relations, research, and project management experience. Outstanding written, oral, and interpersonal skills in interactions with senior management. Emphasis on marketing, event management, and corporate identity.

_____PROFESSIONAL EXPERIENCE_____

CITIBANK, New York, NY   2001 to Present
Marketing Consultant
- Researched, wrote copy, and coordinated with global senior management and design team launch of new web site.
- Developed internal communications strategy, including internet promotion and articles in monthly corporate magazines, to generate cross-divisional business opportunities.
- Created media relations program, securing favorable mention in leading financial and trade publications, including *The Wall Street Journal, Buyouts, Private Equity Analyst, European Venture Capital Journal, and Investment Dealers Digest.*

BANK OF AMERICA, San Francisco, CA   1999 to May 2001
Marketing & Communications Manager
- Created and produced marketing materials.
- Led web site development for launch of new private equity fund focused on direct marketing companies.
- Managed media relations program. Composed and distributed press releases; contacted financial and trade press to secure favorable mention of M&A transactions in leading publications. Press coverage led directly to $35 million private equity investment.
- Secured and conducted speaking engagements at international industry conferences, with top-rated presentation appearing as article in trade association quarterly for senior management.

FINANCIAL SOFTWARE ASSOCIATES, Palo Alto, CA   1998 to 1999
Client Communications Consultant
- Developed marketing materials for equity and fixed income product lines for technology company selling analytical software to financial services institutions and consultants.

BEAR, STEARNS & CO., New York, NY   1996 to 1998
Special Projects Manager
- Provided strategic and tactical support to Director of Marketing at securities clearing unit with leading market share.

Tomlinson's revised resume is now entirely in Garamond. The document is attractive to the eye, and it encourages readership.

Harding R. Tomlinson
35 Morton St.
New York, NY 10012

212-677-6443
Hrtom@aol.com

MARKETING COMMUNICATIONS—Financial Services

Marketing • Event Management • Corporate Identity • Public Relations

- Repeated successes with world-recognized financial organizations, including Citibank and Bank of America.
- Instrumental in launch of new web site for Citibank, with activities including securing publicity in leading publications such as "The Wall Street Journal" and "Buyout."
- Directed development of web site for new Bank of America private equity fund—managed media relations program that generated $35 million in private equity investment.
- Planned and implemented communications program for Bear Stearns that contributed to 90% client retention rate in competitive market.

EXPERIENCE

Citibank, New York, NY. 2001 - Present
Marketing Consultant

- Researched, wrote copy, and coordinated with global senior management and design team the launch of new web site.
- Developed internal communications strategy, including internet promotion and articles in monthly corporate magazines, to generate cross-divisional business opportunities.
- Created media relations program, securing favorable mention in leading financial and trade publications, including "The Wall Street Journal," "Buyouts," "Private Equity Analyst," "European Venture Capital Journal," and "Investment Dealers Digest."

Bank of America, San Francisco, CA. 1999 - 2001
Marketing & Communications Manager

- Created and produced marketing materials.
- Led web site development for launch of new private equity fund focused on direct marketing companies.
- Managed media relations program. Composed and distributed press releases, plus contacted financial and trade press to secure favorable mention of M&A transactions in leading publications. Press coverage led directly to $35 million private equity investment.
- Secured and conducted speaking engagements at international industry conferences, with top-rated presentation appearing as article in trade association quarterly for senior management.

Financial Software Associates, Palo Alto, CA. 1998 - 1999
Client Communications Consultant

- Developed marketing materials for equity and fixed income product lines for technology company selling analytical software to financial services institutions and consultants.

Bear, Stearns & Co., New York, NY. 1996 - 1998
Special Projects Manager

- Provided strategic and tactical support to Director of Marketing at securities clearing unit with leading market share.
- Wrote articles and edited newsletters distributed to executives at over 400 clients and senior management of firm. Edited quarterly newsletter of articles by external attorneys and accountants, distributed to senior executives at over 2000 clients. Communications activities contributed to 90% client retention rate in competitive market.
- Organized program, recruited 70 speakers for 30 sessions, and created all written materials within budget for annual 2-day conference for 600 senior executives of client firms.

Problem 35: Using Extra Large Type

Another device for gaining readers' attention, which is used by Vanderway in this resume, is to use large type. This backfires because it produces a juvenile look.

ROGER A. VANDERWAY

1863 Gulf Gate Drive • Sarasota, FL 34231

(941) 921-6502

EXPERIENCE

Batson & Cook, Atlanta, GA. 1998 - 2002

90-year-old, $400 million nationwide general contractor.

General Carpenter Foreman / Field Superintendent

Sarasota, FL. July 1999 - 2002

- Transferred to Sarasota with Job Superintendent and Assistant Job Superintendent to begin luxury, high-rise "Renaissance" project.
- Played key role in site preparation, then supervised subcontractors, including engineering layout, carpentry, iron workers, electricians, plumbers, concrete finishers, HVAC, painting, and fire / sprinkler.
- Poured 30,000 sq. yds. of concrete in 100 days—won first bonus ever paid to a Field Superintendent.
- Oversaw 12 direct reports and crews of up to 100.
- Interfaced with engineers, architects, surveyors, building authority personnel, and owners' representatives.

Atlanta, GA. 1998 - July 1999

- Supervised construction of 18-story office building.
- Oversaw all subcontractors, including daily crews of up to 100.
- Interfaced with engineers, architects, surveyors, building authority personnel, and owners' representatives.

West Georgia Construction, Atlanta, GA. 1996 - 1998

Owner / Manager

- Performed carpentry subcontracting work on single-family homes and Publix supermarkets through Keene Construction Co., a General Contractor.
- Employed full-time crew of up to 8.

1988 - 1996: Carpenter Foreman for several Georgia companies. Projects included high-rises, mid-rises, the Georgia Dome, banks, parking decks, supermarkets, schools, sewer treatment plants, weapons testing facility, prison, and warehouse.

1983 - 1988: Lead Carpenter, Carpenter, Carpenter Helper - various companies.

EDUCATION

AGC workshops; Batson & Cook-sponsored training; high-school diploma.

The type in the makeover is now a standard size, which gives the resume a digni-fied, professional appearance.

Roger A. Vanderway
1863 Gulf Gate Drive
Sarasota, FL 34231

Tel: (941) 921-6502

CONSTRUCTION MANAGEMENT

- Won first bonus ever paid to Field Superintendent in history of 90-year-old, $400 million general contractor.
- Set company record for pouring 30,000 sq. yds. of concrete in 100 days.
- Recognized by building inspectors and subcontractors' supervisors as most knowledgeable man on the site.
- Continuously sought after by Superintendents for construction knowledge, management abilities, and record of completing projects on time, within budget, and according to specifications.

EXPERIENCE

Batson & Cook, Atlanta, GA. 1998 - 2002

90-year-old, $400 million nationwide general contractor.

General Carpenter Foreman / Field Superintendent

Sarasota, FL. July 1999 - 2002

- Transferred to Sarasota with Job Superintendent and Assistant Job Superintendent to begin luxury, high-rise "Renaissance" project.
- Played key role in site preparation, then supervised subcontractors, including engineering layout, carpentry, iron workers, electricians, plumbers, concrete finishers, HVAC, painting, and fire / sprinkler.
- Poured 30,000 sq. yds. of concrete in 100 days—won first-ever bonus paid to Field Superintendent.
- Oversaw 12 direct reports and crews of up to 100.
- Interfaced with engineers, architects, surveyors, building authority personnel, and owners' representatives.

Atlanta, GA. 1998 - July 1999

- Supervised construction of 18-story office building.
- Oversaw all subcontractors, including daily crews of up to 100.
- Interfaced with engineers, architects, surveyors, building authority personnel, and owners' representatives.

West Georgia Construction, Atlanta, GA. 1996 - 1998

Owner / Manager

- Performed carpentry subcontracting work on single-family homes and Publix supermarkets through Keene Construction Co., General Contractor.
- Employed full-time crew of up to 8.

1988 - 1996: Held position of Carpenter Foreman for various Georgia companies. Projects included high-rises, mid-rises, the Georgia Dome, banks, parking decks, supermarkets, schools, sewer treatment plants, and a weapons testing facility, state prison, and warehouse.

1983 - 1988: Held positions of Lead Carpenter, Carpenter, Carpenter Helper.

EDUCATION

AGC workshops, Batson & Cook-sponsored training, high-school diploma.

Problems with Composition/Appearance/Formatting in Resumes

161

Problem 36: Using Too Small Type

Believing that it's important for his resume to be only one page long, Baranowicz uses very small type. This will cost him an untold number of interviews because people don't like to have to squint in order to read a resume.

Arthur Baranowicz

1705 California St. • Redwood Shores, CA 94065 • (650) 245-3298 • abaranowicz@pacbell.net

EXPERIENCE

Games.com, Alameda, CA. 2000 to 2002

Division of Hasbro, chartered with creating largest and most exciting community-based games web site in the world, with exclusive license to Milton Bradley, Parker Bros., and Atari brands, including most popular board and arcade games of all time: Monopoly, Scrabble, Sorry, BattleShip, Asteroids, Centipede.

Senior Software Engineer

- Performed design and development of both website and games.
- Played key role in turnaround of R&D organization severely behind schedule due to technical obstacles.
- Achieved both live and beta milestones on schedule.

Electronic Arts, Redwood City, CA. 1993 to 1999

World's leading interactive entertainment software company.

Senior Software Engineer

- Key member of product development team that won Paladin Cup award for outstanding technology development in architecting and implementing brand-new 3-D engine, 1994.
- Additional projects included:

Tiger Woods & PGA Tour Products

- Member of console development team for EASPORTS Tiger Woods products.
- Played leading role in developing and architecting *The Internet Tour,* Electronic Arts' first online multiplayer tournament.
- Instrumental in development of company's first web site for PGA Tour products.

Tiger Woods '99 Playstation

- Played key role in architecting new 3D engine and data format to allow full-motion cameras in Playstation game engine, while retaining compatibility with existing course data.

PGA Tour 486, PGA Tour '96

- Lead Software Engineer for PC-based PGA Tour products from 1993-1996, including OEM versions, add-on course disks, and derivative products. Managed 1-5 engineers.
- Designed and implemented new 3D engine. Developed art and video production processes, including blue-screened golfers, 24-bit scanned art, and color reduction across all platforms.
- Consulted on software adaptations to Mac, 3DO, Sony Playstation (PSX), and Sega Genesis platforms.
- Won several awards from major gaming magazines for outstanding new products as well as best golf simulation, PGA Tour 486.

RasterOps Corp., Santa Clara, CA. 1989 to 1993

Company pioneered 24-bit color desktop publishing and multimedia systems, developing first 24-bit color displays for Macintosh.

Software Engineer

- Developed MS Windows, DOS, OS/2, and other OEM projects, including imbedded microprocessors and digital live video.
- Responsibilities included extensive device driver and application programming, BIOS and firmware development for various multi-processor products, as well as architecture and administration of ethernet network consisting of DOS, Windows 3.x/NT, Mac, and UNIX clients.
- Successfully developed products including Paintboard-PC ISA 24-bit frame buffer, 1024MC MCA 24-bit frame buffer, CorrectColor Calibrator, RS24 IBM RS6000 24-bit frame buffer, CorrectPrint 300 Dye-sub printer, and 16PC TARGA compatible frame buffer.

Metamorphose Engineering, Inc., Los Altos, CA. 1986 to 1989

Hardware and software development company engaged in live video capture and desktop imaging for the PC.

Software Engineer

- Worked on software design and development as well as test processes.
- Worked on design team for TARGA-compatible and 34010-based true-color frame buffers. Worked extensively on live video application development and low level firmware and driver development. Also developed applications to integrate these components into workstations for various markets, ranging from video editing/production to animation to hair salons.

Activision, Inc., Mountain View, CA. 1984 to 1986

Leading third-party developer, producer, and distributor of video games.

Software Designer

- Designed software for and programmed video games, with successes including "Murder on the Mississippi," "Little Computer People," "Ghostbusters," and "Zengi."

Atari Corp., New York, NY. 1983

Leading developer, manufacturer, and distributor of video games.

Software Engineer

- Developed video game software and new proprietary hardware technology to accelerate games on Atari 2600 Video Computer System.
- Created new computer add-on and developed video game titles to take advantage of new technology, including the arcade hit *Robotron.*

The revised resume uses a traditional type size. The fact that the resume is two pages long will be no deterrent at all.

Arthur Baranowicz
1705 California St.
Redwood Shores, CA 94065

(650) 245-3298
abaranowicz@pacbell.net

SOFTWARE DEVELOPMENT
Interactive Entertainment • Multimedia Development.

- Instrumental in turning around Hasbro's games web site that had been stalled in development.
- Key member of award-winning teams designing and developing 27 interactive products, including "Tiger Woods," "PGA Tour," "Little Computer People," "Ghostbusters," and "Zengi."
- Vast experience in software development, including architecture, design, and scheduling. Responsible for many successful leading-edge software and hardware products on platforms from Atari 2600 to Playstation to PC's and the Internet.

EXPERIENCE

Games.com, Alameda, CA. 2000 - 2002

Division of Hasbro, chartered with creating largest and most exciting community-based games web site in the world, with exclusive license to Milton Bradley, Parker Bros., and Atari brands, including most popular board and arcade games of all time: Monopoly, Scrabble, Sorry, BattleShip, Asteroids, Centipede.

Senior Software Engineer

- Performed design and development of both website and games.
- Played key role in turnaround of R&D organization severely behind schedule due to technical obstacles.
- Achieved both live and beta milestones on schedule.

Electronic Arts, Redwood City, CA. 1993 - 1999

World's leading interactive entertainment software company.

Senior Software Engineer

- Key member of product development team that won Paladin Cup award for outstanding technology development in architecting and implementing brand-new 3-D engine, 1994.
- Additional projects included:

Tiger Woods & PGA Tour Products
- Member of console development team for EASPORTS Tiger Woods products.
- Played leading role in developing and architecting "The Internet Tour," Electronic Arts' first online multiplayer tournament.
- Instrumental in development of company's first web site for PGA Tour products.

Tiger Woods '99 Playstation
- Played key role in architecting new 3D engine and data format to allow full-motion cameras in Playstation game engine, while retaining compatibility with existing course data.

PGA Tour 486, PGA Tour '96
- Lead Software Engineer for PC-based PGA Tour products from 1993-1996, including OEM versions, add-on course disks, and derivative products. Managed 1-5 engineers.
- Designed and implemented new 3D engine. Developed art and video production processes, including blue-screened golfers, 24-bit scanned art, and color reduction across all platforms.
- Consulted on software adaptations to Mac, 3DO, Sony Playstation (PSX), and Sega Genesis platforms.
- Won several awards from major gaming magazines for outstanding new products as well as best golf simulation, PGA Tour 486.

RasterOps Corp., Santa Clara, CA. 1989 - 1993

Company pioneered 24-bit color desktop publishing and multimedia systems, developing first 24-bit color displays for Macintosh.

Software Engineer

- Developed MS Windows, DOS, OS/2, and other OEM projects, including imbedded microprocessors and digital live video.
- Responsibilities included extensive device driver and application programming, BIOS and firmware development for various multi-processor products, as well as architecture and administration of ethernet network consisting of DOS, Windows 3.x/NT, Mac, and UNIX clients.

Problems with Composition/Appearance/Formatting in Resumes

163

Problem 37: Writing a One-Page Accomplishments-Focused Resume

This widely used one-page format has two problems: (1) it's impossible to tell when the exciting accomplishments appearing in the top half of the document took place, and (2) the resume omits key information so that it will be only one page long.

GEORGE Y. LENNOX

402 9th St.
East Hoboken, NJ 07030

(201) 659-6526
Glennox3@netscape.net

Senior Executive skilled in P&L management, operations, strategic planning, and business development in diverse industries.
- Revamped production operations to enable 278% sales increase in 3 years, achieving record profit level.
- Added $1.5 million to bottom line in 1 year through continuous cost reductions.
- Created strategy to enter competitive new market, adding 10% to total sales within 3 years.

Proven ability in change management, turnarounds, start-ups, productivity improvement, and business process reengineering.
- Increased inventory turns from 1.4 to 14 per year.
- Achieved profitable multiyear fixed price contract with largest customer by lowering labor costs.
- Developed national award-winning employee suggestion program to improve company processes (78+% participation).
- Guided team in implementing new integrated management information system package within 5 months.

Results-oriented, multifaceted leader with broad-based business acumen. Strong communication, team-building, problem-solving, organizational, motivational, and interpersonal skills.

BS, Mechanical Engineering, Temple University.
Excellent health; enjoy sports. Married, 2 sons. Willing to relocate.

PROFESSIONAL EXPERIENCE

INTERNATIONAL TEMPERATURE CONTROL SYSTEMS, INC., Chester, NJ.   1996 - 2002
Privately held, employee-owned manufacturer of high-tech temperature control systems for the aerospace industry.
Director of Operations
- Directed turnaround and achieved record profits.
- Changed company focus to customer service orientation; reduced costs and maintained 99.7% acceptance rate.
- $1 million new product sales achieved in 8 months by refocusing product support into business development strategy.
- Reduced medical insurance costs by 20% for 2 consecutive years through direct negotiations.

TECHNOLOGY DISPLAY SYSTEMS, INC., Fayetteville, SC.   1988 - 1996
International manufacturer of display technology products with annual sales in excess of $500 million; ISO 9001 and ISO 14001 certification.
Operations Manager - Fayetteville, 1991 - 1996
- Led relocation and facility design team for new 110,000 sq. ft. facility, missing no delivery dates despite 25% increase in sales.
- Increased sales 31% and 18% during 2 years of construction and relocation.
- $2 million cut in material purchases (lead time cut from 4 months to 4 weeks) by bringing outside process in-house.
- Decreased rework from 10% to 1%.

Supervisor of Operations, 1988 - 1991
- Reduced employee turnover rate from 60% to 10% per year through instituting innovative compensation program.

UNITED FREEZER & STORAGE COMPANY, Youngstown, OH.   1985 - 1988
Company provided nationwide distribution for GM, Rubbermaid, and PPG Industries.
Contracts Manager
- Reduced delivery delinquencies from 50% to less than 2% during sales growth of 59%.

Rewritten according to the guidelines set forth in Part I, Lennox's resume has the excitement of the original version but none of its liabilities. It also contains important additional information concerning responsibilities and accomplishments.

George Y. Lennox
402 9th St.
East Hoboken, NJ 07030

(201) 659-6526
Glennox3@netscape.net

SENIOR EXECUTIVE—OPERATIONS

Strategic Planning • Process Reengineering • Productivity Improvement • Turnarounds

- Introduced numerous changes in manufacturing, resulting in increased productivity and profitability:
  - Revamped manufacturing to turn around company with declining sales, enabling 278% sales increase in 3 years to record profit level.
  - Increased inventory turns 900% and reduced rework 90%.
  - Decreased employee turnover 67%, plus won 2 national awards for employee motivation / involvement.

A visionary operations executive and skilled change agent who combines manufacturing expertise with broad strengths in human resources development and maximization. Recognized as an exceptional mentor and motivator who optimizes staff performance through fostering a supportive, empowering management style. Tireless in the pursuit of quality production processes, maximum growth, and profitability.

EXPERIENCE

International Temperature Control Systems, Inc., Chester, NJ. 1996 - 2002

Privately held, employee-owned manufacturer of high-tech temperature control systems for the aerospace industry.

Director of Operations

Complete responsibility for manufacturing, manufacturing engineering, quality engineering, product assurance engineering, human resources, management information systems, facilities, and shipping and receiving. Oversaw 110 personnel, including 7 managers, and reported to C.E.O. Served as Corporate Director and member of Executive Committee.

- Played key role in turning around company with declining sales—changed culture from autocratic to team-based, plus reengineered departments to create customer-driven focus, supporting 278% sales increase in 3 years and attainment of record profits.
- Grew profits $1.5 million through instituting rigorous cost-reduction program, including 13% reduction in labor expenses.
- Created rapid-prototype development team, enabling entry into new market and new sales equaling 10% of corporate revenues.
- Increased inventory turns from 1.4 to 14 through decreasing process time and increasing flow rates, while maintaining 99.7% customer acceptance rate.
- Introduced continuous improvement and employee motivation programs that reduced turnover from 60% to 20%, plus won 2 national awards from Employee Involvement Association for employees' interest in improving company, with over 78% making suggestions for change.
- Transformed product support function to business development initiative, delivering $1 million in new sales.
- Reduced medical costs 20% plus created and managed MIS Department.

Technology Display Systems, Inc., Fayetteville, SC. 1988 - 1996

International manufacturer of display technology products with annual sales in excess of $500 million.

Operations Manager - Fayetteville, 1991 - 1996

Responsible for production, inventory control, QC / QA, purchasing, and shipping and receiving. Oversaw 250 personnel through 6 direct reports. Reported to VP - Operations.

- Led relocation and facility design team for new 110,000 sq. ft. facility, missing no delivery dates despite 25% increase in sales.
- Increased sales 31% and 18% during 2 years of construction and relocation.
- Reduced material purchases $2 million, while reducing lead time from 4 months to 4 weeks by bringing outside

Problem 38: Experience Presented in Paragraph Form and Without Bullets

In this resume, Beanstock describes her experience in paragraph form instead of with individual statements preceded by bullets. As a result, her accomplishments are buried within the text, and the resume has no impact.

Barbara J. Beanstock
18 Old Stump Drive
Gig Harbor, WA 98332
(253) 851-4189
BJB74@aol.com

Summary:

Professional and effective leader focused on people, quality, and results.

Experience:

KWIK-SHOP STORES, Seattle, WA. Jan/99 - present
Privately held regional convenience store chain.

Director of Operations, Feb/01 - present

P&L responsibility for day-to-day operations of 30 stores with run rate of $15 million in merchandise sales, $13.5 million in fuel sales, and approximately $18 million in lottery sales and money orders.

Opened 3 new stores generating average annual volumes of $700,000 in merchandise sales and 2 million gallons in fuel sales. Developed remodel budgets and layouts for 3 additional sites.

Director of Transition - Acquisition Department, Nov/00 - Feb/01

Responsible for development and implementation of transition plans to integrate 2 acquisitions into parent organization, with activities including operations, marketing, accounting, IT, legal, real estate, and gasoline. One plan ensured continuation of smooth operations while closing corporate office to save over $300,000, while second plan assimilated 3 stores from day 1 due to closure of office.

Director of Marketing, Apr/99 - Nov/00

Responsible for 25 stores, with activities including the selection, pricing, promotion, and planogramming of all products as well as negotiating vendor and supplier contracts, implementing all corporate marketing and merchandising programs, plus managing store implementation, execution, and training through network of field merchandisers. Oversaw 5 direct reports and reported to Division President.

Inherited neglected marketing function. Created formal department through hiring personnel, setting up operating and reporting processes, plus implementing an effective price book, resulting in increasing margins from 32% to 34%. Instituted systems for managing branded and proprietary food service programs for all units. Oversaw store remodeling, plus conducted grand openings. Consolidated 3 separate MIS systems into 1. Supervised all aspects of support for scanning in each location.

SHORE STOP CORPORATION, Salisbury, MD. Aug/97 - Apr/99

$250 million, 81-store chain and the dominant retail marketer on eastern shores of Delaware, Maryland, and Virginia.

Director of Retail

Promoted with responsibilities of operations, facility maintenance, and human resources in addition to marketing. Planned and administered $4 million annual capital expenditure budget. Oversaw 700 personnel through directs reports including Directors of Training and Operations, and Managers of Marketing, Food Service, and Administration. Held P&L responsibility and reported to President.

Developed and implemented strategic and tactical business plans, resulting in 33% increase in EBITDA while growing same store sales more than 10%. Reduced operating costs 5%, decreased inventory shrink 50%, and lowered supply and utility expenses 10%. Improved appearance of stores, plus developed and implemented labor

Presented on separate lines and preceded by bullets, Beanstock's accomplishments are prominent and effective in the makeover.

Barbara J. Beanstock
18 Old Stump Drive
Gig Harbor, WA 98332

(253) 851-4189
BJB74@aol.com

MULTI-UNIT RETAILING EXECUTIVE—Convenience Stores

P&L • Marketing • Operations • Acquisitions / Divestitures • Food & Automotive Products

- Built strong marketing department, expanding margins from 32% to 34% at 25 units.
- Developed and implemented strategic growth plan for 81-store chain, increasing EBITDA 33% while growing same store sales 10%.
- Instituted marketing program at 50-store chain that grew merchandise sales 12% and margin dollars 17% over previous year. Planned and launched Discount Cigarette Stop that improved sales of all merchandise 8-fold.

An innovative and energetic leader, skilled communicator / team builder, and adept negotiator. Recognized for broad strengths in strategic planning, marketing, merchandising, staffing, training, and human resources development and maximization. Proven ability to analyze operations and markets, then introduce strategic and tactical solutions that improve competitive performance while growing revenues and profits. MBA.

EXPERIENCE

Kwik-Shop Stores, Seattle, WA. 1999 - present
Privately held regional convenience store chain.

Director of Operations, February 2001 - present
P&L responsibility for day-to-day operations of 30 stores with run rate of $15 million in merchandise sales, $13.5 million in fuel sales, and approximately $18 million in lottery sales and money orders.

- Opened 3 new stores generating average annual volumes of $700,000 in merchandise sales and 2 million gallons in fuel sales.
- Developed remodel budgets and layouts for 3 additional sites.

Director of Transition - Acquisition Department, 2000 - 2001
Responsible for development and implementation of transition plans to integrate 2 acquisitions into parent organization, with activities including operations, marketing, accounting, IT, legal, real estate, and gasoline.

- Created plan that ensured continuation of smooth operations while closing corporate office to save over $300,000
- Developed second plan that enabled assimilation of 3 stores from day 1 due to closure of office.

Director of Marketing, 1999 - 2000
Responsible for 25 stores, with activities including the selection, pricing, promotion, and planogramming of all products as well as negotiating vendor and supplier contracts, implementing all corporate marketing and merchandising programs, plus managing store implementation, execution, and training through network of field merchandisers. Oversaw 5 direct reports and reported to Division President.

- Inherited neglected marketing function. Created formal department through hiring personnel, setting up operating and reporting processes, plus implementing an effective price book, resulting in increasing margins from 32% to 34%.
- Instituted systems for managing branded and proprietary food service programs for all units.
- Oversaw store remodeling, plus conducted grand openings.
- Consolidated 3 separate MIS systems into 1.
- Supervised all aspects of support for scanning in each location.

Problem 39: Utilizing a Two-Column, Multiple-Font Format

Offered by a few career marketing firms, this visually striking resume features a two-column approach with both vertical and horizontal lines. The resume's complex format is its nemesis. Its dizzying layout makes for a disjointed read with no focus or impact. Nothing stands out that immediately gains the reader's attention.

● ● ● ● ● ● ● ●

Walter D. Parsons

WDParsons2000@aol.com

25 Berkeley Rd.
Elyria, OH 44035
(440) 366-3812

OBJECTIVE:

Seeking challenge and reward in a senior-level sales position; offer strong skills in marketing, operations, and strategy—all wrapped up with a bias for action and intensity that is unparalleled.

QUALIFICATIONS SUMMARY:

Experienced enterprise executive offering multidisciplinary capabilities coupled with the inclination to lead and inspire multidirectional teams within a business-to-business environment.

EXPERTISE:

Holistic business approach empowered by an exceptional combination of strategic marketing, operational, and sales management skills.

Proven customer acceptance, valid across multiple domestic markets.

Solution conceptualization and direct application of strategic abilities and insights.

EDUCATION:

Mechanical Engineering & Technology, University of Akron

● ● ● ● ● ● ● ●

PROFESSIONAL EXPERIENCE

National Bearings, Inc.   Cleveland, OH   2000 - Present

Manufacturer of specialty bearings selling to OEMs in diverse domestic and international markets.

Sales Manager

- Responsible for strategic planning, sales and marketing, and customer service in North America. Oversee 37 manufacturer's reps and 2 inside sales/customer service personnel. Report to COO.
- Generated 2002 run rate 21% ahead of 2001 level.
- Achieved 98% of goal in 2001 despite industry sales declining 20%.
- Grew 2000 sales 13% over previous year, versus industry growth rate of only 4%.
  - Redirected strategic growth plan, including upgrading rep organization and leading company into new markets.
  - Developed and implemented targeted marketing campaigns.

Steel & Metallurgical Co.   Youngstown, OH   1996 - 2000

Technical sales and service organization representing diverse product line used in manufacture of steel- and metallurgical-related products.

Sales Manager, Eastern Region, 1997 - 2000

Represented 9 manufacturers, responsible for sales to molten metal industry in Ohio, Pennsylvania, Delaware, Maryland, New Jersey, West Virginia, and Kentucky.

- Transformed underperforming territory from last in U.S. to #1, growing sales more than 300%.
- Performed extensive prospecting and landed new accounts.

Sales Engineer, Eastern Region, 1996 - 1997

- Grew sales 300% within 18 months, then generated 16% increase final 6 months.
- Increased business with existing customer base plus landed new accounts.

Takara Belmont USA, Inc.   Akron, OH   1994 - 1996

$2 billion worldwide leader in equipment and furnishings for salon industry.

Regional Sales Engineer

- Responsible for sales in Michigan, Pennsylvania, West Virginia, Kentucky, Indiana, and Ohio, overseeing network of distributors.

With the information organized according to the traditional format and the resume beginning with a powerful introductory section, the document is now easy to read and makes a convincing presentation of Parsons's capability.

Walter D. Parsons
25 Berkeley Rd.
Elyria, OH 44035

(440) 366-3812
WDParsons2000@aol.com

SALES & MARKETING EXECUTIVE

Strategic Planning • Turnaround Management • Industrial Products

- Led nationwide sales for manufacturer of specialty bearings, dramatically increasing revenues and outperforming industry growth rate 10-fold.
- Transformed rep firm's eastern region from worst in nation to #1, growing sales over 300%; earlier during tenure, increased sales 300% within 18 months, then an additional 16% the final 6 months.

An accomplished sales executive skilled at prospecting, accessing key decision makers, and closing business. Recognized for strengths in consultative / solutions sales, selling in fast-paced, rapidly changing markets, winning business at accounts previously dominated by the competition, as well as developing long-term relationships with customers built on trust and exceptional service. Proven ability to motivate and manage high-performance sales teams.

EXPERIENCE

National Bearings, Inc., Cleveland, OH. 2000 - Present
Manufacturer of specialty bearings selling to OEMs in diverse domestic and international markets.

Sales Manager

Responsible for strategic planning, sales and marketing, and customer service in North America. Oversaw 37 manufacturer's reps and 2 inside sales / customer service personnel. Report to COO.

- Generated 2002 run rate 21% ahead of 2001 level.
- Achieved 98% of goal in 2001 despite industry sales declining 20%.
- Grew 2000 sales 13% over previous year, versus industry growth rate of only 4%.
  - Redirected strategic growth plan, including upgrading rep organization and leading company into new markets.
  - Developed and implemented targeted marketing campaigns.

Steel & Metallurgical Co., Youngstown, OH. 1996 - 2000
Technical sales and service organization representing diverse product line used in manufacture of steel- and metallurgical-related products.

Sales Manager - Eastern Region, 1997 - 2000
Represented 9 manufacturers, responsible for sales to molten metal industry in Ohio, Pennsylvania, Delaware, Maryland, New Jersey, West Virginia, and Kentucky.

- Transformed underperforming territory from last in U.S. to #1, growing sales more than 300%.
- Performed extensive prospecting and landed new accounts.

Sales Engineer - Eastern Region, 1996 - 1997

- Grew sales 300% within 18 months, then generated 16% increase the final 6 months.
- Increased business with existing customer base plus landed new accounts.

Takara Belmont USA, Inc., Akron, OH. 1994 - 1996
$2 billion worldwide leader in equipment and furnishings for salon industry.

Regional Sales Engineer

Responsible for sales in Michigan, Pennsylvania, West Virginia, Kentucky, Indiana, and Ohio, overseeing network of distributors.

Problem 40: Utilizing the Functional Format

In this resume, a reader can't tell where or when the accomplishments occurred. As a result, few interviews will come Cheng's way.

CHIN "CHUCK" Y. CHENG

30567 Caliente Way • Fremont, CA 94539 • (510) 490-4389 • cychen@aol.com

SUMMARY
Business management professional with significant accomplishments in planning, developing, and implementing business plans for products and services to increase sales and profits. Recognized for achievements in management, marketing, and sales, with broad strengths in:

- Business and marketing plan authorship
- Distributor management
- Market research
- Marketing
- New hire recruitment and training
- New product introductions

- Pricing
- Product management
- Profit and loss management
- Sales and operations planning
- Sales training
- Sales management

EXPERIENCE SUMMARY

MANAGEMENT

- Assumed all business responsibilities for a used equipment business and took it from less than $1 million in annual revenue to a $9 million business while increasing margins from 12% to almost 50% in a two-year period. Transformed business from brokerage operation to full buy / rebuild / upgrade / sell organization.
- Managed program to refurbish discontinued product that resulted in $2.8 million in revenue, then closed sale for restarting product line, achieving new equipment sales of over $10 million.
- Recruited, trained, and managed new hires. Managed all aspects of training and development up to initial field assignment.
- Created full remanufacturing business through expanding products from "as is" resale to fully remanufactured equipment for 3 major product lines.
- Directed marketing communications, including trade publication relations, advertising, trade shows, and regional marketing and technical exhibitions.
- Managed sales and marketing initiatives worldwide and exceeded financial objectives every quarter, achieving gains as large as 160% of plan.
- Managed technical training, plus upgraded the selling capability of field sales representatives. This organization had more than 100 field sales representatives selling 5 major product lines.
- Negotiated the contract, closed the sale, and managed the staffing and implementation of more than 110 service and support contracts with major international customers. The scope of these contracts ranged from periodic service calls to some worth more than $4 million in annual revenue with more than 17 on-site employees. Dramatically improved presentations to customers as well as sales engineers' and service engineers' follow-up activities.
- Received award for "Best Performance Over Quota for Regional Sales Manager."

SALES

- Received significant sales awards for gains at major accounts such as IBM, Motorola, Texas Instruments, Defense Mapping Agency, Veterans Administration, and Digital Equipment Corp. Multiple sales assignments with all territories showing significant growth. Called on customers of all sizes in various industries.
- Managed five of the nine North American distributors, growing business of all assigned distributors by 10%. These distributors accounted for sales of $11 million in 1995 and had growth 5% higher than the total division. Concurrently, expanded market share from 46% to 55%. Provided leadership, guidance, technical and sales support, which increased sales, market share, and earnings.

- Enhanced distributor network by eliminating underperforming account. Selected and trained new distributors as a replacement.
- Successfully developed a new merchandising booklet program, along with a team selling approach to grow sales. The merchandising booklet is now utilized throughout the Electronics Business Unit.

MARKETING

- Full marketing responsibility for electronic products:
  - Defined strategies and programs, then managed implementation to attain goals for both new and existing products.
  - Performed competitive analysis and market research.
  - Conducted pricing studies.
  - Planned and coordinated exhibits at trade shows.
  - Managed new product launch.
  - Oversaw design and production of collateral materials.
- Planned and implemented all marketing initiatives for $37 million product line. Introduced new product, directing all phases from concept and determination of resource needs to full commercialization. Product launch further contributed to increased market share.

EMPLOYMENT HISTORY

Semiconductor Processing, Inc., Mt. View, CA. 1997 - 2002
    Business Manager - Remanufactured Equipment Business, Worldwide. 1999 - 2002
    Sales & Operations Manager - Value Added Products and Services Division. 1997 - 1998
E.I. DuPont de Nemours and Company, Wilmington, DE. 1978 - 1996
    Western Distributor Manager - Printed Circuit Materials, Western U.S. & Canada. 1994 - 1996
    Product Manager - Electronics Department, U.S. & Canada. 1990 - 1994
    Personnel Consultant - Electronics Department, Wilmington, DE. 1988 - 1990
    Sales Specialist, Photo Products Department, Southern U.S. 1985 - 1988
    Field Sales Representative, Texas and Georgia. 1978 - 1985

EDUCATION

MBA, Wilmington College.
BS, Business Administration, University of Delaware.

MILITARY

Captain, Infantry, United States Army, Active Duty for two years
Various assignments, including 101st Airborne Division

In the revised resume, Cheng's experience is presented according to employer, eliminating the problem.

Chin "Chuck" Y. Cheng
30567 Caliente Way
Fremont, CA 94539

(510) 490-4389
cychen@aol.com

BUSINESS MANAGEMENT

P&L • Organizational Reengineering • Sales & Marketing • Global Distribution • Manufacturing

- Grew equipment refurbishing business from annual sales of less than $1 million to $9 million level during 2-year period; consistently exceeded quarterly goals, achieving as high as 160%, plus increased margins from 12% to almost 50%.
- Expanded service / support business from 70 contracts to over 110, winning "Best Performance Over Quota for Regional Sales Manager."
- Managed distributor network for DuPont, driving market share of printed circuit materials from 46% to 55% and exceeding division growth by over 5%.
- Won multiple DuPont sales awards for growing volume at leading accounts, including IBM, Motorola, Texas Instruments, and Digital Equipment Corporation.

An innovative and energetic leader, skilled communicator / team builder, and adept negotiator. Proven ability to analyze businesses, products, markets, and growth opportunities, then introduce strategic and tactical solutions that improve competitive performance while increasing sales, market share, and profits. MBA.

EXPERIENCE

Semiconductor Processing, Inc., Mt. View, CA. 1997 - 2002

Leading manufacturer of semiconductor assembly equipment with annual sales of $555 million.

Business Manager - Re-Manufactured Equipment Business, 1999 - 2002

P&L responsibility for all operations in this matrix organization, with direct reports including Manufacturing Program Manager and Sales Planner. Held dotted line responsibility for 12-person worldwide sales organization, requiring extensive travel to Asia. Reported to Director of Value Added Products and Services (VAPS) Division.

- Grew business from less than $1 million in annual revenue to $9 million level, while driving margins from 12% to almost 50% during 2-year period.
  - Transformed business from brokerage operation to full buy / rebuild / upgrade / sell organization.
- Managed program to refurbish discontinued product that resulted in $2.8 million in revenue, then closed sale for restarting product line, ultimately achieving new equipment sales of over $10 million.
- Expanded products from "as is" resale to fully remanufactured equipment for 3 major product lines, creating full remanufacturing business.
- Managed sales and marketing initiatives worldwide and exceeded financial objectives every quarter, achieving gains as large as 160% of plan.

Sales and Operations Manager - Value-Added Products & Services, 1997 - 1998

Managed sales, staffing, and execution efforts for service contracts in the U.S. and Europe. Oversaw 8 U.S. sales engineers and 5 European distributors on dotted line basis. Reported to VP for Value Added Products & Services.

- Expanded business from under 70 service and support contracts to more than 110, catering to major international customer base. Contracts ranged from periodic service calls to more than $4 million in annual revenue with over 17 on-site employees.
  - Dramatically improved presentations to customers as well as follow-up activities of sales and service engineers.
- Received award for "Best Performance Over Quota for Regional Sales Manager," 1997.

E.I. DuPont de Nemours and Company, Wilmington, DE. 1978 - 1996

Leading global manufacturer and distributor of diverse line of chemicals and synthetic products.

Western Distributor Manager - Printed Circuit Materials, 1994 - 1996

Provided leadership, guidance, and technical / sales support, managing 5 of the 9 North American distributors.

- Grew business of all assigned distributors by 10%, achieving $11 million annual level and exceeding overall division growth by more than 5%; concurrently, expanded market share from 46% to 55%.
- Enhanced distributor network by eliminating underperforming account. Selected and trained new distributors as a replacement.

Product Manager, Electronics Department, 1990 - 1994

Full product marketing ownership for key products. Defined strategies and programs, plus managed implementation to attain goals.

- Planned and implemented all marketing initiatives for $37 million product line. Introduced new product, directing all phases from concept and determination of resource needs to full commercialization. Product launch further contributed to increased market share.
- Developed new merchandizing booklet program along with team-selling approach to grow sales. Booklet is utilized today throughout business unit.

Personnel Consultant - Electronics Department, Wilmington, DE. 1988 - 1990

Managed Sales Division's training, marketing communications, and recruiting activities.

- Recruited, trained, and managed new hires through initial field assignment.
- Directed marketing communications activities, including trade publication relations, advertising, trade shows, and regional marketing and technical exhibitions.
- Managed training to enhance and upgrade sales and technical selling skills for over 100 field sales representatives responsible for 5 major product lines.

Sales Specialist - Photo Products Department, Various Southeast Locations. 1985 - 1988

- Called on diversified customer base and significantly grew sales in all territories.
- Won numerous sales awards for growing business at key accounts, including IBM, Motorola, Texas Instruments, Defense Mapping Agency, Veterans Administration, and Digital Equipment Corporation.

Field Sales Representative, Texas and Georgia. 1978 - 1985

EDUCATION

MBA, Wilmington College.
BS, Business Administration, University of Delaware.

Problem 41: Utilizing the Accomplishments Format

This type of resume presents the same problem as the functional format: You can't tell where and when successes occurred. Very few people read it as a result.

Lawrence N. Orange

3 Pond Avenue • Brookline, MA 02445 • (617) 566-6310 • Lnol@attbi.com

---

Objective

Management position in a larger organization where the Human Resources function is enfranchised and its focus is on initiatives that increase managerial effectiveness and ensure cost sensitive programs that support the organization's profitability objectives.

Professional Summary

Results-oriented, self-motivated Human Resources generalist possessing the depth of knowledge, decision-making ability, and execution skills required to successfully define and implement the structural and process changes or program cost controls required in "HR Function Start-ups," "Business Turnarounds," and "M&A Integration" situations.

Human Resources Expertise

• Recruiting & Staffing	• Benefits & Compensation	• Management Training
• Performance Management	• Motivation & Development	• Morale Development
• Policies & Procedures	• Safety & Security	• Union Avoidance

Accomplishments

- Started up and managed a company's first Human Resources Department.
- Revamped recruiting and staffing procedures, saving $680,000 annually.
- Replaced senior management staff, personally recruiting the CFO and VPs of Engineering, Manufacturing, Marketing, and Sales, as well as 2 Division General Managers.
- Revised recruiting methods, decreasing hiring cycle 50% and saving $150,000 a year.
- Developed and instituted Executive Management Succession Plan.
- Reduced healthcare plan costs 20%, saving $575,000 annually, with no reduction in coverage or increase in cost to employees.
- Obtained $185,000 cash rebate from healthcare plan providers for claims overpayment.
- Changed 401k retirement plan provider, reducing costs 85% and saving $150,000 a year.
- Renegotiated benefit contracts, saving 20%, or $175,000 annually.
- Brought management training in-house, saving $140,000 a year.
- Implemented supervisory training, decreasing turnover rate from 65% to 20% and resulting in contested unemployment claims dropping from average of 124 per year to 4.
- Established Employee Basic Skills Training Program via $120,000 state grant.
- Instituted Management Skills Training Program.
- Defined and implemented programs that attracted more experienced and talented management and improved skills of existing management.
- Reduced turnover rate from 40% to 17%.
- Reduced temporary labor costs 80%, or $1.9 million; short-term disability costs 67%, or $356,000; payroll service costs 45%, or $45,000; obtained 25% unemployment tax rate reduction, saving $50,000 annually.
- Implemented pay structure, employment offer controls, and merit increase guidelines, saving $660,000 a year.
- Established controls on utilization of contract labor and consultants, saving $450,000 annually.
- Introduced company vision and values statement, re-invigorated Employee Activity Committee (participation increased 65%), and established company news magazine (both hardcopy and online).
- Revised safety investigation methods, reducing lost-time accidents 60% per year.
- Identified and thwarted local Teamsters' attempt to organize drivers.
- Detected and eliminated IBEW's attempt to organize assembly workers.
- Assumed responsibility for all facilities; renegotiated leases, saving $150,000 a year.
- Managed relocation of New York organization to Massachusetts, winning 95% acceptance from employees.
- Introduced company's first policies, pay structure, and performance review systems, obtaining 100% merit increase budget compliance for 3 consecutive years, saving $280,000 annually.
- Implemented Performance & Conduct Management programs, resulting in zero third-party claims for 2 years.

Employment Background

Analytic Systems, Waltham, MA. 2000 - Present

Director of Human Resources at this $150 million developer and manufacturer of production metrology and inspection systems for the semiconductor industry, with 600 employees and 3 manufacturing facilities in Massachusetts and Arizona plus 5 service centers in the US, Europe, and the Far East.

Organizational Challenge: Business Turnaround. Organization unable to achieve profit goals and losing market share to competitors, attributable to excessive operating costs, high turnover of key employees, marginal management skills, outdated performance measurement systems, fragmented organizational structures, and loss of employee confidence/low morale.

Human Resources Charter: To define and implement those changes in program costs as well as drivers of turnover, organizational structure, management operating methods, management development and employee dissatisfaction required to improve company's performance and profits.

Brewster & Hamilton, Lexington, MA. 1999 - 2000

Contract Management Consultant at this management consulting firm providing organizations with human resources expertise in benefits, compensation, recruiting and staffing, and employee relations.

- Engagements included managing Micrion Corporation's local acquisition integration of FEI and establishing and staffing a permanent employment and recruiting function for WebCT.

Northeast Food Products, Inc., Boston, MA. 1995 - 1999

Director of Human Resources at this $400 million manufacturer, distributor, and retailer of food products, with 1400 employees, 400 commercial vehicles, 2 manufacturing facilities, 4 distribution depots, and 60 retail stores.

Organizational Challenge: Business Turnaround. Consolidation of regional operators eroding organization's ability to compete and sustain profitability; owners desired to position business for merger with or acquisition by a regional or national competitor.

Human Resources Charter: To correct or eliminate program costs and management or organizational issues that reduce company's attractiveness or perceived value as a merger / acquisition candidate.

D / A Industries, Inc., Fall River, MA. 1989 - 1995

Senior Human Resources Manager at this $75 million manufacturer of PC-based data acquisition products, with 500 employees located in Massachusetts and New York.

Organizational Challenge: M&A integration / HR start-up involving two recently acquired technology businesses located in Massachusetts and New York; both organizations exhibited pronounced, widespread resistance to corporate headquarters' business growth and acquisition ROI objectives.

Human Resources Charter: To establish HR function, plus define and implement programs and processes that support corporate consolidation efforts and synergy initiatives.

Massachusetts Plastics, Inc., Framingham, MA. 1988 - 1989

Divisional Human Resources Manager at this $100 million manufacturer of custom and precision technology-related, injection-molded products, with 1000 employees in 2 Massachusetts manufacturing facilities.

Organizational Challenge: Business Turnaround. Company's growth rate was exceeding competency and skills of its manufacturing line management, with unmet production goals, high employee turnover, and union organizing threat.

Human Resources Charter: To define and implement programs that attract more experienced management, develop and improve skills of existing management, eliminate drivers of turnover, and stop union threat.

Previously, held increasingly responsible HR positions with Tau-tron, Genrad, Gould Modicon, and Prime Computer.

EDUCATION

B.A., Framingham State College, Framingham, MA.

With the problem eliminated, Orange's revised resume will be received with enthusiasm due to his outstanding background and accomplishments in the human resources field.

Lawrence N. Orange
3 Pond Avenue
Brookline, MA 02445

(617) 566-6310
Lnol@attbi.com

HUMAN RESOURCES EXECUTIVE

- **Recruitment**
- **Performance Management**
- **Training**

- **Compensation & Benefits**
- **Safety & Security**
- **Union Avoidance**

- A history of success starting up and managing HR departments as well as playing key roles in turning around underperforming companies and integrating acquisitions into operations.

- Expert at developing and implementing programs, processes, and controls that achieve dramatic cost savings, with representative successes including the following savings: staffing - 25%, training - 45%, healthcare plans - 30%, 401k retirement plan providers - 85%, temporary labor - 80%, short-term disability - 67%, and payroll services - 45%.

- Decreased hiring cycle as much as 50%, reduced turnover rate 69%, and decreased lost-time accidents 60%.

A visionary HR leader and partner to senior business line executives. Recognized for broad strengths in developing HR processes that improve productivity, quality, revenues, and profits while reducing operating costs. An accomplished strategist and change agent skilled at building successful relationships organization-wide, including providing executive consulting and coaching to support top management in attainment of corporate and departmental goals.

EXPERIENCE

Analytic Systems, Waltham, MA. 2000 - Present

$150 million developer and manufacturer of production metrology and inspection systems for the semiconductor industry, with 600 employees and 3 manufacturing facilities in Massachusetts and Arizona plus 5 service centers in the US, Europe, and the Far East.

Director of Human Resources

Played key role in turning around organization failing to meet profit goals and losing market share due to excessive operating costs, high turnover of key employees, marginal management skills, outdated performance measurement systems, fragmented organizational structures, and loss of employee confidence / low morale. Developed and implemented numerous processes, resulting in dramatic improvement in organization's competitive performance.

- Reduced healthcare plan costs 20%, saving $575,000 annually, with no reduction in coverage or increase in cost to employees.
- Obtained $185,000 cash rebate from healthcare plan providers for claims overpayment.
- Changed 401k retirement plan provider, reducing costs 85% and saving $150,000 a year.
- Brought management training in-house, saving $140,000 a year, or 45%.
- Revamped recruiting and staffing procedures, saving $680,000 annually, or 25%.
- Reduced turnover rate from 40% to 17%.
- Implemented pay structure, employment offer controls, and merit increase guidelines, saving $660,000 a year.
- Replaced senior management staff, personally recruiting CFO and VPs of Engineering, Manufacturing, Marketing, and Sales, as well as 2 Division General Managers.
- Established controls on utilization of contract labor and consultants, saving $450,000 annually.
- Developed and instituted Executive Management Succession Plan.
- Introduced company vision and values statement, re-invigorated Employee Activity Committee (participation increased 65%), and established company news magazine (both hardcopy and online).

Brewster & Hamilton, Lexington, MA. 1999 - 2000

Management consulting firm providing organizations with human resources expertise in benefits, compensation, recruiting and staffing, and employee relations.

Contract Management Consultant

- Engagements included managing Micrion Corporation's local acquisition integration of FEI and establishing and staffing a permanent employment and recruiting function for WebCT.

Northeast Food Products, Inc., Boston, MA. 1995 - 1999

$400 million manufacturer, distributor, and retailer of food products, with 1400 employees, 400 commercial vehicles, 2 manufacturing facilities, 4 distribution depots, and 60 retail stores.

Director of Human Resources

Hired to achieve major cost reductions at this underperforming company and position organization for merger or acquisition by a regional or national competitor.

- Developed and implemented sweeping changes that resulted in dramatic annual cost reductions: temporary labor costs - 80%, or $1.9 million; short-term disability costs - 67%, or $356,000; healthcare costs - 30%, or $700,000; payroll service costs - 45%, or $45,000; obtained 25% unemployment tax rate reduction, saving $50,000 annually.
- Implemented supervisory training, decreasing turnover rate from 65% to 20% and resulting in contested unemployment claims dropping from average of 124 per year to 4.
- Established Employee Basic Skills Training Program via $120,000 state grant.
- Implemented Performance & Conduct Management programs, resulting in zero third-party claims for 2 years.
- Identified and thwarted local Teamsters' attempt to organize drivers.

D / A Industries, Inc., Fall River, MA. 1989 - 1995

$75 million manufacturer of PC-based data acquisition products, with 500 employees located in Massachusetts and New York.

Senior Human Resources Manager

Hired to establish HR Department to facilitate 2 recent technology acquisitions, where both companies were exhibiting resistance to parent's growth and ROI goals.

- Managed relocation of New York organization to Massachusetts, winning 95% acceptance from employees.
- Revised recruiting methods, decreasing hiring cycle 50% and saving $150,000 a year.
- Renegotiated benefit contracts, saving 20% or $175,000 annually.
- Revised safety investigation methods, reducing lost-time accidents 60% per year.
- Assumed responsibility for all facilities; renegotiated leases, saving $150,000 a year.
- Introduced company's first policies, pay structure, and performance review systems, obtaining 100% merit increase budget compliance for 3 consecutive years and saving $280,000 annually.
- Detected and eliminated IBEW's attempt to organize assembly workers.
- Instituted Management Skills Training Program.

Massachusetts Plastics, Inc., Framingham, MA. 1988 - 1989

Divisional Human Resources Manager

$100 million manufacturer of custom and precision technology-related, injection-molded products, with 1000 employees in 2 Massachusetts manufacturing facilities.

Hired to resolve problems of unmet production goals, high turnover, and threat of unionization at this company where growth rate was exceeding competency and skill levels of manufacturing line management.

- Defined and implemented programs that attracted more experienced and talented management; improved skills of existing management; eliminated union threat.

Tau-tron Incorporated, Westford, MA. 1984 - 1988

Human Resources Manager

$75 million manufacturer of telecommunication test equipment, with 400 employees.

- Started up and managed company's first Human Resources Department.

Previously, held increasingly responsible HR positions at Genrad, Gould Modicon, and Prime Computer.

EDUCATION

B.A., Framingham State College, Framingham, MA.

Problems with Composition/Appearance/Formatting in Resume

Problem 42: Placing a Border on a Resume

Some job hunters think that an attractive "finishing touch" to their resume is to place a border on it. Unless someone is in an artistic field, this type of presentation is frowned upon and considered to be unprofessional or "unbusinesslike."

JAMES D. GREENBERG
4190 Ramblewood Court
Solon, OH 44139
216-548-4923
Mhdunleavy@earthlink.net

PROFILE

In-depth experience developing and implementing athletic and physical fitness programs. Possess a high energy level with excellent leadership, organizational, and communication skills.

EXPERIENCE

Cleveland Jewish Community Center, Cleveland, OH. January 1995 - December 2002
Program Director
#2 person at the agency, reported to Executive Director with complete responsibility for planning and managing $115,000 budget, creating and implementing over 50 programs, and supervising 2 full-time staffs, 5 part-time staffs, and up to 150 volunteers.
- Directed all health, physical education, and maintenance activities.
- Planned and conducted over 50 programs, including Youth Sports, Men's Basketball Leagues, Golf & Tennis Fund-raisers, Summer Sports Camp, Junior Varsity and Varsity Baseball, and Sports Specialty Camps.
- Organized committees for each event and supervised their activities.
- Raised $120,000 a year through fund-raisers.
- Recruited, hired, trained, scheduled, and supervised up to 150 volunteers.
- Selected as "J.C.C. All-Ohio Conference Kindred Group Leader for Physical Education," 1996 and 1997.

Cleveland Family YMCA, Cleveland, OH. May 1991 - December 1994
Athletic Director
- Directed Youth Sports Program, Teen Program, Parent / Child Program, and Men's Basketball Leagues.
- Managed 4 personnel on Fitness Center staff, plus supervised up to 100 volunteers.
- Featured in "Cleveland Plain Dealer" for outstanding athletic contributions to the community.
- Co-directed annual road race.

Louisville Jewish Community Center, Louisville, KY. September 1986 - March 1991
- Directed Youth Sports Program, B.B.Y.O. Sports Program, Adult Basketball Leagues, Adult Softball Leagues, and Junior Varsity and Varsity Basketball.
- Awarded "Employee of the Year," 1990.
- Chaperoned 30 children during 5-week trip to Israel.
- Taught preschool physical education classes.
- Served as staff liaison for numerous committees.
- Supervised volunteers.

EDUCATION

B.S., Physical Education, Westfield State College, Westfield, MA. 1986
Minor: Recreation; All-American in Track.

With the border removed, the revised resume will meet with no resistance from reviewers.

James D. Greenberg
4190 Ramblewood Court
Solon, OH 44139

216-548-4923
Mhdunleavy@earthlink.com

ATHLETIC & PHYSICAL FITNESS MANAGER

- Developed and introduced over 50 new programs for Cleveland Jewish Community Center during 8-year period.
- Winner of numerous awards for outstanding performance, including "Employee of the Year."
- Featured in "Cleveland Plain Dealer" for key athletic contributions to the community.
- B.S., Physical Education; former All-American track athlete.

An outstanding leader and manager who combines broad strengths in program development / execution with exceptional athletic abilities. Recognized for success in eliciting strong program participation among membership.

EXPERIENCE

Cleveland Jewish Community Center, Cleveland, OH. 1995 - 2002
Program Director

#2 person at the agency, reported to Executive Director with complete responsibility for planning and managing $115,000 budget, creating and implementing over 50 programs, and supervising 2 full-time staffs, 5 part-time staffs, and up to 150 volunteers.

- Directed all health, physical education, and maintenance activities.
- Planned and conducted over 50 programs, including Youth Sports, Men's Basketball Leagues, Golf & Tennis Fund-raisers, Summer Sports Camp, Junior Varsity and Varsity Baseball, and Sports Specialty Camps.
- Organized committees for each event and supervised their activities.
- Raised $120,000 a year through fund-raisers.
- Recruited, hired, trained, scheduled, and supervised volunteer staff.
- Selected as "J.C.C. All-Ohio Conference Kindred Group Leader for Physical Education," 1996 and 1997.

Cleveland Family YMCA, Cleveland, OH. 1991 - 1994
Athletic Director

- Directed Youth Sports Program, Teen Program, Parent / Child Program, and Men's Basketball Leagues.
- Managed 4 personnel on Fitness Center staff, plus supervised up to 100 volunteers.
- Featured in "Cleveland Plain Dealer" for outstanding athletic contributions to the community.
- Taught senior exercise classes.
- Co-directed annual road race.

Louisville Jewish Community Center, Louisville, KY. 1986 - 1991
Assistant Director, Health & Physical Education

- Directed Youth Sports Program, B.B.Y.O. Sports Program, Adult Basketball Leagues, Adult Softball Leagues, and Junior Varsity and Varsity Basketball.
- Awarded "Employee of the Year," 1990.
- Chaperoned 30 children during 5-week trip to Israel.
- Taught preschool physical education classes.
- Served as staff liaison for numerous committees.
- Supervised volunteers.

EDUCATION

B.S., Physical Education, Westfield State College, Westfield, MA. 1986
Minor: Recreation; All-American in Track.

Cover Letter Problems

Problem 43: Writing Too Brief a Letter

Fitch offers no information about herself that makes the reader want to learn more about her. She refers to her past "achievements" and "successes" but fails to say what they are. The letter is really no more than a statement along the lines of "I'm looking for a job, I'm really good, what do you have?"

Helene S. Fitch
2855 Westwoods Circle
Arvada, CO 80007
(303) 463-7912
Hsfitch@yahoo.com

November 4, 2002

Mr. Michael Turner
Rocky Mountain Recruiters, Inc.
1801 Broadway, Suite 810
Denver, CO 80202

Dear Mr. Turner:

I am faxing my resume for your review and consideration. I am confident that my capabilities and past achievements can be easily transferred to make significant contributions to many companies.

My strong commitment to excel, sense of professionalism, and the ability to master new concepts, ideas, and practices have been major factors in my past successes. I respond well to challenges and am known as a team player.

I would appreciate the opportunity to discuss how my qualifications, drive, and enthusiasm can contribute to your clients' success. I look forward to hearing from you so we may set up a convenient time to meet.

Sincerely,

Helene S. Fitch

In her revised letter, Fitch offers a wealth of information about her strengths and accomplishments, ensuring that her resume will be read with enthusiasm.

Helene S. Fitch
2855 Westwoods Circle
Arvada, CO 80007
(303) 463-7912
Hsfitch@yahoo.com

November 4, 2002

Mr. Michael Turner
Rocky Mountain Recruiters, Inc.
1801 Broadway, Suite 810
Denver, CO 80202

Dear Mr. Turner:

I have 12 years' experience as an administrative assistant, where I have provided outstanding support to corporate officers and their staff. With boundless energy and enthusiasm for my work, I have been repeatedly told by supervisors and peers that I have a knack for "creating calm out of chaos." I'm currently seeking a new position and am enclosing my resume for your review. Key highlights include:

- Computer proficient, with strengths in Word and Excel.
- An outstanding communicator who has the flexibility to work effectively with a wide variety of people.
- Skilled at working under pressure, deadlines, and in fast-paced environments.
- Well-organized, attentive to detail, with excellent follow-through.
- Developed a records-management system that reduced the time required to access information by 50%.
- Created a project-management system for a department that was so successful it was adopted throughout the multi-division corporation.
- Tripled the rate for successful collections.

I pride myself on my ability to work independently, always completing projects on time. Often, I have to handle several different tasks simultaneously, and I have no problem juggling them. I always deliver top-quality work.

Please contact me at your convenience if you need any additional information. Otherwise, I look forward to hearing from you when you have a position for which my background is appropriate.

Thank you in advance for reviewing my credentials.

Sincerely,

Helene S. Fitch

Problem 44: Omitting Accomplishments and Stating Only Responsibilities

In this letter, Gerringer doesn't discuss any of his successes, which prevents his cover letter from having impact.

Hayden N. Gerringer
2299 Rolling Pine Drive
West Bloomfield, MI 48323
(248) 366-6790
Haydeng@attbi.com

October 15, 2002

Mr. Thomas P. Strickland
Vice President of Sales
Advanced Systems Concepts, Inc.
1150 Griswold
Detroit, MI 48226

Dear Mr. Strickland:

Throughout my 15-year career, I have held progressively responsible positions in sales, sales training, and sales management. Employers have included manufacturers, resellers, and service organizations that have been in both traditional and high-technology businesses.

I am well aware of the great strides your company has been making, especially in penetrating the explosive healthcare market, and would like to speak with you about how my background could contribute to your company's growth. My resume is enclosed for your review.

Briefly, as sales manager for a software developer, I held complete responsibility for establishing sales goals, developing and implementing the sales strategy, setting pricing, plus directing sales channel development and management, sales force recruitment/training/motivation, as well as customer service. I quickly won recognition as an energetic, results-oriented leader who drove the company to new levels of success.

As sales trainer for a manufacturer of bearings with nationwide distribution, I defined the company's training needs, identified and utilized outsourced sales training programs, created in-house training programs, plus monitored improvement in sales performance. I trained most individuals at the corporate headquarters but performed extensive travel working with the sales force in the field as well as coaching district and regional managers on how to develop their sales personnel. My activities played a key role in the company's growth.

I would like to meet with you to discuss how my background could be of value to your company and will call your office next week to follow up. Thank you in advance for reviewing my resume.

Sincerely,

Hayden N. Gerringer

By including his successes in his revised cover letter, readers see the enormous contributions Gerringer has made at his employers and will be eager to read his resume.

Hayden N. Gerringer
2299 Rolling Pine Drive
West Bloomfield, MI 48323
(248) 366-6790
Haydeng@attbi.com

October 15, 2002

Mr. Thomas P. Strickland
Vice President of Sales
Advanced Systems Concepts, Inc.
1150 Griswold
Detroit, MI 48226

Dear Mr. Strickland:

I'm an accomplished sales executive with a record of success in both sales training and field sales management. I have made important changes at my last two employers that drove both organizations to record revenue levels. At the present time I'm confidentially seeking a new opportunity and challenge and would like to meet with you to discuss how my background could play a key role in your growth and future plans. My resume is enclosed for your review. Select highlights include:

- Joined a software developer as sales manager and grew sales 300% in 2 years, achieving 150% of goal and record sales.
- Redirected the sales strategy from focusing on small businesses to targeting key vertical markets, especially healthcare and financial services.
- Replaced 75% of the sales force through recruiting and hiring sales executives with target market experience.
- Aligned pricing with market conditions, expanding margins 20%.

- Previously, held the position of sales trainer for a reseller of computer components and systems, holding nationwide training responsibility. Developed and implemented programs that led to a 25% increase in sales within a 14-month period while reducing turnover 35%. Both were record levels.
- Rigorously analyzed training needs, then developed programs for both new hires and experienced personnel.
- Trained individuals at corporate headquarters, plus traveled throughout the U.S. to work with sales reps in the field.
- Coached district and regional sales managers on effective ways to further develop their teams.

I feel that my successes in sales training and sales management would enable me to make immediate and significant contributions to your company. I would welcome the opportunity to meet with you and will call your office next week to discuss the appropriate next step. Thank you in advance for reviewing my credentials.

Sincerely,

Hayden N. Gerringer

Problem 45: Writing a Letter Devoid of Enthusiasm

While d'Agostino is on the right track by citing impressive accomplishments, the brevity and tone of this letter are such that he shows no enthusiasm for his work. Prospective employers seek out individuals who are excited about what they do and who will bring vitality and energy to their job.

Paul d'Agostino
14203 Flint St.
Overland Park, KS 66221
(913) 681-9216

January 17, 2003

Mr. Maurice de Rouget
General Manager
Chez Richard
2 Pershing Square
Kansas City, MO 64108

Dear Mr. de Rouget:

I am a superb chef with over 20 years' experience, and am currently seeking a new position. My resume is enclosed for your review. The following will give you a good idea of what I can offer your restaurant:

• Managed fine-dining kitchens that served up to 450 guests per night.
• Reduced food and labor costs up to 20% and 15%, respectively.
• Created award-winning specials.

The enclosed resume discusses my experience in detail. Thank you in advance for reviewing my background, and I look forward to hearing from you concerning an interview.

Sincerely,

Paul d'Agostino

The makeover conveys a chef who is not only extremely capable but also very interested in his work and proud of his successes.

Paul d'Agostino
14203 Flint St.
Overland Park, KS 66221
(913) 681-9216

January 17, 2003

Mr. Maurice de Rouget
General Manager
Chez Richard
2 Pershing Square
Kansas City, MO 64108

Dear Mr. de Rouget:

My background includes over 20 years' experience as a chef, with French and Italian cuisines my specialties. I'm currently seeking a position with a fine-dining restaurant and am enclosing my resume for your review. Highlights from my experience include:

- Managed fine-dining kitchens that served up to 450 guests per night.
- Created award-winning specials that were incorporated into the menu by popular demand.
- Secured new purveyors and negotiated contracts that reduced food costs 20%.
- Reduced labor costs 15%.
- Planned and set up kitchens for new restaurants plus made dramatic improvements to existing kitchens.
- Skilled at hiring and retaining outstanding kitchen staffs, with turnover significantly below the industry standard.
- Graduate of the Culinary Institute of America.

I take great pride in my ability to operate a kitchen that adheres to the highest culinary, safety, and cleanliness standards while meeting the established profit goal. Owners and general mangers have continuously praised me on my ability to combine culinary excellence with strong business skills.

Thank you in advance for reviewing my background. I look forward to meeting you at your earliest convenience.

Sincerely,

Paul d'Agostino

Problem 46: Beginning a Letter with Philosophical, Global Statements

Some job hunters feel that an effective way to attract readers' attention, as well as show what great thinkers they are, is to begin their letter by discussing challenging issues being confronted by the country or the business world. This approach, which Lawson uses in this letter, backfires. These people appear to be arrogant and pompous as they lecture the reader.

Arthur F. Lawson
5601 Midway Drive
Huntington Beach, CA 92648
(714) 749-8028
Lawson_af@yahoo.com

October 12, 2002

Mr. Scott R. Fielding
Chief Executive Officer
10900 Wilshire Blvd.
Barrenger Industries, Inc.
Los Angeles, CA 90024

Dear Mr. Fielding:

Vision. Leadership. Innovation. These are the qualities that corporations are seeking today due to the troubled times in which we live. With the strength of the economic recovery in doubt and the executive brass lacking credibility with the American people, Corporate America is facing one of the greatest challenges since The Great Depression. Companies need proven executives with integrity, who can identify existing problems as well as growth opportunities, then effect the changes necessary to rise above the competition and drive their organization to new levels of success. I am such an executive.

My background includes a history of achievement in starting up new companies, turning around virtually bankrupt organizations, plus growing the top and bottom lines at already profitable enterprises. My successes embrace multiple industries: electronics, traditional manufacturing, and financial services. It's of little import to me what a product or service is. The key to success is understanding business and its key drivers.

An entrepreneurial leader, critical thinker, outstanding problem solver, and adept corporate strategist, I would welcome the opportunity to talk to you about how my background and accomplishments could be put to use to help grow your company. My resume is enclosed for your review.

Thank you in advance for reviewing my credentials. I look forward to your reply.

Sincerely,

Arthur S. Lawson

By omitting the first paragraph and expanding on the second, especially detailing his successes in turning around and starting up companies, Lawson demonstrates his capability and virtually guarantees that readers will turn right to his resume.

Arthur F. Lawson
5601 Midway Drive
Huntington Beach, CA 92648
(714) 749-8028
Lawson_af@yahoo.com

October 12, 2002

Mr. Scott R. Fielding
Chief Executive Officer
10900 Wilshire Blvd.
Barrenger Industries, Inc.
Los Angeles, CA 90024

Dear Mr. Fielding:

I'm an accomplished general management executive with multi-industry experience, including electronics, traditional manufacturing, and financial services. Key strengths include idea generation, strategic planning, start-ups, and turnarounds. At the present time I'm exploring career opportunities on a confidential basis and would like to meet with you to discuss how my background could play a key role in your growth and future plans. My resume is enclosed for your review. Select highlights include:

- Acquired a failing toy manufacturer, then reengineered the organization, generated a profit within 6 months, and successfully sold the company 12 months later at a 150% premium to purchase price. This was accomplished with no experience in the industry.
- Co-founded a loan management company that specialized in student loan receivables originated and subsequently charged off by lending institutions. Grew the business to 18,000 accounts valued at over $66 million, then sold the company to a large competitor.
- Restructured the Asia-Pacific operations of a manufacturer of electronic products and components, delivering 2 consecutive years of profits after 8 years of losses. Grew sales 62% in a market growing less than 7% annually.

I take great pride in my entrepreneurial talents as well as ability to succeed in highly diverse industries. I would like to meet with you to discuss how my breadth and depth of experience could be of value to one of the Barrenger companies.

Thank you in advance for reviewing my credentials. I look forward to your reply.

Sincerely,

Arthur F. Lawson

Problem 47: Providing a Career Summary in Chronological Order

Like some job hunters, Gupta uses his cover letter to summarize his entire career, starting with his first employer and focusing on responsibilities versus accomplishments. By beginning with the least important part of his background and providing a weak discussion on his successes, he gives readers no incentive to read his resume.

Ranjan R. Gupta
350 First Avenue, Apt. 14A
New York, NY 10010
(212) 475-1302
rrgupta@juno.com

February 8, 2003

Mr. John S. Oliver
SpencerStuart
277 Park Ave., 29th Floor
New York, NY 10172

Dear Mr. Oliver:

Attached, please find a copy of my resume for your review and consideration.

I am a computer professional with over 20 years of experience in various facets of the computing profession. I began my career at Bell Labs as a Member of the Technical Staff involved in data communications projects such as the DataPhone II private network and CCITT performance specification development relating to error detection rates and the development of the technology enabling high-speed data communications over ordinary phone lines.

I went on to work for a small firm, Axxess Information Systems, where I created a technical support call center and an education department responsible for supporting and training university professionals in the use of the Academic Institution Management System developed by the company. The company became one of the nation's top three software providers of the system and enjoyed an outstanding reputation for its high-quality technical support and training.

After Axxess, I joined Computer Concepts, a start-up software firm specializing in turnkey computing solutions primarily for the medical and insurance industries. I performed functions ranging from software sales to programming to supporting daily operations. I was responsible for $5 million of high-margin sales annually.

After Computer Concepts was sold, I performed "hands on" management roles with Isos Technology and Data General in their Professional Services Groups, building highly profitable practices for both companies.

My next employer was Fargo Systems, where I was Chief Technical Officer and VP - Technical Services. After the company was sold, I joined Saks Fifth Avenue, where I currently work. I have held management positions responsible for the maintenance and development of retail applications.

I hold an M.S. in Engineering Management and a B.S. in Computer Science.

With a wealth of both management and technical experience, I bring a great deal to companies seeking to grow their IT function. My income is in the $185,000 a year area.

Thank you in advance for reviewing my resume. I look forward to hearing from you.

Sincerely,

Ranjan R. Gupta

Gupta's revised cover letter omits the chronological discussion of his background and is also accomplishments-driven, providing a compelling case for reading his resume.

Ranjan R. Gupta
350 First Avenue, Apt. 14A
New York, NY 10010
(212) 475-1302
rrgupta@juno.com

February 8, 2003

Mr. John S. Oliver
SpencerStuart
277 Park Ave., 29th Floor
New York, NY 10172

Dear Mr. Oliver:

I'm an accomplished IT executive with a record of success in the development and management of large-scale software systems, with activities including project planning, computer programming and engineering, and new product development. At the present time I'm exploring career opportunities on a confidential basis and would like to apprise you of my background. My resume is enclosed for your review. Select highlights include:

- Established and managed engineering groups of up to 18 personnel, plus led organizations of up to 32 professionals, responsible for sales, marketing, and technical activities.
- Held diverse responsibilities, including developing and maintaining software applications, supporting user populations with customized application solutions, developing e-commerce sites and applications, creating migration methodologies, plus developing new products that have generated up to $5 million in annual revenues.
- Hardware background includes medium- to large-scale IBM, DEC, Honeywell, Prime, and Data General systems as well as the IBM PC.
- Software has consisted of C and C++, Data Basic, Microsoft Basic, Fortran, COBOL, RPG II and III, PL/1, Visual Basic, Simscript II.5, Ratran IV, Snobol, APL, ADA, and numerous assemblers.
- Operating environments have included DOS, Windows, UNIX, CMS, Primos, NT, and CITRIX.
- Databases have comprised Ramis, Oracle, Informix, Ingres, Access, Microsoft SQL, PICK and Advanced PICK, uniVerse, Unidata, D3, PI and PI-OPEN, and Sybase.
- I hold an M.S. in Engineering Management and a B.S. in Computer Science.

Many of my accomplishments resulted from building dedicated and motivated teams that supported me in my mission. I have the proven ability to recognize and attract top talent as well as create an environment where people work with commitment to achieve established goals.

In short, I combine outstanding human relations skills with the resourcefulness, drive, and technical / management knowledge that are required to propel an IT organization to the next level of success and profitability. My income is in the $185,000 a year area.

Please contact me at your convenience if you need any additional information. Otherwise, I look forward to hearing from you when my background is appropriate for a search assignment.

Thank you in advance for reviewing my credentials. I look forward to your reply and a personal meeting.

Sincerely,

Ranjan R. Gupta

Problem 48: Offering a Narrative Presentation
with Excessive Use of "I" and "My"

Bertram's letter has two problems: (1) it's written in a narrative style that automatically buries the accomplishments within the text; and (2) it uses "I" and "My" excessively, which makes for boring reading.

Raymond M. Bertram
9 Wandsworth Bridge Sway
Lutherville, MD 21093
(410) 825-7601
Rbertram@home.com

January 16, 2003

Mr. Jeffrey Dillon
Director, Department of Botany
University of Florida
P.O. Box 118526
Gainesville, FL 32611

Dear Mr. Dillon:

I am submitting my resume for your review for the position of Forestry Supervisor.

I am a degreed Forester/Supervisor with diverse experience, including managing government contracts and hazardous tree appraisals, developing and administering line-clearance inspection programs, creating and conducting tree-trimming and vegetation management programs, plus planning and managing budgets. I have supervised up to 12 personnel. I am recognized for my strengths in forest-fire fighting, land surveying, and writing/securing federal government grants. My educational training includes degrees in both Soil Science and Forest Management/Recreation. I am also a Certified Arborist with the International Society of Arboriculture. Additionally, I would like you to know that my attributes include dedication and commitment with the ability to adapt to changing environments while meeting all requirements and challenges.

I have been responsible for appraisals for up to 1300 miles of road rights-of-way and have managed tree-trimming and vegetation programs that have reduced power outages as much as 35%. I even developed a nationally recognized public relations program for the removal of hazardous trees. I have also planned and administered budgets as large as $2 million. My enclosed resume elaborates on these experiences plus discusses other aspects of my background.

Thank you in advance for your time and consideration. I look forward to your reply and a personal meeting.

Sincerely,

Raymond M. Bertram

By using bulleted statements in addition to narrative paragraphs, the revised letter is now interesting to read, Bertram's key accomplishments are prominent, and "I" and "My" are not overused.

Raymond M. Bertram
9 Wandsworth Bridge Sway
Lutherville, MD 21093
(410) 825-7601
Rbertram@home.com

January 16, 2003

Mr. Jeffrey Dillon
Director, Department of Botany
University of Florida
P.O. Box 118526
Gainesville, FL 32611

Dear Mr. Dillon:

I'm an accomplished Forestry Supervisor with a record of success in government contracts, hazardous tree appraisals, and line-clearance-inspection, tree-trimming, and vegetation-management programs. At the present time, I'm exploring career opportunities on a confidential basis and would like to meet with you to discuss how my background could be of value to your department. My resume is enclosed for your review. Select highlights include:

- Management responsibility for up to 12 personnel.
- Broad strengths in forest-fire fighting, land surveying, and writing/securing federal government grants.
- Responsible for appraisals for up to 1300 miles of road rights-of-way.
- Managed tree-trimming and vegetation programs that have reduced power outages as much as 35%.
- Developed a nationally recognized public relations program for the removal of hazardous trees.
- Planned and administered budgets as large as $2 million.
- B.S. degrees in both Soil Science and Forest Management/Recreation.
- Certified Arborist with the International Society of Arboriculture.

I am recognized as a dedicated and committed leader with the ability to adapt to changing environments while meeting all requirements and challenges.

I feel confident that my background and successes would enable me to make immediate contributions to The Department of Botany and its numerous programs. I look forward to discussing my experience with you during a personal interview. Thank you in advance for reviewing my credentials.

Sincerely,

Raymond M. Bertram

Problem 49: Focusing on Personal Needs, Not on Value Being Offered

The focus of this cover letter is what Boylan wants from a company, not what he can offer an organization. This self-serving attitude is a turnoff to many resume reviewers.

Robert A. Boylan
1 Leavitt Street
Hingham, MA 02043
(781) 749-1558
Rbtab@hotmail.com

March 17, 2003

Mr. Jack Mohan
Management Recruiters, International, Inc.
607 Boylston St.
Boston, MA 02116

Dear Mr. Mohan:

I'm seeking a manufacturing engineering opportunity with a progressive, growth-oriented company that is recognized in its industry for both innovation and outstanding product quality. The company will consider human resources to be its most valuable asset, plus encourage professional and personal growth through providing a nurturing and empowering work setting. Additionally, the company will have a promote-from-within policy as well as a comprehensive benefits package. My resume is enclosed for your review.

In exchange for the above, I offer outstanding strengths in manufacturing engineering, with a record of achievement in new process and equipment design, cost reduction, productivity enhancement, and inventory management. My contributions at each of my employers have played a key role in the organization's growth to the next level of success.

I am recognized as a team player with a high energy level and burning desire to maximize a company's productivity and operating efficiency. Throughout my career supervisors have cited me for my innovation and hard work. I am certain that when you have a position for which my background is appropriate, your client will want to meet me and hire me.

Thank you in advance for reviewing my credentials. I will call you next week to discuss the appropriate next step.

Sincerely,

Robert A. Boylan

The rewritten cover letter focuses on the value that Boylan brings to companies, which will prompt reviewers to read his resume.

Robert A. Boylan
1 Leavitt Street
Hingham, MA 02043
(781) 749-1558
Rbtab@hotmail.com

March 17, 2003

Mr. Jack Mohan
Management Recruiters, International, Inc.
607 Boylston St.
Boston, MA 02116

Dear Mr. Mohan:

I'm an accomplished manufacturing engineer with a record of success in the electronics industry, with employers producing both high-volume products and custom systems. At the present time, I'm seeking a new opportunity and challenge and am enclosing my resume for your review. Key highlights from my background include:

- Developed and implemented new manufacturing processes that decreased cycle time 15%.
- Designed production equipment that improved quality 10%.
- Introduced assembly procedures that reduced labor costs 12%.
- Created inventory management initiatives that increased annual turns 25%.

I am recognized as a team player with a high energy level and burning desire to maximize a company's productivity and operating efficiency. Throughout my career supervisors have cited me for my innovation and hard work. I am certain that when you have a position for which my background is appropriate, your client will want to meet me and hire me.

Thank you in advance for reviewing my credentials. I will call you next week to discuss the appropriate next step.

Sincerely,

Robert A. Boylan

Problem 50: Writing a Two-Page Letter

Many people won't take the time to read a two-page cover letter, so Owen does nothing to invite readership of his resume.

Harry R. Owens
104 Harvest Commons
Westport, CT 06880
(203) 222-9121
Hrowens@aol.com

March 22, 2003

Mr. Todd Tillinghast
Sr. VP - Information Technology
Paddington Partners
One Landmark Square
Stamford, CT 06901

Dear Mr. Tillinghast:

I'm a senior management executive with a record of achievement in IT consulting, offering expertise in strategic enterprise solutions. Key strengths include P&L management, strategic planning, sales and marketing, business development, strategic alliances, start-up operations, and turnaround management, with both domestic and international experience. I've been following your company very closely, and am aware of your outstanding successes. I would like to meet with you to discuss how my experience could play a key role in your growth and future plans. My resume is enclosed for your review, with select highlights including:

Big 5 Consulting Background

I was fortunate to have played a key role in starting up and managing PriceWaterhouseCoopers' regional enterprise solutions practice, which focused on the employee side of the enterprise portal expanding to business partners and customers. Under my leadership and direct involvement, we sold over $65 million in services to Fortune 500 clients at the "C" level within an eight-month period. Capitalizing on my successes there, I was given the opportunity to create a global mid-market enterprise solution with select vendors and market the solution globally.

Entrepreneurial Experience / Start-ups / Turnaround Management

My ability to recognize opportunity and capitalize on it is what motivated me start up two companies as well as make major contributions in turning around underperforming companies. Both start-ups won sizable customer bases, generated profitable revenues, and were then successfully sold to larger organizations, one of which was PriceWaterhouseCoopers. The first start-up was an ISP, where I generated first-year revenues of almost $2 million, then sold the business for $3 million. The second start-up operation was a KPMG Peat Marwick regional PeopleSoft business, where I produced almost $24 million in revenues over a two-year period. The turnarounds that I have orchestrated resulted from investors contacting me to make sweeping changes in their high-tech businesses so they could recoup their losses. The most successful venture was turning around a bankrupt VPN within one year, where I grew services revenues from $300,000 to $3 million within six months and delivered a 36% net operating profit margin. I then played a leading role in selling the business for over $10 million.

Proven Record Across All Major Corporate Functions

My background consists of years of successful business strategy and technological engagements covering a wide variety of products in diverse industries. With the proven ability to quickly understand a company's operating environment, combined with extensive IT consulting experience, I bring both strategic direction and technological expertise to the table. My referenceable clients include Yahoo, Hewlett-Packard, Washington Mutual Bank, Boeing, Exxon/Mobil, JC Penney, Pier 1 Imports, State Farm Insurance, McDonalds Corp., Daimler/Chrysler, TRW, the US Department of Energy, and The Williams Companies.

International Experience

Leading the global mid-market enterprise solutions team at PwC, I established sales channels and operations for our solution in Canada, the United States, Australia, The European Union, Brazil, and South Africa.

Educational Background

I hold an MBA, an M.S. in Computer Science, and a BSEE.

I feel there is great synergy between my experience and the direction in which Paddington Partners is going. Believing that my wealth of IT experience combined with strategic, organizational, and leadership strengths would enable me to make contributions in several key areas, I would like to meet with you to discuss how I might be of value to your organization. I will call you next week to discuss the appropriate next step.

Thank you in advance for reviewing my credentials.

Very truly yours,

Harry R. Owens

Streamlined to one page, the rewritten cover letter will be read and so will the resume.

Harry R. Owens
104 Harvest Commons
Westport, CT 06880
(203) 222-9121
Hrowens@aol.com

March 22, 2003

Mr. Todd Tillinghast
Sr. VP - Information Technology
Paddington Partners
One Landmark Square
Stamford, CT 06901

Dear Mr. Tillinghast:

I'm a senior management executive with a record of achievement in IT consulting, with great interest and expertise in strategic enterprise solutions. Key strengths include P&L management, strategic planning, sales and marketing, business development, strategic alliances, start-up operations, and turnaround management, with both domestic and international experience. I've been following your company very closely, and am aware of your outstanding successes. I would like to meet with you to discuss how my experience could play a key role in your growth and future plans. My resume is enclosed for your review, with select highlights including:

- 10+ years' experience in the information management and consulting field, driving the growth of consulting firms plus providing topflight service delivery, with emphasis on enterprise portal solutions, implementing ERP packages, and offering package or custom solutions to businesses. Expert at HRMS (PeopleSoft) and financial products.
- Started up and managed PriceWaterhouseCoopers' Midwest enterprise solutions practice—sold over $65 million in services within 8 months to Fortune 50-500 clients, then created a global mid-market enterprise solution and marketed services worldwide.
- Helped start up an ISP, delivered first-year revenues of $1.9 million, then sold the business for almost $3 million.
- Turned around a bankrupt VPN in 1 year, growing services revenues from $300,000 to $3 million within 6 months and delivering a 36% net operating profit margin. Instrumental in selling the business for over $10 million.
- Established KPMG Peat Marwick's PeopleSoft business in the Southwest, generating almost $24 million in revenues over 2 years.
- I hold an MBA, M.S. in Computer Science, and a BSEE degree.

I feel there is great synergy between my experience and the direction in which Paddington Partners is going. Believing that my wealth of IT experience combined with strategic, organizational, and leadership strengths would enable me to make contributions in several key areas, I would like to meet with you to discuss how I might be of value to your organization. I will call you early next week to discuss the appropriate next step. Thank you in advance for reviewing my credentials.

Very truly yours,

Harry R. Owens

INDEX

ABOUT THE AUTHOR

John Marcus is a nationally recognized career coach and author who is widely regarded as the best resume writer in the business. His previous books include *The Complete Job Interview Handbook* and *The Résumé Doctor*. He lives in Sarasota, Florida, from where he writes resumes for clients nationwide.